CAPRICORN
RHYMING DICTIONARY

Capricorn
Rhyming Dictionary

(AID TO RHYME)

by
Bessie G. Redfield

CAPRICORN BOOKS EDITION
G. P. PUTNAM'S SONS NEW YORK

Capricorn Books Edition, 1965

Seventh Impression

SBN: 399-50200-9

by
Bessie G. Redfield

Copyright, 1938
by
Bessie G. Redfield

To

WILLIAM THOMPSON REDFIELD

MADE IN THE UNITED STATES OF AMERICA

HOW TO USE THIS BOOK

The reader will notice the carefully arranged groupings of the words, and their endings, which are specifically placed for his convenience. For instance, the endings of each group of words are in the left column, and the references are in the right-hand column in smaller type under *see,* with suffixes which are added to make plurals, or different tenses of verbs. Thus any word with *ly* refers to **E** group of words, and *en* to those ending in **EN**; also that words with the same endings, but pronounced differently are starred thus *. When pronounced more than one way, the star is repeated, as, for example, in **OUGH**, which has five different pronunciations.

CAPRICORN
RHYMING DICTIONARY

A SOUNDS

Appliqué, attaché, au fait, ballet, **A***
bébé, béret, bouquet, buffet, cabriolet, *see*
cachet, café, chalet, cliché, consommé, AY
coryphée, coupé, crochet, croquet, curé, EIGH
décolleté, déplumé, distrait, épée, ex- EY*
tempore, fiancée, foyer, glacé, gourmet, UAY
lettre de cachet, Madame de Sévigné, UET**
maté, matinée, mauvais, mêlée, métier, S-AISE
moiré, naïveté, narghile, née, névé,
O.K., padre, papiermâché, passé, per
se, Pompeii, protégée, purée, quai, re-
poussé, requiescat in pace, résumé, re-
troussé, réveillé, risqué, roué, sachet,
sesame, soirée, sujet, toupet, ukulele,
visé

Addenda, Ætna, Agra, Agrippa, **A****
Ahura Mazda, akasha, Alaska, alfalfa, *see*
Alhambra, Amalthæa, amoeba, am- ABRA
pulla, anaconda, anathema, Androm- ACA
eda, apocrypha, aqua, aqua vitæ, ADA
Aquila, arietta, Atahualpa, Atlanta, AGA
Attila, Ayesha, Ba, Barbarossa, Beer- AH
sheba, Bermuda, bertha, beta, biretta, ALA
Bogota, bonanza, Borsippa, Brahma, ALPHA
Buddha, Burma, Calcutta, calla, Ca- AMA

4

nova, Caracalla, caramba, Casabianca, **A****
Casanova, cascara, Cassandra, catal- ANA
pa, Catawba, Cleopatra, Clytemnestra, ANDA
cobra, comma, contra, copra, Cordova, ANNA
corolla, Cuba, delta, deva, dharma, di- ANZA
gamma, dilemma, dogma, Durga, éclat, ARA
Electra, eureka, Europa, ex cathedra, ATA
extra, farina, fauna, felucca, fra, AVA
Frigga, Gæa, gamma, Ganesa, Garuda, AWAY
geisha, Geneva, Golgotha, grandpa, AY
hacienda, hagiographa, ha-ha, Hecuba, AYA
Hiawatha, Hybla, impedimenta, Inca, EA
Indra, infanta, influenza, infra, jinrick- EBRA
sha, Joppa, Judæa, Ka, Kaaba, kalpa, EDDA
Kamchatka, kappa, Karma, kibla, ELLA
Krishna, Lady Godiva, larva, Laura, EMA
Leda, Lhassa, Libra, Lyra, ma, Ma- ENA
deira, magenta, Magna Charta, Ma- ENNA
hadeva, mahatma, malacca, Malta, ERA
mama, Manila, mantra, marimba, ESTA
Marpessa, Mazeppa, mazurka, mea IA
culpa, Mecca, mesa, miasma, Minerva, ICA
Minnehaha, Mona Lisa, Mount Shasta, IGMA
Mylitta, naphtha, Nova Zembla, IKA
Odessa, okra, Omaha, omega, operetta, ILLA
orchestra, Ouida, ouija, pa, Padua, IMA
pagoda, palestra, Palmyra, pampa, INA
papa, pasha, peseta, piazza, Pietà, IRA
Pisa, polka, puma, pupa, Pyrrha, Ra, ISTA
regatta, Rig-Veda, rotunda, savanna, ITA
Scylla, Seneca, seta, Sheba, Shiva, OA
sierra, Smyrna, soda, sofa, spa, Sparta, ODA
Spinoza, Sumatra, sura, syringa, taf- OGA
feta, Tampa, tapioca, ta-ta, terra OLA
firma, St. Theresa, Topeka, tuba, OMA
tundra, ultra, umbra, Ursa, Valhalla, ONA
Vega, vendetta, Venezuela, veranda, ONDA

vice-versa, viva, vodka, Volga, Voluspa, yucca, Zarathustra

A**
ONNA
ORA
OSA
OTA
ULA
UMBRA
USA
YA
YDRA

Baal, kraal, kursaal, Transvaal

AAL
see
AL

Ab, Ahab, blab, cab, confab, crab, dab, drab, gab, grab, hissing-crab, jab, Moab, nab, Punjab, Queen Mab, Rahab, sand-dab, scab, slab, stab, tab, taxi-cab

AB*
see
ARAB

Squab, swab

AB**
see
OB

Babble, dabble, gabble, grabble, rabble, scrabble, squabble

ABBLE
see
EL
LE

Cabby, drabby, flabby, scabby, tabby

ABBY
see
E**

Astrolabe

ABE
see

Abel, Babel, label

ABEL
see
EL
LE

Able, adorable, affable, allowable, amicable, answerable, arable, assessable, available, breakable, cable, calculable, capable, censurable, commendable, commensurable, comparable, conceivable, consolable, constable, delectable, demonstrable, deplorable, desirable, despicable, detachable, disable, disputable, durable, enable, escapable, estimable, evaporable, execrable, explicable, fable, formidable, friable, gable, get-at-able, hall-table, immeasurable, immutable, impassable, impeccable, impenetrable, imperishable, implacable, impracticable, impregnable, improbable, inalienable, inapplicable, incalculable, incapable, incommensurable, incomparable, inconsolable, incontestable, indefatigable, indefinable, indemonstrable, indescribable, indispensable, indisputable, ineffable, ineradicable, inexcusable, inexorable, inflammable, inscrutable, inseparable, insurmountable, interminable, invaluable, inviolable, invulnerable, irrefragable, irrefutable, irrevocable, jumpable, knowable, laudable, likable, lovable, memorable, monosyllable, mutable, navigable, notable, palatable, palpable, parable, pardonable, passable, peccable, perishable, pleasurable, polysyllable, portable,

ABLE
see
EABLE
EL
ERABLE
IABLE
ITABLE
LE
UABLE
y-ABLY

practicable, pregnable, presentable, printable, probable, punishable, questionable, readable, reasonable, receptable, redoubtable, refutable, regrettable, removable, resolvable, retable, Round Table, revocable, sable, scrutable, seasonable, spankable, stable, surmountable, syllable, table, tarnishable, taxable, teachable, tenable, terminable, time-table, tractable, unable, unassailable, unavoidable, unbearable, unbelievable, undiminishable, unfathomable, unmentionable, unprintable, unseasonable, unshakable, unspeakable, unstable, unstridable, unsurpassable, unwarrantable, usable, vegetable, vocable, vulnerable, warrantable

ABLE

Ably, adorably, amicably, favorably, inevitably, irrevocably, irritably, justifiably, preferably, presumably, unspeakably

ABLY
see
E**
ABLE-*y*

Baboo, bugaboo, taboo

ABOO
see
OO

Abracadabra, candelabra

ABRA
see
A**

Danse macabre

ABRE
see

Almanac, Armagnac, Balzac, bivouac, bric-à-brac, cognac, cul-de-sac, ipecac, lac, lilac, Pachamac, Potomac,

AC
see
ACH*

sandarac, Saranac, shellac, sumac, tabac

AC
ACK
AK
IAC

Alpaca, cloaca, paca, portulaca, Titicaca

ACA
see
A**

Ace, Alsace, anchoring-place, apace, beardless-face, birthplace, brace, chimney-place, commonplace, deface, disgrace, displace, dough-face, dwelling-place, efface, embrace, face, furnace, gold-lace, grace, grimace, hiding-place, Horace, interlace, interspace, lace, mace, macrimé lace, marketplace, menace, misplace, necklace, open-face, pace, palace, place, point lace, poker-face, populace, preface, Queen Anne's lace, race, refuge-place, replace, resting-place, retrace, Samothrace, scapegrace, shame-face, solace, space, surface, tailrace, terrace, trace, trystingplace, unlace, wheyface

ACE
see
ASE*
ed-AIST
ASTE-*d*
s-IS**
IZ

Adjacent, complacent

ACENT
see
ENT

Bach, Bel-Merodach, Meshach, Shadrach, stomach, sumach

ACH*
see
AC
ACK

Detach, spinach

ACH**
see
ATCH*

Apache, cache, moustache, pistache **ACHE***
see
ASH*

Ache, head-ache, heart-ache **ACHE****
see
AKE

Drachm **ACHM**
see
AM

Steam-yacht, yacht **ACHT**
see
OT

Audacious, contumacious, curva- **ACIOUS**
cious, edacious, efficacious, fumacious, *see*
gracious, loquacious, mendacious, mor- IOUS
dacious, perspicacious, pertinacious, OUS
predacious, pugnacious, rapacious, sa-
gacious, sequacious, spacious, vera-
cious, vivacious, voracious

Capacity, mendacity, opacity, pers- **ACITY**
picacity, pertinacity, pugnacity, ra- *see*
pacity, sagacity, tenacity, veracity, E**
vivacity, voracity ITY

Aback, Adirondack, alack, apple- **ACK**
jack, attack, back, bareback, black, *see*
bookrack, bookstack, bootblack, boot- AC
jack, canvasback, clack, come-back, ACH*
Cossack, crack, cracker-jack, dirt- AK
track, drawback, flapjack, flashback,
full back, gimcrack, greenback, grip-
sack, gunnysack, hack, hackmatack,

hardtack, hat-rack, haversack, hay-rack, high-low-jack, hi-jack, horseback, hunchback, Jack, knack, knapsack, knick-knack, lack, lampblack, leather-back, lumberjack, pack, paddywhack, pickaback, pitch-black, quack, quarter-back, rack, ransack, razorback, rick-rack, sack, setback, shack, shoe-black, sidetrack, slack, slap jack, smack, smoke-stack, snack, spur-track, squir-rel-track, stack, steeple-jack, switch-back, tack, tamarack, thumb-tack, thwack, toast-rack, track, tricktrack, Union Jack, unpack, whack, wisecrack, wrack, zwieback

ACK

Blacken, bracken, slacken

ACKEN
see
EN

Backer, blacker, cannon-cracker, cracker, Georgia cracker, hi-jacker, nutcracker, slacker

ACKER
see
ER

Blue-jacket, bracket, jacket, mon-key-jacket, packet, pea-jacket, racket, strait-jacket

ACKET
see
ET

Cackle, crackle, grackle, ramshackle, shackle, tackle

ACKLE
see
EL
LE

Barracks

ACKS
see
ACK-*s*

Barnacle, binnacle, debacle, manacle, miracle, obstacle, oracle, pinnacle, receptacle, spectacle, tabernacle, tentacle

ACLE
see
EL
LE

Acre, God's acre, massacre, nacre, simulacre, wiseacre

ACRE
see
ER

Abstract, act, attract, bract, cataract, compact, contract, counteract, detract, distract, enact, exact, extract, fact, impact, inexact, intact, interact, matter-of-fact, pact, protract, react, refract, retract, riot-act, Stamp Act, subtract, tact, tract, transact

ACT
see
ACK-*ed*
ed-EAD*
ED
S-AC-S
ACH*-S
ACK-S
AX

Didactic, lactic, prophylactic, tactic

ACTIC
see
IC

Actor, chiropractor, detractor, extractor, factor, tractor

ACTOR
see
OR

Accuracy, adequacy, advocacy, aristocracy, celibacy, confederacy, contumacy, democracy, diplomacy, effeminacy, fallacy, gynecocracy, illiteracy, intimacy, lacy, legacy, literacy, lunacy, obstinacy, papacy, pharmacy, plutocracy, privacy, racy, supremacy, theocracy

ACY
see
E**
ICACY
IRACY

Accad, ad., bad, Bagdad, ballad, brad, cad, Carlsbad, clad, dad, doodad, egad, fad, farad, footpad, forbad, gad, Galahad, glad, had, ironclad, Jehad, lad, lily-pad, mad, mail-clad, monad, olive-clad, pad, sad, salad, shad, Sinbad, snowclad, stark-mad, steel-clad, tetrad, Trinidad, Upanishad, velvet-clad

AD*
see
ADE**
AID***
IAD
YAD

Wad

AD**
see
OD

Armada, Canada, cicada, Granada, Haggada, posada, Torquemada

ADA
see
A**

Add

ADD
see
AD

Addle, paddle, saddle, skedaddle, staddle, straddle, swaddle, twaddle, waddle

ADDLE
see
EL
LE

Abrade, accolade, ambuscade, arcade, balustrade, barricade, blade, blockade, brigade, brocade, cannonade, cascade, cavalcade, centigrade, charade, cockade, colonnade, crusade, deadly nightshade, decade, degrade, escalade, escapade, esplanade, evade, everglade, facade, fade, free-trade, fusillade, glade, harlequinade, homemade, invade, jade, lade, lampshade,

ADE*
see
AID
ENADE
UADE
S-ADES**

lemonade, marmalade, masquerade, nightshade, orangeade, palisade, parade, pasquinade, pervade, pomade, readymade, renegade, retrograde, rhodomantade, shade, shoulder-blade, spade, stockade, sunshade, tirade, trade, wade, well-made **ADE***

Comrade, Scheherazade **ADE****
see
AD

Crusader, masquerader, trader **ADER**
see
ER

Alcibiades, Cyclades, Hades, Hippotades, Miltiades, Pleiades **ADES***
see
EA*-*s*
EASE

Crusades, palisades **ADES****
see
ADE*-*s*

Badge, cadge, Madge **ADGE**
see

Monadic, nomadic, sporadic **ADIC**
see
IC

Avocado, bastinado, bravado, Colorado, comerado, crusado, desperado, El Dorado, mikado, prado, renegado, stoccado, tornado **ADO**
see
O*

Ambassador, conquistador, depre-
dator, Ecuador, Labrador, matador,
picador, San Salvador, toreador

ADOR
see
OR

Arcady, lady, landlady, malady,
milady, shady

ADY
see
E**

Algæ, antennæ, arbor-vitæ, brae,
Danæ, dies iræ, dramatis personæ,
horæ, lapus linguæ, larvæ, lingnum
vitæ, minutiæ, Mycenæ, Parcæ, sundæ,
Thermopylæ

Æ
see
E*

Azrael, Ishmael, Israel, Jael,
Michael, Raphael

AEL
see
EL
LE

Chafe, safe, unsafe, vouchsafe

AFE*
see
AIF

Carafe

AFE**
see
AFF

Chaff, distaff, draff, Falstaff, flag-
staff, gaff, pikestaff, pilgrim staff, riff-
raff, sclaff, shandy gaff, staff, working-
staff

AFF
see
AFE**
AFFE
ALF
APH

Giraffe

AFFE
see
AFE**

Abaft, aft, aircraft, anti-aircraft, craft, daft, draft, fore and aft, graft, haft, handicraft, kingcraft, priestcraft, quaft, shaft, statecraft, waft, witchcraft

AFT
see
APH-*ed*
AUGHT**

After, hereafter, rafter, thereafter

AFTER
see
ER

Bag, beanbag, black flag, blueflag, brag, brain-fag, button-bag, carpetbag, crag, ditty-bag, drag, dufflebag, fag, flag, gag, hag, handbag, juttingcrag, lag, mailbag, money-bag, nag, rag, ragtag, saddlebag, sag, saltbag, sandbag, scallawag, scrag, shag, slag, sleeping-bag, snag, stag, starry flag, tag, wag, water-bag, wig-wag, zigzag

AG
see

Malaga, Naga, rutabaga, saga

AGA
see
A**

Adage, advantage, age, anchorage, appendage, assemblage, baggage, bandage, birdcage, bondage, boscage, cabbage, cage, Carthage, cartilage, classic-age, cleavage, coinage, coldstorage, cordage, cottage, courage, cribbage, damage, dangerous age, discourage, disparage, dosage, drainage, encourage, enrage, ensilage, equipage, espionage, flowering sage, forage, frontage, fruitage, fuselage, garbage, Golden Age, greengage, Greenwich Village, herbage, heritage, homage, hos-

AGE*
see
AUGE
EAGE
EDGE
EGE
ERAGE
IAGE
ORAGE
OTAGE
UAGE
s-ES*

tage, image, leafage, leakage, luggage, **AGE***
manage, middle age, mismanage, mort-
gage, mucilage, nonage, orphanage,
ossifrage, outrage, package, page, par-
entage, parsonage, pasturage, patron-
age, percentage, pilgrimage, pillage,
plumage, portage, postage, pottage,
presage, rage, rampage, ravage, rum-
mage, sabotage, sage, salvage, sausage,
savage, saxifrage, scrimmage, scrum-
mage, scutage, seepage, sewage, short-
age, shrinkage, silage, skunkcabbage,
smallage, spoilage, stage, steerage,
stone age, stoppage, storage, suffrage,
tallage, tankage, tillage, title-page,
tutelage, umbrage, upstage, usage,
vantage, vassalage, vicarage, village,
vintage, visage, voyage, wage, wolfish-
rage, wreckage

Appanage, badinage, bon voyage, **AGE****
boscage, camouflage, entourage, es- *see*
pionage, feuillage, garage, massage,
ménage, mirage, persiflage, personage

Agent, press-agent **AGENT**
see
ENT

Dowager, lager, manager, old stager, **AGER**
onager, tanager, wager *see*
ER

Diaphragm **AGM**
see
AM

Champagne, Charlemagne, Bretagne **AGNE**
see
AIN

Ago, archipelago, dago, farrago, **AGO**
Iago, lumbago, plumbago, sago, solid- *see*
ago, virago, years-ago O*

Aragon, Dagon, dragon, flagon, **AGON**
hexagon, octagon, paragon, pentagon, *see*
snapdragon, tarragon, tetragon, wagon, AN**
waterwagon ON

Anagram, diagram, pentagram **AGRAM**
see
AM

Hague, plague, Prague, vague **AGUE***
see
EG

Colleague, league **AGUE****
see
UE**

Ague, argue **AGUE*****
see
U*

Asparagus, sarcophagus, Tagus **AGUS**
see
US

Abdullah, ah, amah, bah, Beulah, **AH**
bismillah, blah, cheetah, dahabeeyah, *see*
Deborah, fellah, Gomorrah, howdah, A**
hurrah, huzzah, Jehovah, Jonah, jub- IAH

bah, Judah, kiblah, maharajah, Ma- **AH**
nassah, Menephtah, Methuselah,
Micah, Mizpah, mullah, Noah, pah,
Pisgah, Ptah, purdah, rajah, Rizpah,
Rosh Hashanah, Selah, shah, Shah-
Namah, Shekinah, Shenandoah, shil-
lelah, sirrah, Terah, Torah, yeah

Adonai, caravanserai, El Shaddai, **AI**
Mordecai, Shanghai, Sinai *see*
I*

Aramaic, archaic, Hebraic, laic, **AIC**
Lamaic, mosaic, prosaic, Romaic, vol- *see*
taic IC

Afraid, aid, air-raid, bondmaid, **AID***
braid, handmaid, inlaid, laid, maid, *see*
mermaid, milkmaid, overpaid, paid, ADE*
plaid, poorly-paid, raid, repaid, sea- AY-*ed*
maid, shepherd's plaid, staid, unpaid,
upbraid, waylaid

Aforesaid, said, Thebaid, unsaid **AID***
see
EAD*

Naif, waif **AIF**
see
AFE*

Arraign, campaign **AIGN**
see
AIN

Straight **AIGHT**
see
ATE

Haik

AIK
see
IKE

Ail, assail, avail, bail, bewail, black-
mail, bobtail, cat-tail, cocktail, curtail,
derail, detail, dinner-pail, dovetail,
draggle-tail, entail, fail, fan-mail, fan-
tail, flail, foxtail, frail, grail, hail, hand-
rail, hangnail, hobnail, jail, mail, main-
sail, mare's tail, monorail, nail, oxtail,
pail, pigtail, pintail, prevail, quail, rail,
remail, retail, ringtail, sail, silver nail,
slaptail, snail, stay-sail, swallow-tail,
taffrail, tail, tattered-sail, thumbnail,
trail, travail, vail, wagtail, wail, wassail

AIL
see
ALE
EIL

Blackmailer, trailer

AILER
see
ER

Acclaim, aim, claim, declaim, dis-
claim, Ephraim, exclaim, maim, Miz-
raim, proclaim, quitclaim, reclaim

AIM
see
AME*

Abstain, again, amain, appertain, at-
tain, bargain, blain, boatswain, brain,
Cain, captain, certain, chain, chamber-
lain, chaplain, chieftain, chilblain,
come-again, complain, constrain, con-
tain, coxswain, cross-grain, curtain,
detain, disdain, domain, drain, drop
curtain, enchain, endless-chain, enter-
tain, explain, fain, foreordain, foun-
tain, gain, grain, ingrain, legerdemain,
main, maintain, Mark Twain, mountain, obtain, ordain, pain, pattering-

AIN
see
AGNE
AIGN
AINE
ANE
EIGN
EIN

rain, plain, plantain, porcelain, pre-ordain, purslain, quatrain, rain, rattle-brain, refrain, regain, remain, restrain, retain, sea-captain, simple-swain, soda-fountain, Spain, Spanish Main, stain, St. Germain, strain, sustain, suzerain, swain, tent-curtain, terrain, train, twain, vain, vervain, villain, weather stain

AIN

Aquitaine, chatelaine, cocaine, Lor-raine, migraine, moraine, ptomaine

AINE
see
AIN

Aint, aquaint, complaint, constraint, faint, liveries-quaint, paint, patron saint, plaint, quaint, restraint, saint, self-restraint, taint, warpaint

AINT
see
EINT
ly-E**

Affair, air, armchair, backstair, bath chair, camel's hair, campchair, chair, Corsair, debonair, éclair, fair, flair, hair, horsehair, impair, kinky hair, lair, maidenhair, Mayfair, mid air, mohair, open-air, pair, repair, rocking-chair, sedan-chair, stair, study-chair, unfair, Vanity Fair, Windsor chair

AIR
see
AIRE
ARE*
EAR**
EIR*

Brumaire, debonaire, doctrinaire, Frimaire, legionnaire, millionaire, mul-timillionaire, questionnaire, savoir faire, secretaire, solitaire, Vendemaire, vin ordinaire, Voltaire

AIRE
see
AIR

Bairn, cairn, Pitcairn

AIRN
see

Airy, dairy, fairy, hairy	**AIRY** *see* E**
Dais, Sais	**AIS*** *see* IS*
Calais, Rabelais	**AIS**** *see* A*
Braise, chaise, malaise, Marseillaise, mayonnaise, Père-la-Chaise, polonaise, postchaise, praise, raise, self-praise	**AISE** *see* AISSE A*-*s* AIZE ASE** AY-*s* EIGH-*s*
Archaism, Hebraism, Judaism, Lamaism	**AISM** *see* ISM
Bouillabaisse, caisse	**AISSE** *see* AISE
Waist, wasp-waist	**AIST** *see* ASTE
Bait, bull bait, fishbait, gait, plait, portrait, strait, wait, whitebait	**AIT** *see* ATE

Bull baiter, congress gaiter, gaiter, waiter **AITER**
see
ER

Faith, water-wraith, wraith **AITH***
see

Saith **AITH****
see
ETH

Glaive, naive, waive **AIVE**
see
AVE*

Baize, maize **AIZE**
see
AISE

Al Borak, Barak, Irak, Karnak, kodak, yak, yashmak **AK**
see
AC
ACH*
ACK

Air-brake, bake, betake, brake, cake, canebrake, clambake, coasterbrake, cornflake, drake, earthquake, fake, flake, forsake, gartersnake, give and take, griddlecake, handshake, intake, keepsake, kittiwake, lake, make, mandrake, mercy-sake, mistake, namesake, overtake, pancake, partake, quake, rake, rattlesnake, retake, saffron cake, sake, sea-snake, shake, sheep-bake, sheldrake, shortcake, snake, snowflake, **AKE**
see
ACHE**
AQUE**
EAK**

spake, stake, sweepstake, take, tipsy-cake, undertake, wide-awake **AKE**

Awaken, betaken, mistaken, taken, wind-shaken **AKEN**
see
EN

Baker, breaker, caretaker, dress-maker, haymaker, jail-breaker, law-breaker, maker, matchmaker, peace-maker, Quaker, sailmaker, Shaker, shoemaker, spinnaker, tentmaker, un-dertaker **AKER**
see
ER

Abnormal, abysmal, admiral, adum-bral, antidotal, antipodal, apocryphal, arbital, astral, austral, autumnal, avowal, Bengal, betrayal, betrothal, cabal, carnal, cathedral, caudal, cen-tral, cerebral, cloistral, coastal, colos-sal, corral, crystal, demoniacal, de-posal, dihedral, disavowal, dismal, dis-missal, dorsal, ducal, enthral, epochal, feudal, Fingal, Funchal, gal, gyral, herbal, integral, interval, isothermal, jackal, Jubal, lachrymal, lethal, Luper-cal, madrigal, magistral, mammal, marshal, medal, missal, mistral, modal, narwhal, nasal, naval, offal, orchestral, pal, papal, Parsifal, paschal, pedal, panal, portrayal, postal, prodigal, pro-posal, Provençal, quintal, rascal, rear-admiral, rebuttal, rehearsal, renewal, reprisal, reversal, rock-crystal, sacer-dotal, sandal, scandal, seneschal, se-pulchral, signal, spectral, spiral, spousal, storm-signal, survival, synagogal, Taj **AL**
see
AAL
ANAL
EAL
EGAL
ENAL
ENTAL
ERAL
ERIAL
ERNAL
ESTAL
ETAL
EVAL
IAL
IBAL
ICAL
IDAL
IMAL
INAL
ION-*al*
IPAL
ITAL

Mahal, teetotal, thermal, total, tribunal, triumphal, universal, upheaval, vandal, vassal, verbal, withdrawal, withal

AL
IVAL
OCAL
ONAL
OPAL
ORAL
ORMAL
ORTAL
OVAL
OYAL
UAL
UGAL
URAL
URNAL
USAL
UTAL
ly-E**
s-ALS

Cabala, gala, Kalevala, Guatemala, Jumala, La Scala, marsala, Sakuntala, Shambhala

ALA
see
A**

Talc

ALC
see

Bald, emerald, herald, piebald, ribald, scald, skald

ALD
see
ALL-*ed*
AUL-*ed*

Heraldry, ribaldry

ALDRY
see
E**

Airedale, ale, bale, chippendale, dale, exhale, farthingale, female, gale, gunwale, hale, impale, inhale, kale,

ALE
see
AIL

male, martingale, musicale, nightingale, pale, percale, regale, rummagesale, sale, scale, shale, stale, swale, tale, telltale, vale, whale, wholesale, Yale

ALE
EIL

Equivalent, prevalent

ALENT
see
ENT

Aleph

ALEPH
see
IPH

Behalf, calf, half, half and half, sea calf

ALF
see
APH

Ali, Bali, Bengali, Kali, Somali

ALI
see
I**

Australia, bacchanalia, paraphernalia, parentalia, penetralia, regalia, saturnalia, Thalia, Vestalia

ALIA
see
IA

Invalid, squalid, valid

ALID
see
ID

Aurora borealis, chrysalis, Count de Gabalis, cum grano salis, digitalis, oxalis

ALIS
see
IS*

Bilingualism, fatalism, formalism, idealism, imperialism, individualism, nationalism, rationalism, revivalism, royalism, socialism, vandalism

ALISM
see
ISM

Abnormality, actuality, banality, beastiality, carnality, conviviality, duality, equality, eternality, ethereality, fatality, finality, formality, frugality, generality, hospitality, inequality, intellectuality, liberality, locality, mentality, modality, mortality, municipality, neutrality, normality, originality, partiality, personality, plurality, potentiality, principality, prodigality, quality, rascality, reality, speciality, substantiality, technicality, tonality, totality, triviality, vitality

ALITY
see
E**
ITY

Equalize, idealize, immortalize, individualize, legalize, localize, materialize, moralize, mortalize, neutralize, penalize, rationalize, realize, scandalize, signalize, specialize, tantalize, visualize, vocalize

ALIZE
see
IZE

Balk, beanstalk, cakewalk, calk, chalk, cornstalk, intermittent talk, jaywalk, rope-walk, sheep-walk, sidewalk, small-talk, stalk, talk, walk

ALK
see
AWK

All, appall, ball, banquet-hall, baseball, basketball, befall, bird-call, blackball, bookstall, bugle-call, button-ball, call, carry-all, catcall, Chinese Wall, clarion-call, coffee-stall, Cornwall, croquet-ball, dancehall, downfall, enthrall, eyeball, fall, fish-ball, footfall, forestall, fruit-stall, gall, hall, highball, hold-all, install, mall, mudwall, music-hall, musketball, nightfall, overall, pall, pitfall, prison-wall, puffball,

ALL*
see
AUL
AWL
ed-ALD
y-E**
ALLY

rainfall, recall, roll call, sea-wall, small, **ALL***
spit ball, squall, stall, stonewall, tall,
tapestried-wall, tea-ball, thrall, wall,
waterfall, windfall

Shall   **ALL****
                                             see
                                             AL

Callow, fallow, hallow, mallow,   **ALLOW**
marsh mallow, sallow, shallow, tallow,   *see*
wallow   OW*

Ally, cynically, dally, diametrically,   **ALLY**
dilly-dally, eternally, graphically,   *see*
ideally, mathematically, morally, oc-   E****
casionally, paradoxically, personally,
pragmatically, prosaically, rally, ras-
cally, reverentially, rurally, sally,
shilly-shally, stoically, tally, techni-
cally, totally, typically, tyrannically,
vitally

Balm, becalm, calm, doum palm,   **ALM**
embalm, palm, psalm   *see*
                                             UALM

Buffalo, halo, water-buffalo   **ALO**
                                             see
                                             O*

Anomalous, bicephalous, jealous,   **ALOUS**
megacephalous, scandalous   *see*
                                             OUS

Alp, scalp   **ALP**
                                             see

Alpha	**ALPHA** *see* A**
Cavalry, chivalry, rivalry	**ALRY** *see* E**
Annals, cymbals	**ALS** *see* AL-*S*
Alt, asphalt, basalt, cobalt, exalt, halt, malt, rock salt, salt, sea-salt, shalt, smalt, spring-halt	**ALT** *see* AULT *S*-ALTZ
Healthy, stealthy, wealthy	**ALTHY** *see* E**
Alto, contralto, Rialto	**ALTO** *see* O*
Casualty, fealty, loyalty, mayoralty, penalty, realty, royalty, salty, vice-royalty	**ALTY** *see* E**
Waltz	**ALTZ** *see* ALT-*S*
Bucephalus, Dædalus, Heliogabalus, Sardanapalus, Tantalus	**ALUS** *see* US

Bivalve, calve, halve, needle valve, salve, valve

ALVE
see

Abraham, Adam, Adullam, am, amalgam, balsam, bantam, bedlam, beldam, buckram, cablegram, cam, clam, Coulee Dam, cram, dam, dram, Durham, epigram, flotsam, gam, gingham, gram, grand-slam, ham, Hiram, I am, imam, Islam, jam, jetsam, jimjam, lam, macadam, madam, mantram, marconigram, milldam, Omar Khayyam, pam, praam, pram, quandam, ram, Rustam, salaam, scram, sham, Siam, slam, Surinam, swam, sweet-marjoram, telegram, Uncle Sam, wham

AM
see
AGM
AGRAM
AMB
AMME
AMN
ASM
OGRAM

Aceldama, Alabama, Bahama, cyclorama, Dalai Lama, drama, Fujiyama, Gautama, Kama, lama, llama, mama, melodrama, pajama, Panama, panorama, pranayama, Rama, Yama, Yokohama

AMA
see
A**

Dithyramb, iamb, jamb, lamb

AMB
see
AM

Amble, bramble, preamble, scramble, shamble

AMBLE
see
EL
LE

Aflame, blame, came, candle-flame, dame, defame, fame, flame, frame, game, hallowed-flame, hame, inflame,

AME*
see
AIM

lame, name, nickname, oriflame, over-came, pen-name, same, selfsame, shame, stepdame, surname, tame **AME***
AIME

Madame, Notre Dame **AME****
see
AM

Camel, caramel, enamel **AMEL**
see
EL
LE

Amen, cyclamen, stamen, Tutank-hamen **AMEN**
see
EN

Armament, filament, firmament, la-ment, ligament, lineament, medica-ment, ornament, parliament, predica-ment, sacrament, temperament, testa-ment, tournament **AMENT**
see
ENT

Gossamer, steamer, streamer, tamer **AMER**
see
ER

Adamic, balsamic, ceramic, dynam-ic, hydrodynamic, panoramic **AMIC**
see
IC

Benjamin, gamin **AMIN**
see
IN

Gramme, oriflamme, programme **AMME**
see
AM

Damn   **AMN**
see
AM

Amor, clamor, enamor   **AMOR**
see
OR

Aid-de-camp, champ, clamp, cramp, damp, decamp, encamp, firedamp, glow-worm's lamp, lamp, postage-stamp, ramp, safety-lamp, scamp, spirit-lamp, stamp, tamp, tramp, vamp   **AMP***
see

Dismal Swamp, swamp   **AMP****
see
OMP

Pampa, Tampa   **AMPA**
see
A**

Damper, hamper, pamper, scamper, tamper   **AMPER**
see
ER

Ample, example, sample, trample   **AMPLE**
see
EL
LE

Campus, grampus, hippocampus   **AMPUS**
see
US

Calamus, hippopotamus, ignoramus, mandamus, Morituri Salutamus, Nostradamus   **AMUS**
see
US

Bigamy, foamy, infamy, monogamy, poetogamy, polygamy, thingamy

AMY
see
E**

Afghan, Ahriman, Alaskan, Alderbaran, alderman, astrakhan, azan, backwoodsman, Balkan, ban, banyan, barrel-organ, began, birdman, bogeyman, Brahman, bran, brogan, bushman, Caliban, can, cancan, capstan, caravan, catamaran, cattleman, caveman, Chinaman, clan, clansman, clergyman, corban, courlan, Cretan, divan, dolman, draftsman, dustpan, Elizabethan, Etruscan, everyman, fan, fantan, fellowman, fireman, fisherman, foreman, Franciscan, freshman, fryingpan, Genghis Khan, gentleman, G-man, Gulistan, hackman, hardpan, harmattan, harridan, helmsman, heman, henchman, Heshvan, highwayman, Hindustan, horseman, hot-watercan, human, husbandman, inhuman, interurban, Iran, Ispahan, Jordan, kaftan, Kashan, khan, Khorassan, Ku-Klux-Klan, Kurdistan, layman, leman, leviathan, Libyan, longshoreman, madman, Magellan, man, marksman, marzipan, medicine-man, merchantman, middleman, midshipman, minute-man, molluscan, Musselman, Naaman, news organ, Nisan, Norman, Norseman, organ, orphan, Oscan, oysterman, pagan, pan, pavan, pecan, Peter Pan, plan, policeman, postman, Pullman, quartan, raglan, ragman, Ramadan, ran, randan, rataplan, rat-

AN*
see
ARIAN
ATAN
EAN**
EDIAN
ERAN
ESAN
IAN
ICAN
ICIAN
IGAN
ISAN
ITAN
OMAN
UAN

tan, redan, Redman, reman, rifleman, **AN***
Roman, rowan, sacristan, sampan,
sandman, sauce-pan, scan, Scotsman,
seaman, sedan, shaman, showman,
silvan, slogan, snowman, Solyman,
Soudan, span, Spartan, spick and span,
spokesman, St. Dunstan, steersman,
stewpan, suburban, suffragan, sultan,
suntan, superhuman, superman,
switchman, sylvan, talisman, tattan,
than, Theban, Tibetan, tincan, Titan,
toboggan, toucan, Trajan, Uhlan,
watchman, Welshman, yeggman, yeoman, Zoan

Swan, wan **AN****
see
ON
UAN

Ana, Apollonius of Tyanna, arcana, **ANA**
banana, bandana, Cana, Diana, dulci- *see*
ana, Ecbatana, fata morgana, Guiana, A**
gymkhana, Havana, iguana, lantana,
liana, Louisiana, mañana, Narayana,
Nirvana, quotidiana, Ramayana, sul-
tana, vox humana

Bacchanal, banal, canal **ANAL**
see
AL

Charabanc, franc **ANC**
see
ANK

Abeyance, abidance, abundance, acquaintance, admittance, advance, aidance, allowance, ambulance, annoyance, appearance, appurtenance, arrogance, askance, assistance, assurance, attendance, avoidance, balance, barn dance, bechance, buoyance, chance, circumstance, clairvoyance, clearance, concomitance, concordance, connivance, contra-dance, contrivance, conveyance, countenance, country dance, dance, discordance, dissonance, distance, disturbance, durance, elegance, encumbrance, endurance, enhance, entrance, extravagance, finance, for instance, fragrance, France, freelance, furtherance, glance, governance, grievance, guidance, hindrance, ignorance, importance, inelegance, inheritance, instance, insurance, jubilance, lance, maintenance, mischance, misfeasance, monstrance, morrice-dance, nonchalance, nuisance, obeisance, observance, ordinance, ordnance, outdistance, overbalance, parlance, penance, perchance, performance, perseverance, petulance, pittance, prance, predominance, protuberance, quittance, reappearance, reconnaisance, redundance, relevance, reluctance, remembrance, remittance, remonstrance, renaissance, repugnance, resemblance, resonance, riddance, romance, semblance, severance, shawl-dance, sibilance, significance, stance, substance, sun-dance, superabundance, surveillance, temperance, tolerance, trance, unbalance, ut-

ANCE
see
ANSE
ANT*-*s*
ENCE
ENSE
ENT-*s*
IANCE
IENCE
UANCE

terance, valance, vengeance, vigilance, war-dance **ANCE**

Blanch, branch, olive-branch, ranch **ANCH***
see
ANCHE

Stanch **ANCH****
see
AUNCH

Avalanche, carte blanche, Comanche **ANCHE**
see
ANCH*

Blatancy, buoyancy, chiromancy, dactylomancy, discrepancy, expectancy, fancy, flagrancy, flippancy, hesitancy, inconstancy, infancy, necromancy, nonchalancy, occupancy, oneiromancy, pyromancy, radiancy, redundancy, relevancy, sycophancy, tenacy, truancy, vacancy, vagrancy, vibrancy **ANCY**
see
E**
EE

Aforehand, and, band, beforehand, behindhand, Black Hand, bland, borderland, brand, brigand, cab-stand, command, contraband, countermand, demand, disband, eland, elfland, England, expand, fairyland, Ferdinand, firebrand, flower-land, flowerstand, free-hand, garland, gland, grand, grandstand, grassland, Greenland, hand, headland, highland, Holy Land, husband, Iceland, inkstand, inland, island, land, Lapland, Long Island, **AND***
see
IAND

lowland, mainland, misunderstand, moorland, my-land, mythland, New England, Newfoundland, New Zealand, off-hand, Promised Land, quicksand, remand, reprimand, salt-land, Samarkand, sand, saraband, second-hand, Shetland, shorthand, singing-sand, sleight-of-hand, stand, strand, street-band, Switzerland, tableland, Tallyrand, thousand, underhand, understand, unhand, upland, vandal-hand, warlike-band, washstand, waste-land, withstand, witness-stand, woodland, Zululand

AND*

Gourmand, Roland, wand

AND**
see
OND

Ananda, propaganda, Uganda, veranda

ANDA
see
A**

Alexander, bystander, commander, corriander, gander, grander, Highlander, islander, meander, oleander, pander, philander, pomander, salamander, slander

ANDER*
see
ER

Squander, wander

ANDER**
see
ONDER

Candle, chandle, handle, manhandle, panhandle, rush candle, tallow candle

ANDLE
see
EL
LE

Rembrandt   **ANDT**
                                        see
                                        ANT*

Thousandth   **ANDTH**
                                        see

Apple brandy, bandy, brandy, candy,   **ANDY**
cherry brandy, handy, Normandy,   *see*
rock candy, sandy   E**

Aeroplane, bamboo-cane, bane, bi-   **ANE**
plane, cane, cellophane, chicane, coun- *see*
terpane, crane, Dane, dogbane, ele-   AGNE
campane, fleabane, henbane, humane,   AIGN
hurricane, hydroplane, inane, insane, AIN
lane, mane, marchpane, membrane,   EIGN
monoplane, mundane, pane, plane,   EIN
profane, purslane, sane, soutane, sugar-
cane, supermundane, Tamerlane,
thane, tisane, triplane, urbane, vane,
volplane, wane, wolf's bane, weather-
vane, windowpane

Castanet, planet   **ANET**
                                        see
                                        ET

Bang, boomerang, chain-gang, clang,   **ANG**
fang, gang, hang, hoof-clang, mustang, *see*
orang-outang, out-sang, overhang,   ANGUE
pang, parasang, Penang, rang, sang,   INGUE
shebang, slang, sprang, tang, twang,
whang, whiz-bang, ylang ylang

Arrange, change, derange, estrange,   **ANGE***
exchange, grange, interchange, mange,   *see*
range, strange

Flange, mélange, orange

ANGE**
see

Anger, danger, endanger, manger, moneychanger, ranger

ANGER
see
ER

Angle, bangle, bespangle, dangle, disentangle, entangle, mangle, newfangle, quadrangle, spangle, strangle, tangle, triangle, wangle, wrangle

ANGLE
see
EL
LE

Fandango, mango, tango

ANGO
see
O*

Cangue, gangue, harangue

ANGUE
see
ANG

Anglo-mania, decalcomania, dipsomania, kleptomania, mania, miscellania, Tasmania, Titania, Transjordania, Transylvania, Urania

ANIA
see
IA

Botanic, galvanic, inorganic, interoceanic, mechanic, Messianic, morganic, oceanic, organic, panic, satanic, titanic, transoceanic, volcanic

ANIC
see
IC

Christianity, humanity, inanity, insanity, sanity, urbanity, vanity

ANITY
see
E**
ITY

Bank, blank, clank, crank, Cruikshank, dank, drank, embank, flank, frank, gangplank, hank, lank, mounte-

ANK
see
ANC

bank, plank, point-blank, prank, rank, sank, savings-bank, shank, shrank, spank, stank, swank, tank, thank, yank

ANK
S-ANX

Ankh

ANKH
see
ANK

Longshanks, shanks, spindleshanks

ANKS
see
ANK-S

Anna, canna, hosanna, manna, Polyanna, savanna, Susquehanna

ANNA
see
A**

Banns

ANNS
see
AN-S

Canny, cranny, Fanny, granny, nanny, tyranny, uncanny

ANNY
see
E**

Cinzano, guano, llano, Milano, piano, soprano, volcano

ANO
see
O*

Sans

ANS
see
AN-S

Expanse, manse

ANSE
see
ANCE

Aberrant, abundant, adamant, air-plant, ant, arrant, arrogant, ascendant, aslant, aspirant, benignant, blatant, bon vivant, buoyant, cant, celebrant, chant, claimant, clairvoyant, cogni-zant, confidant, consonant, constant, contestant, cormorant, Corybant, courant, covenant, currant, decant, descant, descendant, discordant, dor-mant, egg-plant, elegant, elephant, emigrant, enchant, equidistant, errant, expectant, extravagant, flagellant, fla-grant, flamboyant, flippant, fondant, fragrant, gallant, gallivant, grant, hierophant, hydrant, ignorant, immi-grant, implant, important, incessant, inconstant, inelegant, infant, inform-ant, instant, irrelevant, jurant, Levant, lieutenant, malignant, merchant, min-istrant, natant, nonchalant, observant, occupant, octant, pant, participant, passant, peasant, pedant, pendant, pennant, petulant, pheasant, pie-plant, plant, pleasant, poignant, postulant, powerplant, predominant, pregnant, protestant, puissant, pursuivant, quad-rant, rant, redundant, regnant, rele-vant, reluctant, remnant, repugnant, resonant, restaurant, resultant, rub-berplant, ruminant, search warrant, sextant, slant, stagnant, supplant, sup-plicant, sycophant, tenant, termagant, tolerant, transplant, trenchant, trium-phant, tyrant, ululant, ungallant, un-important, unpleasant, vacant, va-grant, verdant, vibrant, visitant, war-rant

ANT*
see
ANDT
AUNT
EANT
ERANT
IANT
ICANT
ILANT
ITANT
UANT
ed-ED
ly-E**
S-ANCE
ANSE

Au courant, ci-divant, débutant, en passant, nonchalant, piquant, restaurant, soi-disant, want

ANT**
see
AUNT
ONT**

Andante, ante, bacchante, commandante, corybante, Dante, dilettante

ANTE
see
E*

Amaranth

ANTH
see

Antic, Atlantic, frantic, gigantic, pedantic, romantic, transatlantic, unromantic

ANTIC
see
IC

Canto, Campo Santo, coranto, esperanto

ANTO
see
O*

Errantry, gallantry, infantry, pageantry, pantry, peasantry, pedantry, pleasantry

ANTRY
see
E**

Scanty, shanty, warranty

ANTY
see
E**

Laudanum, tympanum

ANUM
see
UM

Manx, phalanx

ANX
see
ANK-*s*

Any, Bethany, botany, Brittany, company, dittany, epiphany, litany, mahogany, many, miscellany, Ro-

ANY
see
E**

many, Tammany, theophany, Tuscany, **ANY**
zany

Bonanza, esperanza, extravaganza, **ANZA**
stanza *see*
A**

Cacao, cocao, curacao, Mindanao **AO**
see
O*

After-clap, burlap, cap, cat-nap, **AP***
chap, clap, claptrap, crap, earlap, *see*
entrap, enwrap, fill-gap, flap, flytrap, APPE
fool's cap, gap, hanap, handicap, hap, *ed*-APT
Jap, kidnap, knap, kneecap, lap, mad-
cap, mayhap, mishap, mobcap, mouse-
trap, nap, nightcap, on-tap, overlap,
pap, Phrygian cap, pointed-cap, rap,
rattle-trap, red cap, sap, satrap, scrap,
shoulder-strap, skull-cap, slap, snap,
stop-gap, strap, tap, thunder-clap,
trap, Turk's cap, unwrap, Venus's-
flytrap, wrap

Swap **AP****
see
OP

Ape, cape, drape, escape, fire-escape, **APE**
gape, grape, landscape, misshape, nape, *see*
rape, red tape, scrape, shape, ship- EPE
shape, tape

Brown paper, diaper, draper, news- **APER**
paper, paper, rice-paper, sandpaper, *see*
skyscraper, wallpaper ER

Jackanapes

APES
see
APE-*s*

Anemograph, anopisthograph, biograph, bolograph, chronograph, cinematograph, epigraph, epitaph, graph, gyrograph, hectograph, heliograph, hierograph, holograph, lithograph, mimeograph, opistograph, pantograph, paragraph, phonograph, photograph, seraph, stenograph, stylograph, telegraph

APH
see
AFE**
ALF
AUGH
UAFF
ed-AFT
y-APHY

Autobiography, bibliography, biography, cacography, geography, heliography, lexicography, museography, oceanography, orography, orthography, phonography, photography, pyrography, telephotography, topography

APHY
see
E**

Nappe

APPE
see
AP*

Clapper, dapper, flapper, scrapper, snapper, wrapper

APPER
see
ER

Apple, crab apple, dapple, grapple, pineapple, scrapple

APPLE
see
EL
LE

Happy, sappy, scrappy, snappy

APPY
see
E**

Craps, drumtaps, perhaps, snaps, taps

APS
see
AP*-s

Apse, collapse, elapse, lapse, relapse, trapse

APSE
see
AP*-s

Adapt, apt, deep-wrapt, inapt, rapt, slapt, wrapt

APT
see
AP*-*ed*
S-AP*-s

Plaque

AQUE*
see
AC

Opaque

AQUE**
see
AKE

Above par, Adar, afar, Akbar, Alcazar, almemar, altar, antimacassar, astylar, auto-car, avatar, bar, bazaar, beggar, below par, Belshazzar, bipolar, blazing-star, Bolivar, brownsugar, burglar, bursar, Caesar, calabar, calendar, car, caterpillar, cellar, char, cheddar, cigar, cinnabar, coal-tar, cooky-jar, cougar, crockery-jar, crossbar, crowbar, czar, D.A.R., day-star, debar, dog-star, evening-star, Excalibar, exemplar, far, feldspar, gar, Gaspar, Gibraltar, grammar, guitar, Hagar, handle-bar, hangar, horsecar, hussar, interstellar, isobar, Issachar, izar, jack-tar, jaguar, jar, jaunting-car,

AR*
see
ARE**
ARRE
EDAR
IAR
ILAR
OIR**
OLLAR
ULAR
ULGAR
YR
ed-ARD
S-ARS

Julian Calendar, lascar, lazar, Lochin- **AR***
var, lode star, lunar, Macassar, Mada-
gascar, Magyar, Malabar, maple sugar,
mar, medlar, molar, morning-star,
mortar, motor car, nectar, nenuphar,
Ninnar, Omar, par, pedlar, pillar,
Pindar, platform car, polar, Pompey's
Pillar, poplar, Potiphar, realgar, regis-
trar, salt cellar, samovar, sandbar,
scar, scholar, scimitar, Shinar, shoot-
ing-star, side-car, sitar, sleeping-car,
solar, spar, star, stellar, sugar, tar,
tartar, Templar, thus far, Trafalgar,
trolley-car, Vassar, vicar, vinegar,
Zanzibar, Zohar

Civil War, man-of-war, pre-war, war **AR****
see
ATOR
OR

Cithara, dulcamara, Ishvara, mas- **ARA**
cara, Para, Sahara, Sara, solfatara, *see*
Tara, taratantara, tiara A**

Arab, scarab, street-arab **ARAB**
see
AB*

Barb, garb, rhubarb **ARB**
see

Garble, marble, warble **ARBLE**
see
EL
LE

Arc, Joan of Arc, marc **ARC**
see
ARK

Arch, countermarch, larch, march, **ARCH***
outmarch, overarch, parch, starch *see*

Anarch, hierarch, monarch, oligarch, **ARCH****
patriarch, Petrarch, Plutarch, tetrarch *see*
ARK
S-OX

Anarchy, heptarchy, hierarchy, **ARCHY**
monarchy, oligarchy, tetrarchy *see*
E**

Abelard, afterward, Asgard, award, **ARD**
awkward, backward, backyard, bard, *see*
bastard, blizzard, bombard, boulevard, AR*-*ed*
brickyard, buzzard, calling-card, camel- IARD
opard, Camisard, canard, card, chard, UARD
church-yard, costard, coward, custard, *ly*-E**
dastard, discard, disregard, dockyard,
dullard, eastward, forward, foulard,
froward, gizzard, gold standard, green-
sward, haggard, halyard, hap-hazard,
hard, Harvard, hazard, hog's lard,
homeward, inward, izzard, laggard,
lard, leeward, leopard, lizard, mallard,
mansard, Midgard, mustard, nard,
niggard, northward, onward, orchard,
outward, pard, petard, placard, play-
ing-card, pochard, postcard, poultry-
yard, regard, retard, reward, reynard,
Richard, sard, Savoyard, scabbard,

Scotland Yard, seaward, shard, ship- **ARD**
yard, shoreward, skyward, sluggard,
southward, standard, steelyard, stew-
ard, stock-yard, straightforward,
sward, tankard, thee-ward, thither-
ward, toward, trump-card, turkey-
buzzard, upward, us-ward, Utgard,
vineyard, ward, wayward, westward,
windward, wizard, yard

Cowardly, hardly, inwardly, nig-   **ARDLY**
gardly, outwardly   *see*
                                   E**

Aware, bare, beware, blare, care, **ARE***
compare, dare, declare, delftware, *see*
earthenware, ensnare, fanfare, fare, AIR
flare, flatware, glare, hardware, hare, EIR*
insnare, mare, nightmare, pare, pebble- ERE**
ware, plowshare, prepare, rare, scare, IARE
share, snare, spare, square, stoneware,
tableware, tare, threadbare, thorough-
fare, unaware, ware, warfare, wellfare

Are, caviare   **ARE****
                                   see
                                   AR*

Bearer, cupbearer, shearer, tale- **ARER**
bearer, wayfarer, wearer   *see*
                                   ER

Dwarf, scarf, wharf   **ARF**
                                   see

Barge, charge, countercharge, dis- **ARGE**
charge, enlarge, large, marge, over- *see*
charge, recharge, surcharge, ultra-large

Cargo, embargo, largo, supercargo **ARGO**
see
O*

Aria, Ava Maria, cineraria, malaria, **ARIA**
Samaria, wistaria *see*
IA

Abcedarian, agrarian, antiquarian, **ARIAN**
barbarian, humanitarian, librarian, *see*
nonagenarian, proletarian, sectarian, AN*
sexagenarian, utilitarian, vegetarian

Ballbearing, clearing, daring, faring, **ARING**
glaring, hearing, paring, sea-faring *see*
ING

Impresario, Lothario, scenario **ARIO**
see
IO

Apollinaris, Paris, Polaris, Sybaris **ARIS**
see
IS*

Charity, clarity, disparity, hilarity, **ARITY**
irregularity, jocularity, parity, par- *see*
ticularity, peculiarity, polarity, popu- E**
larity, rarity, regularity, similarity,
singularity, solidarity, vulgarity

Ark, bark, birth-mark, book-mark, **ARK**
bulwark, dark, Denmark, disembark, *see*
ear-mark, embark, hark, highwater- ARCH**
mark, landmark, lark, mark, mudlark,
Noah's ark, Ozark, park, Peruvian
bark, pitch dark, pock-mark, post-

mark, quotation-mark, remark, sark, **ARK**
shagbark, shark, shell-bark, skylark,
snark, spark, stark, thumb-mark, tit-
lark, watermark, wood-lark

Carl, gnarl, marl, snarl   **ARL**
see

Early, pearly, popularly, scholarly, **ARLY**
similarly, singularly   *see*
E**

Abandoned farm, alarm, arm, baby **ARM***
farm, charm, disarm, false-alarm, farm, *see*
forearm, harm, unharm   ARME
S-ARMS

Lukewarm, swarm, warm   **ARM****
see
ORM*

Gendarme   **ARME**
see
ARM*

Arms, coat-of-arms, fire-arms, men- **ARMS**
at-arms   *see*
ARM*-*s*

Warmth   **ARMTH**
see

Barn, darn, spun-yarn, tarn, yarn **ARN***
see

Forewarn, warn   **ARN****
see
AWN

Carp, harp, jew's harp, scarp, sharp **ARP***
see

Warp **ARP****
see
ORP

Bizarre, Navarre **ARRE**
see
AR*

Arrow, barrow, drill-barrow, harrow, **ARROW**
marrow, narrow, sparrow, wheel-bar- *see*
row, yarrow OW*

Carry, charry, Du Barry, glengarry, **ARRY**
harry, marry, parry, quarry, remarry, *see*
starry, tarry E**

Champs de Mars, Mars **ARS**
see
AR*-*s*

Marse, parse, sparse **ARSE**
see

Harsh, marsh, salt-marsh **ARSH**
see

Apart, art, black art, braggart, cart, **ART***
chart, counterpart, dart, depart, dog- *see*
cart, Froissart, go-cart, hand-cart, EART
hart, impart, mart, Mozart, ox-cart,
part, pushcart, rampart, smart, start,
tart, upstart, weatherchart

Athwart, stalwart, thwart, wart **ART****
see
ORT

Barter, carter, charter, garter, self-starter, starter

ARTER
see
ER

Swarth

ARTH
see
ORTH*

Carve, starve, wharve

ARVE
see

Adversary, anniversary, apothecary, arbitrary, Barbary, binary, boundary, Calvary, canary, caravansary, cassowary, chary, cinerary, commentary, commissary, constabulary, contemporary, contrary, corollary, customary, dietary, dignitary, disciplinary, dispensary, documentary, dreary, dromedary, Dundreary, eleemosynary, elementary, emissary, fragmentary, functionary, glossary, granary, hoary, honorary, intercalary, involuntary, itinerary, Janizary, lapidary, legendary, library, literary, Mary, mercenary, military, momentary, monetary, notary, ovary, parliamentary, pituitary, planetary, plenary, primary, quandary, quaternary, rosary, rosemary, rotary, rudimentary, salary, sanitary, secondary, secretary, sedentary, solitary, summary, supernumerary, Tartary, temporary, tercentenary, Thackeray, Tipperary, tributary, tutelary, unitary, unwary, vagary, vary, vocabulary, voluntary, votary, wary, Zachary

ARY
see
AIRY
E**
IARY
INARY
ONARY
UARY

Abraxas, alas, Algeciras, arras, Atlas, balsas, Barabbas, Caiaphas, Candlemas, canvas, Carabas, Caracas, Christmas, coal-gas, Cordilleras, Dorcas, embarras, Esdras, fracas, gas, Hatteras, hippocras, Honduras, in vino veritas, Judas, Juventas, Kansas, laughing-gas, Lycidas, madras, Marsyas, Martinmas, Michaelmas, Midas, Mithras, nuda veritas, Pallas, pampas, per fas et nefas, Pocahontas, poison-gas, Puranas, sassafras, St. Nicholas, upas, Ushas, Vedas, Xmas

AS*
see
ASS
EAS
ORAS

As, has, whereas

AS**
see
AZ

Was

AS***
' *see*
AUSE

Airbase, base, bookcase, case, chase, crankcase, debase, erase, lower-case, paper-chase, pillowcase, purchase, show-case, staircase, steeple-chase, suitcase, vanity-case

ASE*
see
ACE
*ed-*AIST
ASTE

Chrysophrase, metaphrase, paraphrase, phase, phrase

ASE**
see
AISE
AZE

Abash, ash, balderdash, bash, brash, calabash, calash, cash, clash, crash, dash, flash, gash, gnash, goulash, hash, lash, mash, mountain ash, nettle rash,

ASH*
see
ACHE*

potash, plash, rash, sash, Shamash, slapdash, slash, smash, soda-ash, spatterdash, splash, succotash, thrash, trash, Wabash

ASH*

Backwash, swash, wash, whitewash

ASH**
see
UASH

Dasher, dishwasher, gate-crasher, haberdasher, potato-masher, rasher

ASHER
see
ER

Aphasia, Asia, Aspasia, athanasia, Australasia, Eurasia, fantasia, paronomasia

ASIA
see
IA

Abrasion, evasion, invasion, occasion, persuasion, pervasion

ASION
see
ION

Amasis, Anabasis, basis, elephantiasis, emphasis, hypostasis, oasis, protasis

ASIS
see
IS*

Ask, bask, cask, damask, flask, gasmask, Iron Mask, mask, task, unmask

ASK
see
ASQUE

Basket, casket, gasket, wastebasket

ASKET
see
ET

Cataplasm, chasm, ectoplasm, enthusiasm, iconoclasm, phantasm, pleonasm, protoplasm, sarcasm, spasm

ASM
see
AM
EM

Diapason, freemason, Jason, mason   **ASON**
see
ON

Asp, clasp, gasp, grasp, handclasp,   **ASP**
hasp, rasp, unclasp, vulture-grasp,   *see*
wasp   *ed*-ED

Basque, casque, masque   **ASQUE**
see
ASK

Applesass, ass, Balaam's ass, bass,   **ASS**
brass, carcass, class, come-to-pass,   *see*
compass, crass, crevass, cuirass, cut-   AS*
lass, eelgrass, embarrass, encompass,   EAS
eye-glass, fieldglass, glass, grass, harass,   IAS
hourglass, isinglass, jackass, looking-
glass, marine glass, marsh-grass, mass,
middle-class, morass, opera-glass, out-
class, overpass, pass, pierglass, plate-
glass, repass, sandglass, sea bass,
sherryglass, spun glass, spy-glass,
stained-glass, sunglass, surpass, trass,
trespass, underpass, upperclass, wind-
lass, wineglass

Demi-tasse, en masse, Montparnasse   **ASSE**
see
AS*
ASS

Brassy, embassy, glassy, massy,   **ASSY**
sassy   *see*
E**

Aghast, avast, ballast, blast, bombast, breakfast, broadcast, cast, contrast, downcast, enthusiast, fast, flabbergast, forecast, foremast, gymnast, half-mast, hast, iconoclast, inballast, jiggermast, jury-mast, last, long last, mast, metaphrast, outcast, outlast, overcast, paraphrast, past, peltast, plastercast, repast, sand-blast, sea-blast, shoemaker's last, steadfast, topmast, vast

AST*
see
ASK-*ed*
ASS-*ed*
ed-ED

Wast

AST**
see
AUST

Baste, chaste, cotton waste, distaste, foretaste, haste, lambaste, paste, post haste, taste, unchaste, waste

ASTE*
see
ACE-*d*
AIST
ASE*-*d*
ed-ED

Caste, half-caste

ASTE**
see
AST

Alabaster, aster, burgomaster, caster, courtplaster, disaster, faster, headmaster, master, piaster, pilaster, plaster, quarter-master, schoolmaster taskmaster, Zoroaster

ASTER
see
ER

Bombastic, drastic, ecclesiastic, elastic, fantastic, mastic, monastic, plastic, sarcastic, scholastic, spastic

ASTIC
see
IC

Ghastly, lastly, vastly **ASTLY**
see
E**

Dynasty, hasty, nasty, pasty, tasty **ASTY**
see
E**

Embrasure, measure, pleasure, tape **ASURE**
measure, treasure *see*
URE

Apostasy, easy, ecstasy, fantasy, **ASY**
free-and-easy, idiosyncrasy, phantasy *see*
E**

Acrobat, aerostat, Allat, Al Sirat, **AT***
Ararat, arhat, aristocrat, assignat, at, *see*
autocrat, automat, baccarat, bat, blat, IAT
bobcat, bodhisat, brat, brick-bat, carat,
cat, caveat, chat, chit-chat, civet cat,
combat, concordat, cravat, cricket-bat,
crush-hat, democrat, diplomat, ducat,
fat, format, ghat, gnat, habitat, hat,
heliostat, hell-cat, Herat, high-hat,
hors de combat, Jack Sprat, Jehosha-
phat, jurat, Kit-cat, Maat, Magnificat,
Monteserrat, mudflat, muscat, musk-
rat, pat, pit-a-pat, plutocrat, pole-cat,
rat, rat-a-tat, Rubaiyat, sat, Shebat,
slat, spat, tat, that, that's that, theo-
crat, thereat, Tiamat, tit-for-tat, tom-
cat, top-hat, vat, wax fat, wharf-rat,
whereat, wildcat, ziggurat

Somewhat, squat, swat, what **AT****
see
IOT

Nougat   **AT*****
see
A**

Automata, cantata, crux-ansata,   **ATA**
data, errata, inamorata, Mahabharata,   *see*
natura naturata, persona grata, pro   A**
rata, sonata, strata, ultimata

Fatal, natal, prenatal   **ATAL**
see
AL

Charlatan, Satan, tarlatan, Yucatan   **ATAN**
see
AN*

Batch, boxing-match, catch, cross-   **ATCH***
patch, dispatch, hatch, latch, lifted-   *see*
latch, match, melon-patch, nuthatch,   ACH**
overmatch, patch, potlatch, safety-
match, scratch, snatch, sulphur match,
thatch, unlatch

Dog-watch, night-watch, stop-   **ATCH****
watch, watch, wrist-watch   *see*
OTCH

Abate, accommodate, adumbrate,   **ATE**
agate, annotate, antedate, ate, bifur-   *see*
cate, billingsgate, bookplate, breast-   AIT
plate, caliphate, carbohydrate, carnate,   AVATE
celebrate, celibate, checkmate, chief   EAT**
mate, cognate, compensate, concen-   EATE
trate, confiscate, conflagrate, conflate,   EBATE

conjugate, co-ordinate, copperplate, correlate, corrugate, coruscate, crate, cremate, date, deflagrate, deflate, demonstrate, desecrate, designate, dictate, dinnerplate, discarnate, distillate, divagate, door-plate, edentate, electroplate, elevate, elongate, elucidate, emigrate, equilibrate, estate, exculpate, exhilarate, expurgate, extirpate, fashionplate, fate, filtrate, first-rate, floodgate, frustrate, gate, Golden Gate, grate, gyrate, hate, helpmate, hibernate, hydrate, illustrate, importunate, impregnate, incarnate, incubate, inculcate, inflate, ingrate, inmate, innate, insenate, instate, insulate, interpenetrate, interrogate, interstate, inundate, late, lucubrate, lustrate, magistrate, magnate, mandate, mate, messmate, methylate, migrate, narrate, negate, Newgate, nictate, nitrate, obfuscate, objurate, orchestrate, ornate, oscillate, ovate, overrate, overstate, palate, pate, penetrate, perpetrate, phosphate, placate, plate, playmate, pomegranate, potentate, promulgate, propagate, prostrate, pulsate, rate, recapitulate, reinstate, remonstrate, roller-skate, rotate, sate, schoolmate, scintillate, second-mate, second-rate, sedate, separate, serrate, skate, slate, sluice-gate, stagnate, stalemate, state, syncopate, tergiversate, tessellate, tinplate, titillate, tollgate, translate, truncate, upto-date, vacate, vacillate, variegate, vegetate, vertebrate, vibrate, Vulgate, wooly-pate

ATE

ECATE
EGATE
EIGHT*
ELATE
ENATE
ERATE
ETE**
IATE
ICATE
IDATE
IGATE
ILATE
IMATE
INATE
IPATE
IRATE
ITATE
IVATE
OATE
OBATE
OCATE
OGATE
OLATE
ONATE
ORATE
OVATE
UATE
ULATE
URATE
S-ATES

Accurately, alternately, desolately, lately, innately, intimately, irately, ornately, passionately, philately, precipitately, sedately, separately, stately

ATELY
see
E**
ELY

Alma-Mater, crater, Dis pater, fire-eater, greater, idolater, later, man-eater, pater, Stabat Mater, sweater, theater

ATER
see
ER

United States

ATES*
see
ATE-*S*

Fides Achates, Harpocrates, Hippocrates, Mithridates, Socrates

ATES**
see
ES

Aftermath, Ardath, bath, bridle-path, by-path, footbath, footpath, Goliath, hath, lath, math, mudbath, path, Sabbath, sandbath, showerbath, sitz-bath, towpath, Turkish-bath, warpath, wrath

ATH
see
OPATH

Bathe, enswathe, lathe, rathe, scathe, spathe, swathe

ATHE
see

Allopathy, antipathy, apathy, homeopathy, neuropathy, sympathy, telepathy

ATHY
see
E**

Amati, Frascati, Haimavati, Illuminati, literati, Parvati, Sarasvati

ATI
see
I**

Acrobatic, anastigmatic, aquatic, aristocratic, aromatic, Asiatic, autocratic, automatic, axiomatic, chromatic, climatic, diplomatic, dogmatic, dramatic, ecstatic, Eleatic, emblematic, emphatic, epigrammatic, erratic, fanatic, fluviatic, hieratic, hypostatic, idiomatic, lunatic, lymphatic, mathematic, melodramatic, miasmatic, morganatic, operatic, phlegmatic, piratic, plutocratic, pneumatic, polychromatic, pragmatic, prismatic, problematic, rheumatic, sabbatic, semi-aquatic, static, systematic, thematic, theocratic, trichromatic

ATIC
see
IC

Literatim, verbatim

ATIM
see
IM

Gelatin, Latin, matin, satin

ATIN
see
IN

Fascinating, grating, hibernating, lubricating, pulsating, rating

ATING
see
ING

Abdication, acclamation, accusation, administration, admiration, adulation, adumbration, affectation, affirmation, agitation, alteration, amplification, animation, appellation, arborization, attenuation, auto-intoxication, avocation, calculation, cantillation, carnation, causation, cessation, circulation, citation, civilization, collation,

ATION
see
IATION
ION

combination, communication, compensation, concatenation, concentration, condemnation, condensation, configuration, confirmation, conformation, conglomeration, congregation, consolation, constellation, consternation, consultation, consummation, contamination, contemplation, coöperation, co-ordination, coronation, corporation, counter-irritation, culmination, dedication, degustation, delegation, deportation, destination, dilapidation, dilation, discrimination, disintegration, dispensation, dissertation, dissipation, distillation, donation, duration, elevation, elimination, elucidation, emanation, embrocation, emigration, emulation, encrustation, enumeration, equation, eradication, estimation, evocation, exaggeration, exaltation, exhiliration, expectation, expiration, exploitation, expostulation, extenuation, exudation, exultation, fixation, flirtation, fluctuation, fornication, fortification, fulmination, fumigation, generalization, gestation, glorification, gradation, graduation, gravitation, gurgitation, gustation, hallucination, hesitation, identification, illation, illumination, illustration, imitation, impersonation, incantation, incarnation, incineration, incrustation, individualization, individuation, inflammation, inflation, information, innovation, insolation, inspiration, installation, insubordination, insulation, interpenetration, interpolation, interpretation, interrogation, in-

ATION

ATION

toxication, inundation, investigation, irritation, isolation, iteration, jubilation, laceration, legation, levitation, libation, liberation, libration, limitation, location, lubrication, lucubration, lustration, manifestation, manipulation, materialization, mediation, meditation, mensuration, migration, miscalculation, miscreation, mitigation, moderation, modulation, mutation, mutilation, natation, nation, negation, notation, nullification, obfuscation, oblation, obligation, observation, occupation, oration, organization, orientation, oscillation, osculation, ossification, ostentation, ovation, pagination, participation, particularization, peculation, peregrination, perspiration, plantation, population, potation, precipitation, predestination, presentation, preservation, privation, probation, proclamation, prolongation, propagation, provocation, publication, pulsation, punctuation, purification, quotation, radiation, ramification, ration, recantation, recapitulation, reclamation, recreation, recrimination, recuperation, reformation, reforestration, refrigeration, regeneration, regimentation, regulation, reincarnation, reiteration, relation, reparation, repastination, representation, reputation, reservation, respiration, resuscitation, revelation, reverberation, revocation, rotation, ruination, salutation, salvation, sanitation, simulation, speculation, stabilization, stagnation, station, stimulation, subordination, supererogation, supplication, tabulation, temptation, tergiversation, tintinnabulation, transfiguration, translation, transmigration, transmogrification, transmutation, transportation, trepidation, tribulation, undulation, unification, vacation, vaccination, valuation, vaticination, vegetation, veneration, ventilation, verification, vexation, vibration, violation, visitation, visualization, vituperation, vocalization, vocation

ATION

Clematis, gratis

ATIS
see
IS*

Affirmative, alternative, causative, communicative, comparative, corroborative, curative, decorative, derivative, evocative, excitative, figurative, formative, germinative, illative, illustrative, imaginative, imperative, initiative, insinuative, laxative, legislative, lucrative, mediative, meditative, modificative, narrative, native, negative, nominative, operative, optative, palliative, predicative, prerogative, preservative, provocative, purgative, putative, relative, remunerative, representative, restorative, sanative, sedative, superlative, talkative, tentative, terminative, vocative

ATIVE
see
IVE**

Agitato, animato, appogiato, ben trovato, Cato, inamorato, obligato, pizzicato, Plato, potato, rabato, staccato, tomato, vibrato

ATO
see
O*

Accelerator, administrator, agitator, alligator, arbitrator, aviator, curator, dictator, educator, elevator, emigrator, equator, escalator, fornicator, generator, gladiator, imperator, impersonator, incinerator, incorporator, incubator, indicator, instigator, insulator, investigator, liberator, lubricator, mediator, moderator, narrator, navigator, nominator, orator, perambulator, percolator, perpetrator, prestidigitator, prevaricator, procrastinator, procurator, prognosticator, promulgator, radiator, refrigerator, senator, spectator, speculator, testator, translator, ventilator, vibrator

ATOR
see
AR**
OAR
OR

Amatory, anticipatory, conservatory, consignatory, dedicatory, depreciatory, derogatory, dilatory, evocatory, feudatory, fumatory, gyratory, indicatory, inflammatory, laboratory, laudatory, lavatory, mandatory, migratory, objurgatory, obligatory, observatory, oratory, predatory, prefatory, preparatory, propitiatory, purgatory, reformatory, respiratory, sudatory, vibratory

ATORY
see
E**
ORY

Amphitheatre, theatre

ATRE
see
ER

Idolatry, ophiolatry, psychiatry

ATRY
see
E**

Captain Marryatt, kilowatt, watt

ATT
see
OT

Batter, chatter, clatter, flatter, hatter, matter, patter, platter, scatter, shatter, smatter, spatter, splatter, subject-matter

ATTER
see
ER

Battle, cattle, prattle, rattle, Seattle, sham-battle, tattle, tittle-tattle, wattle

ATTLE
see
EL
LE

Ageratum, Atum, erratum, pomatum, stratum, substratum, superstratum, ultimatum

ATUM
see
UM

Armature, caricature, creature, curvature, denature, entablature, feature, illnature, immature, judicature, legislature, ligature, literature, mature, miniature, nature, nomenclature, premature, signature, temperature

ATURE
see
EUR

Afflatus, apparatus, hiatus, saleratus, Pisistratus

ATUS
see
US

Esau, Nassau

AU*
see
AW

Esquimau, landau, Pau

AU**
see
O*

Jungfrau, tau **AU*****
see
OW**

Bedaub, daub **AUB**
see
AB**
OB*

Sauce **AUCE**
see
OS*
OSS

Debauch **AUCH**
see

Applaud, defraud, fraud, gaud, laud, **AUD**
maraud, Maud
see
AW-*ed*
ed-ED

Quohaug **AUG**
see
OG

Gauge **AUGE**
see
AGE

Laugh **AUGH***
see
AFE

Faugh **AUGH****
see
AW

Aught, caught, distraught, dread-naught, fearnaught, fraught, naught, onslaught, self-taught, taught, un-taught, well-taught

AUGHT*
see
AUT*
OUGHT

Draught

AUGHT**
see
AFT

Haughty, naughty

AUGHTY
see
E**

Caterwaul, caul, Gaul, haul, maul, overhaul, Paul, Saul

AUL
see
AWL
ed-ALD

Assault, catapault, default, fault, somersault, treasure-vault, vault

AULT
see
ALT
s-ALTZ

Capernaum, meerschaum

AUM
see
UM

Faun, Marble Faun

AUN
see
AWN

Craunch, haunch, launch, paunch, staunch

AUNCH
see
ANCH**

Aunt, daunt, flaunt, gaunt, haunt, jaunt, taunt, vaunt

AUNT
see
ANT**
ed-ED
s-ONSE

Bucentaur, centaur, dinosaur, mino-taur, plesiosaur	**AUR** *see* OR
Epidaurus, ichthyosaurus, plesio-saurus, Taurus, thesaurus	**AURUS** *see* URUS US
Santa Claus	**AUS** *see* AUSE
Applause, because, cause, clause, pause	**AUSE** *see* AUS AW-*s*
Exhaust, Faust, holocaust	**AUST** *see* OST*
Gauze	**AUZE** *see* AUSE
Aeronaut, Argonaut, juggernaut, taut	**AUT*** *see* AUGHT*
Sauerkraut	**AUT*** *see* OUT
Nautch	**AUTCH** *see*

Mauve	**AUVE** *see* OVE*
Slav	**AV** *see* AVE**
Ava, Balaklava, Bhairava, cassava, guava, Java, lava	**AVA** *see* A**
Aggravate, excavate	**AVATE** *see* ATE
Architrave, behave, brainwave, brave, cave, close shave, concave, conclave, crave, deprave, engrave, enslave, forgave, galley-slave, grave, hairwave, heatwave, Hertzian wave, knave, lave, marcel wave, margrave, misbehave, nave, octave, pilgrim-stave, quarry-slave, rave, save, sea-wave, shave, shortwave, slave, stave, tidal wave	**AVE*** *see* AIVE
Have	**AVE**** *see* AV
Caravel, gavel, gravel, navel, ravel, travel, unravel	**AVEL** *see* EL LE
Craven, engraven, haven, heaven, leaven, raven, smooth-shaven	**AVEN** *see* EN

Cadaver, claver, engraver, graver, palaver, quaver, shaver, waver

AVER
see
ER

Gravy, navy, wavy

AVY
see
E**

Blue law, bucksaw, cat's-paw, caw, Choctaw, claw, coleslaw, draw, flaw, forepaw, foresaw, gew-gaw, guffaw, handsaw, haw, hee-haw, in-law, jackdaw, jackstraw, jaw, jig-saw, kickshaw, law, lockjaw, macaw, mackinaw, maw, outlaw, paw, pawpaw, pshaw, raw, rickshaw, Saginaw, Salic Law, scrollsaw, see-saw, straw, taw, thaw, underjaw, Warsaw, withdraw

AW
see
AWE
UAW
ed-AUD
s-AUSE
OR-*s*

Away, caraway, castaway, fadeaway, far-away, fly-away, rockaway, runaway, stayaway, stowaway, straightaway, while away

AWAY
see
A**

Bawdry, tawdry

AWDRY
see
E**

Awe, overawe

AWE
see
AW

Awk, fish-hawk, gawk, henhawk, Mohawk, moulting-hawk, news hawk, sparrowhawk, squawk, tomahawk

AWK
see
ALK
y-E**

Awl, bawl, brawl, cawl, crawl, drawl, goat-shawl, scrawl, shawl, sprawl, trawl, yawl

AWL
see
UALL
ed-ALD

Brawn, dawn, day-dawn, deep-drawn, drawn, false-dawn, fawn, lawn, long-drawn, overdrawn, pawn, prawn, rosy-fingered dawn, sawn, spawn, with-drawn, yawn

AWN
see
ARN**
ONE**
ORN

Ajax, anthrax, anti-climax, battle-ax, bees-wax, borax, climax, flax, Hali-fax, head-tax, income tax, lax, opopa-nax, overtax, Pax, pickax, poll-tax, relax, sealing-wax, smilax, surtax, syn-tax, tax, thorax, toad-flax, wax, zax

AX*
see
AC-*s*
ACHS
ACK-*s*
ACT-*s*

Coax, hoax

AX**
see
OKE-*s*

Affray, airway, allay, All Fool's Day, All Soul's Day, alpha-ray, alway, any-way, Appian Way, arbor day, archway, array, assay, astray, ay, bay, Bay of Biscay, belay, beta-ray, betray, blue-jay, Bombay, Botany, Bay, bray, breakfast tray, by-play, byway, Ca-thay, causeway, Charlotte Corday, clay, cutaway, dapple-gray, daresay, day, decay, defray, delay, disarray, dismay, display, doomsday, doorway, dray, everyday, essay, fast day, fay, field day, flay, foray, fray, Friday, gainsay, gamma-ray, gangway, gay, gray, half-pay, halfway, hatchway,

AY
see
A*
AWAY
EIGH
EY
UAY
UET**
ed-ADE*
AID*
s-A*-*s*
AISE
AIZE
ASE**
AYS

hay, headway, heyday, highway, holi- **AY**
day, horseplay, hurray, inlay, jay,
Judgment-day, lamp-ray, Labor-day,
lay, leeway, mainstay, Malay, Manda-
lay, man Friday, market-day, mascu-
line-array, may, midday, midway,
Milky-Way, miracle-play, mislay,
Monday, Mother's day, natal-day,
nay, noonday, Norway, nosegay, now-
aday, N-ray, Ojibway, outlay, out-of-
the-way, outstay, passageway, Passion
Play, pathway, pay, photo-play, play,
popinjay, portray, pray, prepay, pri-
vate-way, railway, ray, redletter day,
relay, repay, roundelay, runaway, run-
way, Saint's-Day, Saturday, say, shay,
silver-gray, slay, sluice-way, soothsay,
speedway, spillway, splay, spray, stay,
sting ray, stray, subway, Sunday,
sway, tag-day, Thursday, today, To-
kay, Tuesday, ultra violet ray, under-
pay, underway, war-array, water-way,
waylay, Wednesday, welladay, Whit-
sunday, workaday, X-ray, yesterday

Himalaya, Maya **AYA**
see
A**

Assayer, layer, payer, piano-player, **AYER**
prayer, slayer, soothsayer, sprayer, *see*
taxpayer ER

Bygone-days, fable-days, now-a- **AYS**
days, salad days, side-ways *see*
AY-*S*

Alcatraz, Boaz, Shiraz, topaz   **AZ**
see
AS**
AZZ

Ormazd   **AZD**
see

Ablaze, amaze, blaze, craze, daze,   **AZE**
emblaze, faze, gaze, glaze, haze, maze,   *see*
raze, stargaze   AISE
AY-*s*
y-AZY

Bombazine, magazine   **AZINE**
see
INE**

Amazon, blazon, emblazon   **AZON**
see
ON

Jazz   **AZZ**
see
AZ

Crazy, glazy, hazy, lazy   **AZY**
see
E**

E SOUNDS

Acme, adobe, agape, Ananke, ane-
mone, Aphrodite, Ariadne, Astarte,
Ate, be, bene, campanile, Chile, Chloe,
Circe, Comanche, Cybele, Danae,
Daphne, dele, Don Quixote, epitome,
Euterpe, evoe, festina lente, finale,
fricasse, Ganymede, Ge, Gethsemane,
Goethe, he, Hebe, Il Trovatore, King
Rene, Lao-Tse, Lethe, macrame, may-
be, me, m.d., Melpomene, Miserere,
Mitylene, Nepenthe, netsuke, Nike,
Niobe, nota bene, padre, phoebe,
Phryne, Proserpine, Psyche, recipe,
sake, salame, Selene, Semele, sesame,
she, sotto voce, stele, tele, the, tse-tse,
ukulele, Ultima Thule, viva-voce, we,
would-be, Yangtse, ye, Zantippe

E*
see
A*

Abruptly, accordingly, adroitly,
Allegheny, amply, anchovy, angry,
anomaly, army, aunty, avowedly,
baby, badly, bankruptcy, bel-esprit,
belfry, belly, biddy, bigotry, blackly,
blameworthy, Blavatsky, blindly,
bloodthirsty, booby, bossy, brawny,
briskly, buddy, buggy, bunchy, Bur-
gundy, bushy, busy, caddy, calumny,
canopy, certainly, certainty, cheeky,
chiefly, choosy, chunky, clingingly,

E**
see
ABBY
ABLY
ACITY
ACY
ADY
AE
AIN-*ly*
AINT-*ly*
AIRY

clumsy, cocky, colonelcy, conspiracy, controversy, copy, corruptly, country, county, coyly, cozy, crafty, cuppy, curtly, daily, daisy, darkly, deftly, deucedly, dicky, dingy, dirty, doughty, downy, dowry, dreary, drowsy, dumpy, early, easy, eighty, elegy, empty, entreaty, envy, epilepsy, eurythmy, faulty, fifty-fifty, filthy, finicky, fishy, flaky, flatly, fleshy, flimsy, flinty, flossy, flunky, fool-hardy, forestry, forty, frailty, frenzy, freshly, friendly, frisky, frosty, frowsy, fusty, fuzzy, galaxy, garden-party, gaudy, gawky, gayly, ghostly, glossy, godly, goodly, goofy, gossipy, gramercy, greatly, grimy, grisly, grouchy, grumpy, guilty, half-empty, haply, happy-go-lucky, harpy, hazy, heady, healthy, heathenishly, heavy, hoity-toity, honestly, hooky, horny, huffy, husbandry, hypocrisy, idiocy, imperiously, industry, inly, Italy, ivy, jaunty, jelly, jeopardy, Jewry, jiffy, jointly, jolly, jumpy, kilty, kindly, kingly, lanky, larceny, leafy, lethargy, liberty, Lombardy, lousy, lucky, lumpy, lycanthropy, mammy, meaty, mercy, mimicry, minstrelsy, miry, missy, misty, monopoly, mostly, mouldy, muchly, muddy, mumsy, Muscovy, namby-pamby, narrowly, natty, nearly, neatly, neighborly, nervy, newly, newsy, nifty, nightly, nimbly, nippy, noisy, noteworthy, novelty, oily, oozy, orgy, outlawry, overstudy, paddy, palfry, palsy, paltry, panicky, panoply, pansy, partly,

E**

AL-*y*
ALDRY
ALITY
ALLY
ALRY
ALTHY
ALTY
AMY
ANCY
ANDY
ANITY
ANNY
ANT*-*ly*
ANTE
ANTRY
ANTY
ANY
APHY
APPY
ARCHY
ARDLY
ARITY
ARLY
ARRY
ARY
ASSY
ASTLY
ASTY
ASY
ATELY
ATHY
ATORY
ATRY
AUGHTY
AVY
AZY

party, pastry, patty, pebbly, perfidy, perilously, perky, pesky, philanthropy, pigmy, pithy, pixy, plucky, podgy, poky, polyandry, poppy, porphyry, pot-belly, poultry, praiseworthy, priestly, priory, privy, progeny, pudgy, Punch and Judy, puppy, pussy, rainy, raspy, ready, regularly, remedy, revelry, risky, rocky, roughly, ruby, ruddy, Rugby, rusty, rutty, sacristy, saintly, saucy, scaly, scraggy, scratchy, scrawny, scurvy, seaworthy, secretly, sentry, shabby, sharply, sharpy, shifty, shindy, shoddy, sightly, sissy, sketchy, slangy, slightingly, slimy, smithy, smugly, snoozy, snugly, softly, softy, solemnly, sooty, sovereignty, sparingly, speak-easy, spiffy, spongy, sporty, sprightly, spunky, squally, steady, stealthy, stingy, stocky, strategy, study, subsidy, sultry, superbly, surly, suzerainty, swanky, swarthy, tansy, tantivy, tapestry, tawdry, tawny, taxidermy, tetchy, theory, therapy, Thessaly, thinly, third-party, thirty, thorny, thoroughly, thrifty, throaty, tidy, timothy, toady, toby, toddy, tootsy-wootsy, topsy-turvy, trebly, tricky, twenty, ugly, understudy, unearthly, uneasy, unerringly, unfriendly, ungainly, unknowingly, unlucky, unsteady, unwieldy, veery, vestry, villainy, wanly, waxy, wealthy, weary, weekly, wheezy, whimsy, willingly, windy, wintry, wishy-washy, wooly, wordy, wormy, worry, worthy, wrongly, yearly

E**

EA*
EALTH-*y*
ECTLY
ECY
EDY
EE
EEDY
ELRY
ELY
EMY
ENARY
ENCY
ENLY
ENNY
ENTLY
ENTRY
ENTY
ERGY
ERITY
ERLY
ERRY
ERY
ESTY
ESY
ETRY
ETTY
ETY
EVY
EWY
EY**
I**
IARY
IBLY
ICACY
ICITY
ICKLE

E**

ICY
IDITY
IDLY
IE*
IETY
IGHTY
IGY
ILITY
ILLY
ILY
INARY
ING-*ly*
INKY
INNY
INTLY
INY
IPSY
IRACY
IRY
ISH-*ly*
ISKY
ISTRY
ITTY
ITY
IVERY
IVITY
OBBY
OCHE
ODY
OGGY
OGY
OLLY
OLY
OMY
ONLY
ONRY

E**

ONY
OODY
OPHY
OPPY
OQUY
ORITY
ORRY
ORY
OSITY
OSY
OSYNE
OTRY
OUSLY
OWDY
OWLY
OWY
UAL-_y_
UALLY
UARY
UBBY
UGGY
UITY
ULKY
ULLY
ULTY
ULY*
UMMY
UNDRY
UNDY
UNNY
UNY
UPTCY
URDY
URGY
URITY
URLY

E**

- URRY
- URTLY
- URY
- USTY
- USY
- UTTY
- UTY
- YE**
- *S*-EASE*
- IE*-*S*

Beeftea, blue-sea, cambric tea, chart-less sea, choppy sea, Dead Sea, flea, guinea, high-sea, lea, over sea, pea, plea, Red Sea, sea, sweet-pea, tea, undersea, unsailed-sea

EA*
see
E**
S-ADES*
EASE*

Adrastea, area, azalea, Boadicea, Bona Dea, cetacea, Chaldea, Crimea, Ea, Gaea, Galatea, hydrangea, Idumea, kea, Korea, Laodicea, Leucothea, Medea, nausea, panacea, Penthesilea, Rhea, spiræa, trachea

EA**
see
A**

Yea

EA***
see
A*

Changeable, impermeable, ineffaceable, malleable, peaceable, permeable, serviceable, sizeable, traceable, unchangeable

EABLE
see
EL
LE

Peace

EACE
see
EASE**

Beach, bleach, cleach, each, im-
peach, over-reach, peach, preach,
reach, teach

EACH
see
EECH
es-EZ

Beacon, deacon

EACON
see
ON

Arrow-head, balm of Gilead, bed-
spread, bedstead, behead, big-head,
block-head, Book of the Dead, bread,
brownbread, bulkhead, bullhead, cab-
bage-head, copperhead, dead, dead-
head, dread, drowsi-head, dunderhead,
figurehead, forehead, gingerbread, gor-
gon-head, hammer-head, head, hogs-
head, homestead, instead, lead, logger-
head, masthead, Oread, overhead,
overspread, pilot-bread, pinhead, read,
roadstead, Roundhead, saphead, shew-
bread, shortbread, sleepy-head, sore-
head, spearhead, spread, squarehead,
stead, sweetbread, thread, towhead,
tread, turtlehead, unread

EAD*
see
ACT-*ed*

Bead, knead, lead, mead, plead,
read, reread

EAD**
see
EDE

Breadth

EADTH
see
EDTH

Bay-leaf, clover-leaf, fallen-leaf, fig-
leaf, flyleaf, goldleaf, leaf, palm-leaf,
rose-leaf, sheaf

EAF*
see
EEF
IEF
S-EAVE-*S*

Deaf

EAF**
see
EF

Acreage, lineage, mileage

EAGE
see
AGE*

Beagle, eagle, gold-eagle, spread-eagle

EAGLE
see
EL
LE

Beak, bespeak, bleak, creak, freak, grosbeak, leak, outspeak, peak, sneak, speak, spring-aleak, squeak, streak, teak, tweak, weak, wreak

EAK*
see
EAKE
EEK
IQUE

Beefsteak, break, daybreak, heartbreak, outbreak, steak

EAK**
see
AKE

Anneal, appeal, armorial seal, cochineal, commonweal, conceal, congeal, deal, heal, leal, meal, misdeal, New Deal, oatmeal, peal, piecemeal, repeal, reveal, seal, self-heal, solomon's seal, squeal, steal, teal, veal, weal, zeal

EAL*
see
EEL
ILE**
ed-IELD

Realm

EALM
see
ELM

Dealt

EALT
see
ELT

Commonwealth, health, stealth, wealth **EALTH**
see
ly-E**

Beam, bream, coldcream, Cold-stream, cream, crossbeam, day-dream, Devonshire cream, dream, gleam, gulf-stream, hornbeam, ice-cream, mid-stream, moonbeam, ream, scream, seam, steam, stream, sunbeam, team **EAM**
see
EEM
IME**

Bean, bemean, clean, dean, demean, dry-clean, glean, jean, lean, mean, string-bean, unclean, wean, yean **EAN***
see
EEN
INE**

Atlantean, Caribbean, cerulean, ce-tacean, crustacean, Epicurean, Hercu-lean, hyperborean, Korean, Mediter-ranean, mid-ocean, nectarean, ocean, pæan, Promethean, protean, pygmean, subterranean, superterranean, terpsi-chorean, terranean, unknown-ocean **EAN****
see
AN*
EN
IEN*

Miscreant, pageant, recreant, ser-geant **EANT**
see
ANT*

Ash-heap, cheap, heap, leap, neap, reap, sand-heap **EAP**
see
EEP

Appear, blear, clear, crystal-clear, dear, disappear, dog-ear, drear, ear, endear, fear, gear, hear, King Lear, lean-year, leap-year, linear, lunar year, my dear, near, overhear, reappear, rear, sear, smear, solar year, spear, steering-gear, tear, year, yesteryear **EAR***
see
EER
ERE
IER
ed-EARD**

Bear, bugbear, forebear, Great Bear, koala bear, northern-bear, pear, polar-bear, prickly pear, swear, tear, teddy-bear, underwear, wear

EAR**
see
AIR
ARE*

Research, search

EARCH
see
ERCH
IRCH
URCH

Heard, overheard, unheard

EARD*
see
ERD
URD

Beard, Bluebeard, Old Man's beard, shaggy-beard

EARD**
see
EAR*-*ed*

Shakespeare

EARE
see
EER

Earl, mother-of-pearl, pearl, seed-pearl

EARL
see
IRL
URL

Earn, learn, unlearn, yearn

EARN
see
ERN
URN

Hearse, rehearse

EARSE
see
ERCE
ERSE
URSE

Bleeding-heart, broken-heart, faint-heart, heart, inmost-heart, sweetheart **EART**
see
ART*

Dearth, earth, fuller's earth, hearth, unearth **EARTH**
see
ERTH

Æneas, Boreas, pancreas **EAS***
see
AS*

Seven Seas **EAS****
see
ESE

Appease, disease, displease, ease, heartease, please **EASE***
see
ADES*
E*-*s*
EESE*

Axle-grease, cease, crease, decease, decrease, elbow-grease, increase, lease, release, surcease **EASE****
see
EECE
ed-IEST**

Leash **EASH**
see
EESH

High treason, rainy season, reason, season, treason **EASON**
see
ASON
ON

Beast, east, Far East, feast, least, love-feast, Near East, northeast, southeast, yeast

EAST*
see
IEST**
ISTE
YST**

Abreast, breast, redbreast

EAST**
see
EST

Aisle-seat, backseat, bearded-wheat, beat, bleat, box-seat, browbeat, buckwheat, cheat, cleat, countryseat, crabmeat, deadbeat, defeat, drumbeat, eat, entreat, feat, forcemeat, heartbeat, heat, maltreat, meat, mince-meat, mistreat, neat, overeat, peat, repeat, reseat, rustic-seat, seat, sweetmeat, treat, unseat, wheat

EAT*
see
EET
EIT*
ed-ED

Great

EAT**
see
EATE

Sweat, threat

EAT***
see
ET

Aureate, baccalaureate, create, laureate, miscreate, nauseate, permeate, procreate, recreate, roseate

EATE
see
ATE
EAT**

Beneath, bequeath, heath, 'neath, sheath, smoke-wreath, underneath, wreath

EATH*
see
EATHE
EETH

Breath, death | **EATH****
see
AITH**
ETH

Breathe, sheathe, unsheathe, wreathe | **EATHE**
see
EATH*

Cordovan leather, feather, heather, leather, pinfeather, sole leather, weather, white feather | **EATHER**
see
ER

Bandeau, beau, bureau, chateau, manteau, plateau, portmanteau, rondeau, Rousseau, tableau, tonneau, trousseau, weather bureau | **EAU**
see
O*

Bereave, cleave, eave, heave, interweave, leave, sheave, sick-leave, weave | **EAVE**
see
EEVE
EVE
S-EAF*-S

Beaver, weaver | **EAVER**
see
ER

Bab el Mandeb, cobweb, cubeb, deb, Horeb, neb, pleb, Seb, spider-web, web | **EB**
see
EBB

Debate, rebate | **EBATE**
see
ATE

Ebb | **EBB**
see
EB

Glebe, grebe, plebe

EBE
see

Algebra, zebra

EBRA
see
A**

Debt

EBT
see
ET

Aztec, Quebec, sec, spec, Toltec, xebec

EC
see
ECK

Deprecate, Hecate, hypothecate, imprecate

ECATE
see
ATE

Decent, indecent, recent

ECENT
see
ENT

Beck, bedeck, breakneck, by heck, check, crookneck, deck, fleck, flyspeck, gooseneck, henpeck, kopeck, leatherneck, longneck, low-neck, mizzen-deck, neck, peck, pinchbeck, quarter-deck, rebeck, recheck, reck, roughneck, rubberneck, shipwreck, smart-aleck, speck, stiff-neck, swan-neck, upperdeck, wreck

ECK
see
EK
EQUE
ed-ECT
s-EX

Freckle, heckle, speckle

ECKLE
see
EL
LE

Abject, affect, architect, bisect, circumspect, collect, confect, connect, correct, defect, deflect, deject, detect, dialect, direct, disinfect, disrespect, dissect, effect, eject, elect, erect, expect, genuflect, imperfect, incorrect, indirect, infect, inflect, inject, insect, inspect, intellect, intersect, introspect, neglect, object, perfect, pluperfect, prefect, prelect, project, prospect, protect, recollect, reflect, reject, respect, resurrect, retrospect, sect, select, self-respect, stage-effect, stick insect, subject, suspect

ECT
see
ECK-*ed*
S-ECK-S
EX

Correctly, directly, objectly, perfectly ⏎

ECTLY
see
E**

Collector, deflector, detector, director, elector, erector, Hector, inspector, projector, prospector, protector, rector, reflector, sector, stamp-collector, tax-collector

ECTOR
see
OR

Fleecy, prophecy, secrecy

ECY
see
E**

Accented, accosted, accredited, addle-pated, affrighted, aged, agitated, anointed, antiquated, barricaded, bed, beloved, benighted, bigoted, biped, bird-witted, bled, blended, blessed, bloodshed, bobsled, booted, bow-legged, branded, bred, brooded,

ED*
see
AID**
EAD
ID
IED**
UID

bruited, buffeted, carted, catfooted, close-fisted, coasted, cold-blooded, comforted, conceited, confounded, corroded, crabbed, crowned, cursed, darkred, defeated, deflected, disquieted, double-bed, dumbfounded, elated, elected, ended, evil-minded, fairminded, false-hearted, feather-bed, fed, fled, fretted, garden-bed, half-hearted, high-minded, hoisted, home-bred, honeyed, hot-bed, hot-headed, hundred, ill-bred, imbed, inbred, indebted, infrared, invented, jagged, jewel-studded, kilted, kindred, knotted, lamented, learned, led, left-handed, light-footed, long-winded, lowbred, Manfred, milkfed, misled, Mohammed, naked, narrow-minded, newly-wed, nodded, onesided, over-fed, oyster-bed, pixilated, precipated, prompted, quadruped, railroaded, recommended, red, red-handed, reported, resounded, restricted, resuscitated, sacred, Samoyed, shed, shredded, single-bed, single-handed, slab-sided, sled, snowshed, sober-minded, sped, spirited, spoon-fed, spotted, starknaked, stilted, stout-hearted, surefooted, talented, Tancred, thoroughbred, translated, trundle-bed, unabated, unaccented, uncomforted, underbred, underfed, unpolluted, unspotted, unsuited, untested, untranslated, unwarranted, unwed, unwonted, variegated, vested, wafted, watershed, well-fed, whole-hearted, wicked, wooded, woodshed, worsted, wretched, zed

ED*

ACT-*ed*
ANT*-*ed*
ASP-*ed*
AST-*ed*
ASTE-*d*
AUD-*ed*
AUNT-*ed*
EAD*-*ed*
EAT*-*ed*
EDE-*d*
END-*ed*
ET-*ed*
ICT-*ed*
IDE-*d*
IED**
IELD-*ed*
IFT-*ed*
IGHT-*ed*
ILT-*ed*
IT-*ed*
OAST-*ed*
OINT-*ed*
ORD*-*ed*
OST*-*ed*
ULT-*ed*
UTE-*d*

Accursed, airconditioned, Argus-eyed, backed, barelegged, beloved, bereaved, bleached, brazen-faced, breathed, caracoled, cloyed, cowled, cured, curtained, dark-eyed, dead-eyed, delved, deranged, drenched, drowsed, electrotyped, endorsed, enveloped, etched, far-fetched, fettered, flagged, fringed, frog-eyed, full-fledged, gnarled, gypped, hallowed, hardboiled, henpecked, horned, Janus-faced, keyed, landlocked, low-necked, mottled, mullioned, newly-wed, pampered, parcelled, peopled, petered, pillowed, refurbished, reserved, riprapped, rockribbed, scowled, sequestered, shamefaced, skewered, slant-eyed, smacked, snarled, so-called, star-spangled, stitched, strait-laced, stuccoed, swaybacked, tattered, tempered, threecornered, two-faced, unlettered, unpeopled, unreined, unremembered, unscathed, untrammeled, wed, wellgroomed, winced, winged, withered

ED**
see

Edda

EDDA
see
A**

Accede, antecede, cede, centipede, concede, expede, impede, intercede, precede, recede, rede, retrocede, secede, stampede, supersede, Swede, velocipede, Venerable Bede

EDE*
see
EED
ed-ED

Suede

EDE**
see
ADE

Dredge, edge, fledge, foreknowledge, kedge, keen-edge, knowledge, ledge, mountain-edge, on edge, pledge, sedge, selvedge, sledge, waters-edge, wedge

EDGE
see
AGE*
EAGE
EGE
IDGE

Comedian, median, tragedian

EDIAN
see
AN*
IAN

Accredit, credit, edit, discredit

EDIT
see
IT

Credo, teredo, Toledo, torpedo, tuxedo

EDO
see
O*

Hundredth

EDTH
see
EADTH

Aqueduct, deduct

EDUCT
see
UCT

Comedy, higgledy-piggledy, remedy, tragedy

EDY
see
E**

Absentee, agree, alee, apogee, ash-tree, banshee, bee, bootee, Bo-tree, bumblebee, calipee, carefree, Chaldee, Cherokee, chick-a-dee, chimpanzee, coatee, coffee, committee, conferee, Cree, debauchee, devotee, disagree,

EE
see
E**
IGREE
S-IES**
IEZE

divorcee, dungaree, elderberry-tree, **EE**
employee, fancy-free, fee, fiddle-dee-
dee, fig-tree, flee, foresee, free, fricassee,
fringe-tree, Galilee, garnishee, gee,
ghoulish-glee, glee, goatee, grandee,
guarantee, hard-alee, hat-tree, honey-
bee, indorsee, jamboree, jubilee, Judas-
tree, knee, lee, legatee, lessee, levee,
marquee, mulberry-tree, nominee, ogee,
oversee, parent-tree, Parsee, patentee,
Pawnee, payee, Pharisee, pledgee,
pongee, presentee, prithee, puttee,
quilting-bee, rappee, referee, refugee,
repartee, rupee, Sadducee, scot-free,
scree, see, set-free, settee, Shawnee,
shoe-tree, snicker-snee, soiree, spelling-
bee, spondee, spree, squeegee, suttee,
talkee-talkee, tee, te-hee, tepee, thee,
third degree, three, toffee, tree, trustee,
vendee, warrantee, wee, whoopee,
Yankee, Zuyder Zee

Fleece, golden-fleece, Greece **EECE**
see
EESE**

Beech, beseech, breech, leech, **EECH**
screech, speech, village-leech *see*
EACH
es-EZ

Agreed, aniseed, apostle's creed, **EED**
bindweed, birdseed, bleed, breed, *see*
chickweed, cotton-seed, creed, cross- EAD**
breed, decreed, deed, exceed, feed, flax- EDE
seed, freed, full speed, gleed, Godspeed, YD
greed, half-breed, hayseed, heed, in- *ed*-ED
deed, Indian weed, ironweed, jewel- *y*-EEDY

weed, knock-kneed, knotweed, linseed, meed, misdeed, need, overfeed, pigweed, pokeweed, poppy-seed, proceed, reed, screed, seaweed, seed, sneezeweed, speed, steed, stinkweed, succeed, title-deed, tobacco-weed, treed, tweed, weak-kneed, weed, whispering-reed **EED**

Darning needle, pine needle, needle, wheedle
EEDLE
see
EL
LE

Greedy, needy, reedy, seedy, speedy, weedy
EEDY
see
E**

Beef, coral-reef, reef, shereef
EEF
see
IEF

Cheek, cleek, creek, Greek, hide-and-seek, leek, meek, next-week, peek, reek, seek, sleek, week
EEK
see
EAK*
IEK
IQUE

Balance-wheel, cartwheel, chain-wheel, cogwheel, creel, despot's heel, eel, emery wheel, feel, Ferris-wheel, flywheel, genteel, heel, high-heel, Jezreel, keel, kneel, millwheel, newsreel, paddle-wheel, peel, potter's wheel, prayer wheel, reel, shabby-genteel, spinning-wheel, steel, Virginia reel, water-wheel, wheel
EEL
see
EAL*
ILE**
ed-IELD

Beseem, deem, esteem, redeem, **EEM**
seem, self-esteem, teem   *see*
                                  EME

Aberdeen, a-tween, baleen, between, **EEN**
bowling green, canteen, careen, Col-   *see*
leen, e'en, eighteen, fellaheen, fifteen,   EAN*
fourteen, go-between, green, Hallow-   ENE
e'en, has-been, keen, lateen, Maureen,   IEN**
might-have-been, nankeen, nineteen,   IENE
ocean-green, overween, Paris-green,   S-EENS
peen, preen, putting green, queen,
sateen, screen, sea-green, seen, seven-
teen, sheen, sixteen, smoke-screen,
spleen, thirteen, tureen, 'tween, ump-
teen, unseen, velveteen, village-green,
ween, wintergreen

Greens, smithereens, teens   **EENS**
                                    see
                                    EEN-*s*

Asleep, Bo-peep, cheep, chimney- **EEP**
sweep, clean sweep, creep, deep, don-   *see*
jon-keep, keep, knee-deep, oversleep,   EAP
peep, sheep, skin-deep, sleep, steep,
sweep, upkeep, weep, well-sweep, Uriah
Heep

Carpet-sweeper, creeper, deeper, **EEPER**
gamekeeper, housekeeper, keeper,   *see*
lighthouse-keeper, office seeker, peeper,   ER
seeker, sky-sleeper, steeper, sweeper

Auctioneer, beer, buccaneer, camel- **EER**
eer, carabineer, career, chanticleer,   *see*
charioteer, cheer, compeer, decreer,   EIR**

deer, domineer, engineer, fallow-deer, freer, gazetteer, ginger-beer, jeer, leer, mountaineer, muleteer, musk-deer, musketeer, mutineer, nearbeer, overseer, peer, pioneer, privateer, profiteer, queer, racketeer, reindeer, rootbeer, seer, sheer, sight-seer, sneer, spruce beer, steer, veer, veneer, volunteer

EER
ERE*
IER**
ed-EARD**

Lees, Maccabees, Pyrenees

EES
see
E**-*s*
EE-*s*
ES*

Cheese, creese, Edam cheese, head-cheese, Swiss cheese

EESE*
see
EASE*
EEZE

Geese

EESE**
see
EASE**
EECE
ESE
IS***

Baksheesh, hasheesh

EESH
see
EASH

Afreet, balance-sheet, beet, bitter-sweet, Blackfeet, crow's-feet, discreet, feet, fleet, greet, indiscreet, meadow-sweet, meet, parakeet, peet, proof-sheet, sheet, skeet, sleet, stern-sheet, stocking-feet, street, sweet, tweet, Wall Street, winding-sheet

EET
see
EIPT
EIT*
ETE*

Dragon's teeth, false teeth, teeth   **EETH**
see
EATH*

Seethe, teethe   **EETHE**
see
EATHE

Beeve, peeve, reeve, sleeve   **EEVE**
see
EIVE

Breeze, faintest-breeze, freeze, land-   **EEZE**
breeze, sneeze, squeeze, sweetscented-   *see*
breeze, wheeze   EASE*
EIZE
IEZE
IE*-*s*

Chef, clef   **EF**
see
EAF

Bereft, cleft, deft, heft, left, reft,   **EFT**
theft, weft   *see*

Defy, liquefy, putrefy, stupefy   **EFY**
see
I*

Bandy-leg, beg, cribbage-peg, dreg,   **EG**
keg, leg, mumbletypeg, nutmeg, peg   *see*
AGUE*
EGG

Illegal, legal, regal, vice-regal   **EGAL**
see
AL

Aggravate, congregate, delegate, legate, relegate, segregate **EGATE**
see
ATE

Allege, college, cortège, privilege, sacrilege **EGE**
see
EDGE
IDGE

China-egg, egg, nest-egg, ostrich-egg, yegg **EGG**
see
EG

Legion, region **EGION**
see
ION

Apothegm, phlegm **EGM**
see
EM

Abednego, alter ego, ego, forego **EGO**
see
O*

Daddylonglegs, dregs, sea-legs **EGS**
see
EG-*s*

Eh, El Gezireh, Gizeh, Nineveh, Tecumseh **EH**
see
A*

Lorelei **EI***
see
I*

Lei, rei **EI****
see
AY

Cassiopeia, hygeia, pharmacopæia **EIA**
see
IA

Nereid, Perseid **EID**
see
ID

Beige **EIGE**
see
EGE

Inveigh, neigh, outweigh, Raleigh, **EIGH**
sleigh, weigh *see*
EY*
ed-AID*

Eight, feather weight, freight, heavy- **EIGHT***
weight, hundred-weight, paperweight, *see*
pennyweight, weight ATE

Height, mountain-height, sleight **EIGHT****
see
IGHT

Deign, feign, foreign, reign, sover- **EIGN**
eign *see*
AIN

Nonpareil, unveil, veil **EIL***
see
AIL
ALE

Ceil **EIL****
see
EEL

Hussein, mullein, protein, Shin Fein, skein, vein **EIN***
see
AIN

Frankenstein, Holstein, Rubenstein, stein **EIN****
see
INE

Seine, vicereine **EINE**
see
AIN–

Being, fleeing, freeing, seeing **EING**
see
ING

Feint **EINT**
see
AINT

Receipt **EIPT**
see
EAT*

Heir, their **EIR***
see
ERE**

Weir **EIR****
see
EAR

Weird	**EIRD** *see* EARD** EAR-*ed*
Edelweiss, gneiss	**EISS** *see* ICE*
Conceit, deceit	**EIT*** *see* ETE
Albeit, counterfeit, forfeit	**EIT**** *see* IT
Deity, homogeneity, ipseity, seity, spontaneity	**EITY** *see* E** ITY
Apperceive, conceive, deceive, perceive, preconceive, receive	**EIVE** *see* IEVE*
Seize	**EIZE** *see* EEZE ES*
Baalbek, Melchizedek, Sebek, topek, trek, Vathek	**EK** *see* ECK
Eke	**EKE** *see* EEK

Angel, apparel, archangel, asphodel, **EL**
barrel, befel, Beth-el, brothel, calomel,   *see*
cancel, cantonflannel, chancel, channel,   ABEL
charnel, chattel, chisel, citadel, compel,   AEL
corbel, counsel, cudgel, damozel, dam-   AMEL
sel, dispel, easel, El, evangel, excel,   AVEL
expel, fardel, flannel, flour-barrel, gam-   ELL
brel, gimel, hazel, hostel, hydromel,   ENNEL
impel, infidel, Israfel, jewel, Jezebel,   EREL
kernel, kummel, lapel, laurel, libel,   ERYL
lintel, marvel, minstrel, missel, model,   EVEL
mongrel, morsel, Mount Carmel, mus-   IEL
catel, mussel, nickel, Noel, panel,   IVEL
parallel, parcel, pastel, personnel, pet-   OVEL
rel, pimpernel, pommel, pretzel, propel,   OWEL
quarrel, rebel, remodel, repel, rondel,   UEL
satchel, scalpel, scoundrel, scrannel,   UNNEL
sentinel, shekel, shrapnel, sorrel, span-   USEL
drel, stormy petrel, tael, tassel, tim-   YL
brel, tinsel, trammel, vessel, wastrel,   *ed*-ELD
weasel, Whitechapel, witch-hazel,   *y*-E**
woodsorrel, yodel, yokel   ELY

Addle, air-castle, amble, ample, **LE**
ankle, Aristotle, astraddle, axle, baffle,   *see*
bamboozle, battle, beagle, beetle,   ABBLE
boodle, bridle, bubble, bugle, bundle,   ABLE
bungle, burble, burgle, carbuncle,   ACKLE
castle, cat's-cradle, cattle, chortle,   ACLE
church-steeple, clientele, cockle, cod-   ADDLE
dle, Constantinople, couple, cradle,   AMBLE
crossword-puzzle, crumple, cuttle,   AMPLE
dawdle, dazzle, decuple, dingle, dis-   ANDLE
mantle, double, embezzle, empurple,   ANGLE
entitle, fettle, foible, fondle, foozle,   APPLE
forecastle, frazzle, gargle, gentle, gur-   ARBLE
gle, haggle, idle, inveigle, jungle,   ATTLE

kindle, kirtle, ladle, mantle, maple,
meddle, mollycoddle, monocle, mottle,
muffle, muscle, myrtle, new-fangle,
noodle, nozzle, octuple, ogle, oodle,
pebble, peddle, peduncle, people, piffle,
pinochle, poodle, purple, quadruple,
quintuple, raffle, rankle, razzle-dazzle,
reshuffle, Roman candle, rubble,
schnozzle, scuffle, septuple, shuffle,
shuttle, snaffle, snuffle, socle, spangle,
sparkle, stag-beetle, staple, startle,
stubble, subtle, supple, temple, tickle,
tinkle, tipple, title, toddle, tousle,
treacle, treadle, treble, trouble, truffle,
trundle, tussle, tweedle, uncle, un-
ruffle, waffle, waggle

LE

EABLE
EAGLE
ECKLE
EEDLE
ELLE
EMBLE
ESTLE
ETTLE
IABLE
IBBLE
IBLE
ICKLE
ICLE
IDDLE
IDLE
IFLE
IGGLE
IMBLE
IMPLE
INDLE
INGLE
INKLE
IPLE
IPPLE
IRCLE
ISTLE
ITTLE
IZZLE
OBBLE
OBLE
OGGLE
OPLE
OSTLE
UBLE
UCKLE
UDDLE

LE
UGGLE
UMBLE
URDLE
URTLE
USTLE
UZZLE
YCLE

Belate, elate, prelate, relate   **ELATE**
see
ATE

Belch, squelch   **ELCH**
see

Beheld, eld, geld, held, meld, upheld, weld, withheld   **ELD**
see
EL-*ed*

Veldt   **ELDT**
see
ELT

Careless, defenceless, gestureless, guileless, homeless, lifeless, measure-less, nevertheless, noiseless, priceless, purposeless, senseless, shameless, shoe-less, spaceless, tasteless, timeless, use-less, vagueless, valueless, verdureless, wireless   **ELESS**
see
ES**
ESCE
ESS

Bandelet, bracelet, corselet, ocelet, omelet, wavelet   **ELET**
see
ET

Delf, elf, herself, himself, itself, my-self, oneself, pantry-shelf, pelf, self, shelf, thing-in-itself, thyself, yourself   **ELF**
see

Twelfth   **ELFTH**
                                       see

Elia, Cordelia, lobelia, Ophelia,   **ELIA**
parahelia   *see*
                                       IA

Goblin, javelin, zeppelin   **ELIN**
                                       see
                                       IN

Elk   **ELK**
                                       see

Alarum-bell, ankle-bell, artesian   **ELL**
well, befell, bell, blue-bell, bombshell,   *see*
buy-and-sell, cell, churchbell, cockle-   EL
shell, convent bell, cowbell, curfewbell,   ELLE
dell, diving-bell, doorbell, dumb-bell,
dwell, eggshell, ell, fare-thee-well, fare-
well, fell, foretell, ground swell, hare-
bell, heather-bell, hell, jell, knell, mis-
spell, nutshell, Oliver Cromwell, over-
sell, pell-mell, quell, resell, retell,
school-bell, seashell, sell, shell, sleigh-
bell, smell, spell, swell, tell, tortoise-
shell, vesper-bell, well, whitewashed-
cell, William Tell, yell

Capella, citronella, fenestrella, Isa-   **ELLA**
bella, nigella, pimpinella, predella,   *see*
prunella, stella, tarantella, umbrella,   A**
villanella

Bagatelle, coutelle, damozelle, fon-   **ELLE**
tanelle, Gabrielle, gazelle, immortelle,   *see*
La Pucelle, mademoiselle, Moselle,   ELL
nacelle, spirituelle, villanelle

Dardanelles
ELLES
see
ELL-*S*

Bookseller, screw propeller, speller, story-teller, teller
ELLER
see
ER

Cello, hello, martello, Othello, punchinello, violoncello
ELLO
see
O*

Bed-fellow, fellow. Longfellow, mellow, yellow
ELLOW
see
O*
OW*

Elm, helm, overwhelm, slippery-elm, St. Anselm, whelm
ELM
see
EALM

Felon, Fenelon, melon, watermelon
ELON
see
ON

Help, kelp, whelp, yelp
ELP
see

Hostelry, jewelry, revelry
ELRY
see
E**

Else
ELSE
see

Belt, delt, dwelt, felt, heartfelt, knelt, lifebelt, melt, pelt, smelt, spelt, welt
ELT
see
EALT

Svelte **ELTE**
see
ELT

Helter-skelter, shelter, swelter, welter **ELTER**
see
ER

Delve, helve, shelve, twelve **ELVE**
see
S-ELVES

Elves, ourselves, selves, shelves, **ELVES**
themselves, yourselves *see*
ELVE-S

Antiquely, blithely, chastely, coarse- **ELY**
ly, comely, completely, concretely, *see*
contumely, conversely, crudely, di- ATELY
vinely, entirely, exquisitely, freely, E**
homely, inanely, infinitely, intuitively, EL-y
lately, leisurely, lithely, loosely, lovely,
merely, naïvely, namely, obliquely,
obtrusively, precisely, princely, pro-
fusely, purely, rarely, relatively, rely,
safely, savagely, scarcely, shapely,
sincerely, solely, sorely, strangely, sub-
limely, supremely, surely, tamely,
tensely, timely, unlovely, untimely,
vaguely, wifely

Ad valorem, anadem, anthem, be- **EM**
gem, cave canem, diadem, emblem, *see*
gem, harem, hem, ibidem, idem, item, AM
Jerusalem, Moslem, poem, postmor- ASM
tem, problem, proem, pro tem, sachem, EGM
Shem, solar system, stem, stratagem, EMN
system, tandem, them, theorem, totem, IAM
Zemzem IEM

Alma Tadema, anathema, cinema, eczema, ulema

EMA
see
A*

December, dismember, ember, member, November, remember, September

EMBER
see
ER

Assemble, dissemble, reassemble, resemble, tremble, tout ensemble

EMBLE
see
EL
LE

Bireme, blaspheme, Carême, extreme, La Bohème, quinquereme, scheme, supreme, theme, trireme

EME
see
EAM
IME**

Accoutrement, achievement, acquirement, amusement, assuagement, at-one-ment, attunement, bereavement, casement, cement, cerement, chastisement, clement, denouement, displacement, divulgement, element, embezzlement, encouragement, enlargement, escapement, excitement, impalement, implement, improvement, inclement, infringement, management, measurement, movement, pavement, postponement, pronouncement, refinement, reimbursement, reinforcement, requirement, retirement, settlement, sub-basement, supplement, tenement, vehement

EMENT
see
ENT

Bessemer, blasphemer, schemer

EMER
see
ER

Condemn, contemn, solemn   **EMN**
see
EM

Demon, lemon   **EMON**
see
ON

Hemp   **EMP**
see

Attempt, contempt, exempt, pre-   **EMPT**
empt, tempt, unkempt   *see*

Academy, alchemy, blasphemy,   **EMY**
Domremy, enemy, Ptolemy   *see*
E**

Aden, ashen, Aten, auf wiedersehen,   **EN**
barren, batten, begotten, beholden,   *see*
bitten, boughten, brazen, brethren,   AMEN
brighten, burden, chicken, chosen,   AKEN
cozen, crestfallen, dampen, darken,   ASTE-*n*
delicatessen, den, dew-beladen, Dolly   AVEN
Varden, dolmen, down-trodden, dozen,   EAN**
Dryden, Eden, embolden, enliven,   EMEN
fatten, fen, flaxen, forbidden, forgot-   ENNE
ten, foughten, frighten, frozen, Galen,   EVEN
garden, gentlemen, glen, glisten, glu-   IEN*
ten, goose-pen, Goshen, gotten, guinea-   IMEN
hen, harden, hasten, heathen, heavy-   IZEN
laden, hen, herb-garden, hidden, hoy-   OGEN
den, Hymen, hyphen, idle-pen, ill-   OKE-*n*
gotten, ken, kindergarten, kinsmen,   OKEN
kitchen, kitten, laden, lengthen, lenten,   OMEN
lessen, lichen, lighten, liken, linden,   OVEN
linen, listen, madden, mad-men, Mag-   UMEN

dalen, maiden, marshy-fen, men, men-haden, mitten, mizzen, moisten, molten, mullen, Munchausen, new-fallen, oaken, oaten, often, olden, open, Origen, overladen, paten, pen, pig-pen, pollen, poverty-stricken, quicken, quill-pen, redden, re-open, risen, roof-garden, rotten, sadden, Saracen, schoolmen, silken, siren, smarten, soften, storm-driven, strength-en, stricken, sudden, sullen, swollen, table-linen, ten, terror-stricken, then, thicken, tungsten, unforsaken, un-loosen, untrodden, vestry-men, vixen, warden, warren, waxen, weather-beat-en, wen, when, whiten, wooden, worm-eaten, wren, written, Yemen, yen

EN
YGEN
ly-E**
s-ENS

Arena, Athena, duena, hyena, no-vena, phenomena, philopena, Porsena, prolegomena, subpœna, verbena

ENA
see
A**

Grenade, hand-grenade, promenade, serenade

ENADE
see
ADE*

Arsenal, Juvenal, phenomenal, venal

ENAL
see
AL

Centenary, mercenary, septenary

ENARY
see
ARY

Hyphenate, oxygenate, rejuvenate, senate

ENATE
see
ATE

Absence, abstinence, acquiescence, adolescence, appetence, back fence, belligerence, cadence, circumference, coincidence, commence, condolence, conference, confidence, continence, corpulence, correspondence, credence, decadence, defence, difference, diffidence, diligence, divergence, divulgence, effulgence, eminence, essence, evidence, excellence, excrescence, fence, Florence, florescence, fraudulence, hence, immanence, impertinence, impotence, impudence, inadvertence, incandescence, incidence, incompetence, inconsequence, independence, indigence, indolence, indulgence, inference, influence, innocence, insistence, intelligence, interference, intumescence, iridescence, irreverence, jurisprudence, lapidescence, magnificence, negligence, non-occurrence, occurrence, offence, omnipotence, omnipresence, opulence, par-excellence, pence, penitence, persistence, Peter-pence, petrescence, phosphorescence, pre-eminence, preference, presence, prevalence, prominence, Provence, providence, prudence, quintessence, recurrence, redolence, reference, reminiscence, renascence, residence, resplendence, resurgence, reticence, reverence, self-defence, senescence, silence, sixpence, snake fence, subsistence, sufferance, thence, tower-of-silence, transference, turbulence, violence, virulence, whence

ENCE
see
ANCE
ANT*-*s*
ENSE
ENT-*s*
IENCE
UENCE

Bench, blench, clench, drench, French, intrench, monkey-wrench,

ENCH
see

oak-bench, quench, retrench, stench, stone-bench, trench, unclench, wench, workbench, wrench   **ENCH**

Agency, appetency, clemency, cogency, cognency, competency, consistency, constituency, contingency, currency, decency, deficiency, delinquency, despondency, efficiency, emergency, exigency, fervency, frequency, impotency, inadvertency, incipiency, inclemency, inconsistency, incumbency, independency, indigency, infrequency, leniency, nascency, patency, permanency, persistency, pertinency, potency, pungency, regency, tendency, transparency   **ENCY**
see
E**

Amend, append, ascend, attend, befriend, bend, blend, candle-end, commend, comprehend, condescend, contend, defend, depend, descend, distend, dividend, emend, end, expend, extend, fend, forfend, friend, Godsend, impend, intend, interblend, legend, lend, mend, offend, pend, perpend, portend, pretend, recommend, rend, reprehend, reverend, send, spend, superintend, suspend, tail-end, tend, transcend, trend, unbend, vend, vilipend, wend, Zend   **END**
see
UEND
ed-ED
ly-E**

Addenda, agenda, hacienda   **ENDA**
see
A**

Bartender, defender, double-ender, engender, expender, fender, gender, lavender, legal-tender, mender, offend-   **ENDER**
see
ER

er, pretender, provender, sea-lavender, **ENDER**
spender, surrender, suspender, tender

Crescendo, diminuendo, innuendo **ENDO**
see
O*

Calends, odds-and-ends **ENDS**
see
END-*S*

Acetylene, contravene, convene, **ENE**
damascene, epicene, ethylene, gan- *see*
grene, hygiene, intervene, kerosene, EEN
Magdalene, Nazarene, Nicene, ob- IEN**
scene, pliocene, pyrene, scene, serene, INE**
supervene

Eye-opener, gardener, listener, scriv- **ENER**
ener *see*
ER

Genet, Plantagenet, tenet **ENET**
see
ET

Ginseng **ENG**
see
ING

Avenge, challenge, lozenge, revenge, **ENGE**
scavenge, Stonehenge *see*

Length, strength, wave-length, **ENGTH**
whole-length *see*

Armenia, gardenia, Iphigenia, millenia, neomania

ENIA
see
IA

Arsenic, eugenic, hygienic, Saracenic, scenic

ENIC
see
IC

Amenity, serenity

ENITY
see
ITY

Evenly, heavenly, keenly, openly, queenly, slovenly, suddenly

ENLY
see
EN-*ly*

Antenna, Avicenna, gehenna, henna, Porsenna, senna, Sienna, Vienna

ENNA
see
ENA

Cayenne, comedienne, Parisienne, tragedienne

ENNE
see
EN

Fennel, kennel

ENNEL
see
EL

Catch-penny, fenny, fippenny, ha'-penny, penny, spinning-jenny

ENNY
see
E**

Amiens, Athens, Camoëns, Dickens, dozens, homo sapiens, lens, nolens volens, wooded glens

ENS
see
EN-*s*

Condense, dense, dispense, expense, **ENSE**
frankincense, horse sense, immense, *see*
incense, intense, license, nonsense, ENCE
offense, pretense, recompense, sense, ENT-*s*
suspense, tense

Censer, condenser, denser **ENSER**
see
ER

Abhorrent, accent, acknowledgment, **ENT**
adjournment, adolescent, adornment, *see*
advent, albescent, alignment, amend- ACENT
ment, annulment, antecedent, apart- AGENT
ment, arborescent, ardent, argent, ALENT
arpent, ascent, astonishment, astring- AMENT
ent, bent, bewilderment, bombard- ECENT
ment, brazen serpent, cent, cerement, EMENT
circumfluent, circumvent, cogent, com- ERENT
ment, competent, consent, consign- ICENT
ment, consistent, content, convergent, IDENT
co-respondent, correspondent, crescent, IENT
current, decadent, descent, deterrent, IMENT
diligent, disalignment, discernment, INENT
discontent, dissent, divergent, em- OLENT
bankment, emulgent, encampment, ONENT
endearment, enjoyment, enrollment, UENT
enthralment, environment, equipment, ULENT
escarpment, establishment, evanescent, ULGENT
event, excellent, existent, extent, fer- UMENT
ment, fervent, foment, fragment, ful- *ly*-ENTLY
filment, gent, Ghent, horrent, ill- *s*-ENCE
content, impellent, impotent, inad-
vertent, incandescent, incoherent, in-
competent, inconsistent, incumbent,
indent, independent, indictment, in-
digent, innocent, insolvent, insurgent,

ENT

intelligent, intent, interlucent, intermittent, intumescent, invent, iridescent, judgment, lambent, latent, latescent, lent, lucent, magnificent, maladjustment, malcontent, nascent, nonexistent, non-payment, oddment, ointment, omnipotent, omnipresent, opalescent, parchment, parent, patent, payment, pendent, penitent, pent, percent, permanent, persistent, phosphorescent, pigment, potent, precedent, present, prevent, prudent, pschent, pungent, punishment, putrescent, quiescent, ravishment, recent, red cent, redolent, refreshment, refringent, refulgent, regent, relent, re-lucent, reminiscent, rent, repellent, repent, resent, resentment, resplendent, respondent, resurgent, retrenchment, rodent, scent, segment, senescent, sent, serpent, shipment, silent, solvent, spent, stringent, student, superincumbent, superintendent, talent, tangent, tent, torment, torrent, transcendent, translucent, transparent, treatment, tumescent, Turkish crescent, unbent, under-current, underwent, unravelment, urgent, vent, vestment, vice-regent, well-content, went

ENTAL
see
AL

Accidental, continental, detrimental, elemental, experimental, fundamental, incidental, instrumental, mental, monumental, occidental, Oriental, ornamental, parental, regimental, rental, sacramental, temperamental, transcontinental

Carpenter, center, enter, re-enter, renter, self-center — **ENTER** *see* ER

Eleventh, n-th, seventh, tenth — **ENTH** *see*

Amentia, dementia — **ENTIA** *see* IA

Eloquently, eminently, frequently, gently, innocently, intently, patiently, penitently, permanently, presently, prominently, prudently — **ENTLY** *see* E** ENT-*ly*

Memento, pimento — **ENTO** *see* O*

Entry, gentry, sentry — **ENTRY** *see* E**

Plenty, twenty, seventy — **ENTY** *see* E**

Borneo, Camdeo, cameo, Galileo, Laus Deo, Leo, Montevideo, nil sine Deo, rodeo, Romeo, vireo — **EO** *see* O*

Sheol — **EOL** *see* OL

Anacreon, bludgeon, burgeon, cameleon, clay pigeon, curmudgeon, dudgeon, dungeon, eon, escutcheon, gal- — **EON** *see* ON leon, Gideon, luncheon, melodeon, Napoleon, neon, Odeon, pantheon, peon, pigeon, stoolpigeon, sturgeon, surgeon, truncheon, widgeon

EON

Alliaceous, aqueous, argillaceous, beauteous, cinereous, consanguineous, contemporaneous, courageous, courteous, erroneous, fabaceous, ferreous, gallinaceous, gaseous, gorgeous, heterogeneous, hideous, homogeneous, igneous, instantaneous, ligneous, malvaceous, miscellaneous, osseous, outrageous, papaveraceous, piteous, righteous, saponaceous, simultaneous, spontaneous, subaqueous, subterraneous, succedaneous, terraqueous, vitreous

EOUS
see
AMUS
EUS*
IOUS
OUS
UOUS
US
ly-OUSLY

Amenhotep, doorstep, footstep, goose step, instep, lockstep, mintjulep, misstep, overstep, pep, prep, quick step, rep, side-step, step, two-step

EP
see
S-EPS

Crêpe

EPE
see
APE

Steppe

EPPE
see
EP

Biceps, corbiesteps, forceps

EPS
see
EP-S

Accept, adept, concept, crept, except, inept, intercept, kept, percept, precept, slept, stept, swept, transept, unkept, well-kept, wept, wind-swept, yclept

EPT
see

Pepys

EPYS
see
EEP-*s*

Cheque

EQUE
see
ECK

Adder, adorer, alter, amber, angel water, antler, archer, artificer, assayer, astrologer, babbler, backwater, badger, Baedeker, banker, banner, banter, barber, bather, bellwether, berserker, billposter, blather, blue-singer, boiler, bolster, boner, booster, bootlegger, bouncer, breakwater, broiler, bungstarter, bunker, butler, buyer, buzzer, caliber, camper, Cancer, canter, Casper, chamber, chandler, chapter, charger, Chaucer, checker, chiseler, choler, chooser, chorister, cipher, clabber, clapper, clinker, cloister, cobbler, conceiver, condoler, confer, conger, consumer, costumer, cowcatcher, coworker, creeper, cricketer, crosser, cruiser, dabster, dagger, dapper, daughter, decanter, deceiver, decipher, differ, dissenter, dodder, draper, drawer, dredger, dresser, dulcimer, duller, duster, eager, Easter, either, elder, embroider, encounter, err,

ER
see
ACKER
ACRE
ADER
AFTER
AGER
AILER
AITER
AKER
AMER
AMPER
ANDER
ANGER
APER
APPER
ARER
ARTER
ARTYR
ASHER
ASTER
ATER
ATRE

Esther, etcher, ether, exploiter, falter, farmer, farther, faster, father, feeler, fibber, fiber, filter, fire-eater, flivver, fodder, follower, forefather, forefinger, forerunner, former, foster, four poster, frankfurter, free-thinker, free trader, fuller, further, gambler, gangster, garner, gather, geyser, Gheber, gibber, golfer, grandfather, greater, greengrocer, grosser, gutter, halter, hammer, hanger, hanker, harder, hawker, hawser, headquarter, heather, heckler, heifer, helicopter, her, hill-climber, holster, hostler, huckster, hunger, idler, importer, improper, infer, inter, jabber, Jacob's ladder, jammer, jasper, jaw-breaker, jaywalker, juggler, kilter, kosher, laborer, ladder, lamplighter, lancer, larder, larger, lather, laughter, launder, lawyer, leader, ledger, leper, lesser, lifer, lighter, linen duster, lobster, loiter, longer, loud speaker, lounger, Luther, madder, man-eater, maneuver, manner, manslaughter, marker, masher, meager, merger, Mesmer, milder, mineral water, minister, minster, miter, monger, monster, mossbunker, mouser, muffler, mummer, murder, necromancer, ne'er, neither, neuter, news-monger, no-whither, officer, oldster, onlooker, ostler, outer, oyster, pacer, panther, partner, passenger, paternoster, pauper, peddler, pepper, performer, pewter, pilfer, pitcher, planter, platter, player, plumber, plunder, plunger, poacher, Poet's Corner, pointer, porker,

ER
ATTER
ATYR
AUR
AVER
AYER
EATHER
EEPER
ELLER
ELTER
EMBER
EMER
ENDER
ENER
ENSER
ENTER
EPHYR
ERER
ERR
ESTER
ETER
ETHER
ETRE
ETTER
EUR
EVER
EWER
IAR
IBRE
ICKER
IDER
IDITY
IER
IFER
IGGER
ILDER
ILER

potato-masher, pouter, preacher, pre-
fer, presbyter, primer, producer,
prompter, proof-reader, propeller,
proper, prosper, psalter, Ptolemy Soter,
pucker, punster, purser, quarter, quicksilver, quitter, racer, rather, rath-
skeller, rattler, reconnoiter, redeemer,
red pepper, reefer, refer, reflector,
reformer, rejoiner, respecter, rhymster,
ringleader, roadster, rooster, rope-
ladder, rose water, roster, rougher,
saber, saucer, saunter, scalper, scandal-
monger, scavenger, scepter, scooter,
scraper, scribbler, scriber, scupper,
seeker, seersucker, seltzer, Sepher,
sepulcher, Shalmaneser, sharpshooter,
sherry cobbler, shockabsorber, shop-
lifter, shopper, shyer, shyster, silver,
simper, slaughter, sleep-walker, slipper,
smarter, smuggler, snubber, snuffer,
soccer, sock-dologer, soda-water, som-
ber, sooner, sou'wester, spanker, spec-
ter, spinster, sprinkler, stage-whisper,
stagger, Star Chamber, star-gazer,
steamboiler, stenographer, stepladder,
stiffer, stomacher, stopper, stretcher,
stroller, sucker, super, sundowner,
supper, sutler, swagger, swashbuckler,
sweater, sweeter, swindler, talebearer,
tallow-chandler, Tam-o'-Shanter, tank-
er, tauter, teacher, teetotaler, temper,
tempter, tether, thaler, Tiber, timer,
tipster, together, toper, tougher, trader,
transfer, transformer, traveler, trick-
ster, trooper, trotter, tumbler, ulster,
upholster, upper, user, usher, vacuum
cleaner, Vancouver, verger, vesper,

ER

ILLER
IMBER
IMMER
INDER
INER
INGER
INKER
INNER
INTER
IPER
IPPER
IR
IRE
ISER
ISHER
ISTER
ITER
ITTER
IVER
IZER
OBBER
OBER
OCKER
OCRE
OER
OFFER
OGRE
OKER
OLDER
OLVER
OMBER
OMER
ONDER
ONER
OOMER
OONER

Vichy water, vintner, voucher, Wagner, waiter, warbler, warder, water, waver, way-farer, Webster, well-wisher, whaler, whimper, whisker, whisper, whiter, whither, wilder, wind-jammer, wine-bibber, wither, woodpecker, wrapper, wrecker, youngster

ER

OPHER
OPPER
ORDER
ORTER
OTHER
OULDER
OUNDER
OUR
OVER
OW*-*er*
OWDER
OWER
UBBER
UCRE
UDDER
UER
UIRE
UMBER
UMNER
UNDER
UR
URER
USTER
UTTER
UVRE
ing-ING
ly-E**

Camera, chimera, cholera, diptera, era, genera, Hera, lepidoptera, opera, Pera, Riviera, Sisera

ERA
see
A**

Conquerable, considerable, discoverable, imponderable, insuperable, intolerable, invulnerable, miserable, prefer-

ERABLE
see
ABLE

able, tolerable, unconquerable, venerable, vulnerable — **ERABLE**

Amperage, average, beverage, brokerage, leverage, peerage, steerage — **ERAGE** *see* AGE*

Collateral, consul-general, ephemeral, equilateral, fal-de-ral, federal, feral, funeral, general, lateral, liberal, literal, mackeral, mineral, numeral, quadrilateral, several, trilateral — **ERAL** *see* AL

Lateran, Lutheran, Teheran, veteran — **ERAN** *see* AN*

Exuberant, intolerant, itinerant, protuberant, tolerant — **ERANT** *see* ANT*

Adulterate, aerate, berate, commiserate, confederate, conglomerate, considerate, degenerate, desperate, enumerate, exaggerate, exasperate, exhilarate, exonerate, exuberate, federate, generate, illiterate, immoderate, incarcerate, incinerate, inconsiderate, intemperate, inveterate, iterate, lacerate, liberate, literate, macerate, moderate, numerate, obliterate, operate, preponderate, recuperate, refrigerate, reiterate, remunerate, reverberate, temperate, tolerate, transliterate, vituperate, vociferate — **ERATE** *see* ATE

Acerb, adverb, herb, kerb, potherb, proverb, reverb, Serb, superb, verb

ERB
see
URB

Coerce, commerce, terce, sesterce

ERCE
see
EARSE
ERSE
URSE

Perch

ERCH
see
IRCH

Cowherd, halberd, herd, potsherd, shepherd, swineherd

ERD
see
EARD
IRD
ORD**
URD

Adhere, ampere, Apollo Belvedere, atmosphere, austere, bathysphere, cashmere, cassimere, cohere, Guinevere, hemisphere, here, inhere, insincere, interfere, mere, Paul Revere, persevere, revere, sere, severe, sincere, sphere, stratosphere

ERE*
see
EER
IER

Anywhere, confrere, elsewhere, ere, everywhere, Folies Bergère, gruyère, nowhere, porte-cochère, somewhere, there, where

ERE**
see
AIR
ARE*
IARE
IERE

Were

ERE***
see
IR

Doggerel, mackerel, pickerel

EREL
see
EL

Adherent, belligerent, coherent, different, incoherent, indifferent, inherent, irreverent, reverent

ERENT
see
ENT

Interferer, loiterer, philanderer, roysterer, sorcerer, wanderer

ERER
see
ER

Entereth, fluttereth, hindereth, lingereth, tendereth

ERETH
see
ETH

Serf

ERF
see
URF

Berg, erg, iceberg, Heidelberg, kilerg, Nuremberg, Venusberg

ERG
see
URG

Absterge, converge, deterge, diverge, emerge, merge, serge, submerge, verge

ERGE
see
IRGE
URGE

Clergy, energy

ERGY
see
E**

Algeria, bacteria, cafeteria, diphtheria, Egeria, hysteria, Iberia, Siberia

ERIA
see
IA

Aerial, immaterial, imperial, material, serial

ERIAL
see
AL
IAL

Atmospheric, choleric, climacteric, congeneric, esoteric, etheric, exoteric, generic, Homeric, mesmeric, neoteric, tumeric, spheric

ERIC
see
IC

Bijouterie, Conciergerie, eerie, Erie, Jacquerie, Janesserie, lingerie, menagerie, reverie

ERIE
see
IE*

Imperil, peril

ERIL
see
IL

Culverin, Erin, glycerin

ERIN
see
IN

Algerine, glycerine, pelerine, tangerine

ERINE
see
INE**

Bickering, burnt-offering, careering, covering, drink-offering, gathering, glistering, glittering, ingathering, loitering, long suffering, muttering, offering, sin-offering, smoldering, tapering, thank-offering, votive offering, wandering, whispering, wool-gathering, westering

ERING
see
ER-*ing*
ING

Ephemeris, Eris, sui generis

ERIS
see
IS*

Cherish, feverish, gibberish, impoverish, pantherish, perish, queerish

ERISH
see
ISH

Demerit, inherit, merit

ERIT
see
IT

Asperity, austerity, celerity, dexterity, insincerity, posterity, prosperity, severity, sincerity, temerity, verity

ERITY
see
ITY

Clerk, beserk, hauberk, jerk, perk

ERK
see
IRK
URK

Merle

ERLE
see
EARL

Cleverly, easterly, elderly, formerly, latterly, meagerly, motherly, northerly, orderly, overly, properly, quarterly, slenderly, soberly, southerly, tenderly, Waverly, westerly

ERLY
see
E**
ER-*ly*

Berm, germ, isotherm, pachyderm, sperm, term, therm

ERM
see
IRM

Altern, bittern, cavern, cistern, cithern, concern, discern, eastern, ern, fern, govern, Hohenzollern, intern, jack-o'lantern, kern, lantern, leathern, lectern, magic lantern, misgovern, modern, northern, pattern, postern,

ERN
see
EARN
ERNE
OURN*
URN

silvern, slattern, southern, stern, sub-
altern, tavern, tern, tree fern, western,
zithern

ERN

Eternal, external, fraternal, infernal,
internal, maternal, paternal, sempiter-
nal, supernal, vernal

ERNAL
see
AL

Interne, Jules Verne, sauterne

ERNE
see
ERN

Bolero, cavalero, Cicero, hero, Nero,
numero, pampero, Prospero, Rio de
Janeiro, sombrero, Trocadero, zero

ERO
see
O*

Acheron, chaperon, Decameron,
hanger-on, heron, Oberon, Percheron

ERON
see
ON

Adulterous, boisterous, cadaverous,
cantankerous, dangerous, dexterous,
generous, lecherous, numerous, ob-
streperous, oderiferous, onerous, pes-
tiferous, ponderous, preposterous, pros-
perous, slanderous, somniferous, splen-
diferous, thunderous, viperous

EROUS
see
OUS

Excerpt

ERPT
see
URP-*ed*

Err

ERR
see
ER

Croix de guerre, nom de guerre, parterre, pied-à-terre

ERRE
see
AIR
ARE*

Berry, blackberry, blueberry, cherry, cranberry, elderberry, equerry, ferry, gooseberry, loganberry, merry, mulberry, raspberry, sherry, spiceberry, strawberry, Tom-and-Jerry

ERRY
see
ERY

Algiers, divers, headquarters, Ghebers, Seven Sleepers, Sicilian Vespers

ERS
see
ER-*s*

Adverse, asperse, converse, disperse, diverse, Erse, immerse, intersperse, inverse, obverse, perverse, reverse, terse, transverse, traverse, universe, verse

ERSE
see
EARSE
ERCE
URSE
*ed-*IRST
ORST

Erst

ERST
see
IRST

Advert, alert, assert, avert, concert, contravert, convert, covert, desert, dessert, disconcert, divert, Egbert, exert, expert, extravert, filbert, inert, insert, introvert, invert, malapert, overt, pert, pervert, re-assert, revert, sherbert, vert

ERT
see
IRT
UIRT
URT

Berth

ERTH
see
IRTH

Liberty, poverty, property

ERTY
see
E**

Cerberus, Hesperus

ERUS
see
US

Conserve, deserve, nerve, observe, preserve, reserve, serve, swerve, un-nerve, unreserve, verve

ERVE
see
URVE

Adultery, anti-slavery, archery, ar-tery, artillery, bakery, battery, blus-tery, brewery, bribery, buffoonery, cajolery, celery, cemetery, chancery, chandlery, chicanery, creamery, crock-ery, cutlery, deanery, debauchery, discovery, distillery, drapery, drudg-ery, effrontery, embroidery, emery, fakery, feathery, fernery, fiery, finery, fippery, fishery, flattery, flummery, foolery, forgery, frippery, gallery, grapery, greenery, grocery, gunnery, haberdashery, hatchery, hosiery, house-wifery, imagery, ironmongery, jewel-lery, jittery, jugglery, knavery, lamas-ery, lathery, leathery, lottery, lubbery, machinery, mastery, millinery, misery, mockery, monastery, mummery, mys-tery, napery, nunnery, nursery, onery, pearl-fishery, peppery, perfumery, pe-riphery, phylactery, pottery, presby-tery, powdery, prudery, psaltery, quackery, query, raillery, recovery, refinery, revery, rockery, roguery, rogues gallery, rookery, scenery, self-

ERY
see
E**
ERRY
IVERY
ORY
OWERY
URY

mastery, shivery, showery, shrubbery, **ERY**
skulduggery, slavery, silvery, slippery,
soldiery, sorcery, spidery, surgery,
thievery, thuggery, tomfoolery, tot-
tery, tracery, treachery, trickery,
trumpery, upholstery, venery, very,
waggery, watery, whispering-gallery,
witchery

    Beryl   **ERYL**
        see
        IL

    Aborigines, Achilles, Albigenses, **ES***
Anchises, Andes, Antilles, antipodes, *see*
Apelles, Archimedes, Ares, Aristides, ADES*
Aristophanes, Artaxerxes, auspices, ATES**
Averroës, Azores, Bacchantes, Benares, EASE
bay-leaves, Bes, Bootes, Buenos Ayres, EES
Celebes, Ceres, Cervantes, Corybantes, EIZE
crevasses, Damocles, Dark Ages, de- ESE
grees, Demosthenes, Dives, doges, IDES*
Dolores, Druses, Empedocles, Epi-
phanes, Erinyes, Euphrates, Ganges,
Graces, Hades, Heracles, Hercules,
Hermes, herpes, Holofernes, lares,
Lemures, Los Angeles, Manes, Me-
phistopheles, Mercedes, Middle Ages,
molasses, Moses, Oannes, oases, omnes,
open spaces, Orestes, penates, Pericles,
Pisces, Praxiteles, Procrustes, Sevres,
similes, Thales, Themistocles, Thersi-
tes, tresses, Ulysses, vortices, Xerxes,
Ximenes

    Ducks-and-drakes, Fates, gules, Guy **ES****
Fawkes, Holmes, Medes, Naples, *see*

Rhodes, skittles, small clothes, stars
and stripes, steppes, Ten Lost Tribes,
Thebes, Wales, wolves

ES**

    Yes

ES***
see
ESCE
ESS

Courtesan, diocesan, parmesan

ESAN
see
AN*

Acquiesce, coalesce, convalesce, ef-
fervesce, effloresce, evanesce, intum-
esce, opalesce

ESCE
see
ES***
ESS

Burmese, Cantonese, Chinese, dio-
cese, Japanese, maltese, manganese,
obese, Pekinese, Portuguese, Siamese,
Singhalese, Sudanese, these, Viennese,
Veronese

ESE
see
EAS**
IECE
IEZE
IS***
ISE***

Beset, boneset, reset

ESET
see
ET

Afresh, enmesh, flesh, fresh, gross-
flesh, horseflesh, mesh, refresh, thresh

ESH
see

Amnesia, anæsthesia, freesia, mag-
nesia, Polynesia, Rhodesia, silesia

ESIA
see
IA

Anamnesis, antithesis, exegesis, Genesis, hypothesis, Lachesis, Nemesis, palingenesis, parenthesis, parthenogenesis, synthesis, telekinesis, thesis

ESIS
see
IS*

Desk, kneeling-desk, office desk

ESK
see
ESQUE

Arabesque, burlesque, grotesque, Moresque, Normanesque, picturesque, romanesque, statuesque

ESQUE
see
ESK

Abbess, abruptness, access, address, agelessness, aggressiveness, aloofness, antiqueness, artfulness, artless, awareness, bashfulness, bitterness, bless, bloodless, bootless, bottomless, boundlessness, brainless, burgess, buttress, calmness, caress, cheerfulness, chess, childishness, childless, closeness, clothespress, cloudless, compress, confess, congress, correctness, countless, cress, cypress, darkness, dauntless, deaconess, diffuseness, digress, dispossess, distress, dress, duchess, dulness, duress, eagerness, earnestness, effortless, egress, empress, enchantress, endless, ess, excess, exhaustless, expertness, express, eye-witness, fathomless, fastness, faultless, fearless, foolishness, footless, forgetfulness, forgiveness, formless, foulness, fruitless, fullness, goddess, godlessness, golden-tress, governess, groundless, guess, hairless, hardness, harness, heiress, helpless, hornless, hostess, huntress, idleness,

ESS
see
ELESS
ES**
ESCE
ESSE
ILESS
INESS
ed-EST

impress, ingress, jazzless, laundress, **ESS**
less, licentiousness, lightness, limitless,
lioness, listless, luckless, matchless,
mattress, meekness, mellowness, mess,
mistress, motionless, mulishness, nak-
edness, nameless, nearness, needless,
negress, ness, nothingness, numberless,
obligingness, obsess, odorless, ogress,
oneness, oppress, overdress, passive-
ness, pathless, peacefulness, peeress,
peerless, perfectness, piggishness, Pilgrim's Progress, poetess, pointless,
possess, powerless, preparedness, pre-
possess, press, priestess, princess, prior-
ess, process, profess, progress, prowess,
pythoness, Queen Bess, quenchless,
questionless, questless, quickness,
quietness, rankness, rashness, rayless,
readdress, recess, reckless, redness,
redress, regardless, regress, repress,
resistless, restless, retrogress, righte-
ousness, rudeness, ruthless, seamless,
seamstress, shadowless, shepherdess,
shiftless, shoreless, shrewdness, shy-
ness, sinless, sleepless, slothfulness,
slyness, sorceress, spaceless, spaceless-
ness, speechless, spotless, stainless,
stewardess, stillness, success, sugarless,
sullenness, sunless, supineness, sup-
press, sweetness, tactless, tenantless,
tenderness, thankless, thickness,
thoughtfulness, thoughtless, thriftless,
thusness, tigress, timeless, timeless-
ness, toothless, traitress, transgress,
treeless, undress, unless, uprightness,
upsidedownness, vagueness, voluptu-
ousness, waitress, wantonness, water-

cress, weakness, weightless, wickedness, **ESS**
wilderness, winepress, witless, witness,
worthless, youthfulness

Finesse, largesse, noblesse   **ESSE**
                                     see
                                     ESS

Accession, cession, concession, con- **ESSION**
fession, depression, digression, expres- *see*
sion, impression, intercession, obses-   ION
sion, precession, procession, profession,
progression, recession, regression, re-
pression, retrocession, retrogression,
session, succession, suppression, trans-
gression

Acid test, addrest, alkahest, alma-   **EST**
gest, arrest, basest, behest, beholdest,   *see*
bendest, best, bitterest, blendest, bless- EAST**
edest, blest, Budapest, cheapest, chest,   ESS-*ed*
chiefest, coarsest, congest, contest,   IEST*
coolest, crest, deprest, describest, de-   UEST
spisest, detest, digest, dishonest, dis-
possest, divest, divinest, drest, driftest,
earnest, enterest, Everest, exactest,
forest, forlornest, frailest, fullest,
genteelest, harvest, honest, horridest,
id est, immodest, implorest, infest,
inquirest, intensest, interest, invest,
jest, keenest, laborest, lest, limberest,
longest, manifest, mare's-nest, mayest,
middle-west, minutest, modest, molest,
nest, obscurest, opprest, palimpsest,
pest, possest, prest, protest, purest,
quietest, reforest, remotest, rest, re-
turnest, rinderpest, robbest, second-

best, shreddest, sincerest, slickest, still-est, stretchest, suggest, swiftest, temp-est, test, thirstest, unblest, unmolest, unrest, urgest, vaguest, vest, west, widest, wildest, wottest, wrest, zest **EST**

Fiesta, podesta, siesta, Vesta, Zend Avesta **ESTA**
see
A**

Festal, pedestal, vestal **ESTAL**
see
AL

Ester, fester, forester, jester, nor'-wester, quester, rhymester, semester, sequester, yester **ESTER**
see
ER

Nestle, pestle, trestle, wrestle **ESTLE**
see
EL
LE

Manifesto, presto **ESTO**
see
O*

Amnesty, dishonesty, honesty, im-modesty, lese-majesty, majesty, mod-esty, travesty, testy **ESTY**
see
E**

Cheesy, courtesy, heresy, poesy, prophesy **ESY**
see
E**

Abet, aigret, alphabet, anchoret, asset, beget, bet, blanket, bonnet, booklet, bouncing-Bet, brevet, Bridget, brisket, brooklet, bucket, budget, buf- **ET**
see
ACKET
ANET

fet, bullet, cabaret, cadet, calumet, chaplet, circlet, claret, cloudlet, comet, cornet, corset, cosset, couplet, court-poet, covet, cresset, crotchet, curb-market, curvet, cygnet, deep-set, dragnet, dulcet, eaglet, egret, Emerald Tablet, emmet, epithet, facet, faucet, ferret, fish-net, flageolet, flibbertigib-bet, floweret, forget, freshet, fret, frisket, gadget, garnet, garret, gas-jet, gauntlet, get, gibbet, giblet, gimlet, goblet, gorget, gusset, hamlet, hatchet, helmet, hic jacet, hornet, inlet, inset, interpret, jennet, jet, junket, kismet, lancet, landaulet, latchet, leaflet, let, leveret, linnet, magnet, mallet, market, met, millet, minaret, moppet, mullet, musket, net, offset, onset, outlet, owlet, pallet, pamphlet, panne velvet, para-pet, pellet, pet, plummet, poet, poke bonnet, posset, privet, prophet, pullet, puppet, quartet, quintet, quodlibet, ratchet, regret, reset, ret, ricochet, ringlet, rivet, russet, scarlet, secret, set, sextet, sherbet, signet, singlet, sonnet, spinet, stet, stockinet, stockmarket, streamlet, sub-let, sunbonnet, sunset, tablet, tabouret, target, tea-set, Tebet, Thibet, thickset, tippet, toilet, To Let, Tophet, trinket, troutlet, turret, ultra-violet, upset, valet, varlet, velvet, videlicet, violet, wallet, wet, whet, wristlet, yet

ET

ASKET
EAT***
EBT
ELET
ENET
ESET
ETTE
ICKET
IDGET
IET
INET
IVET
OCKET
OMET
ONET
OSET
UET*
UGGET
ULET
UMPET
ed-ED

Centripetal, decretal, gun-metal, metal, petal

ETAL
see
AL

Etch, fetch, homestretch, ketch, outstretch, sketch, stretch, vetch, wretch

ETCH
see

Athlete, compete, complete, concrete, Crete, delete, deplete, effete, esthete, incomplete, mete, obsolete, Paraclete, replete, secrete

ETE*
see
EAT*
EET
UITE*

Tête à tête, fête, machete

ETE**
see
ATE

Altimeter, anemometer, barometer, cyclometer, Demeter, deter, diameter, gas-meter, heliometer, hydrometer, kilometer, meter, orometer, pedometer, perimeter, peter, pyrometer, saltpeter, speedometer, thermometer, trumpeter, variometer

ETER
see
ER

Abideth, affordeth, alloweth, Ashtoreth, beginneth, bestoweth, breaketh, chanceth, changeth, compriseth, dwelleth, Elizabeth, encompasseth, fleeth, flieth, gaveth, guideth, howleth, keepeth, lodgeth, loveth, Macbeth, maketh, Nazareth, observeth, seeth, Seth, shibboleth, sleepeth, slideth, taketh, useth, wakeneth, waneth, weepeth

ETH
see
AITH**
EATH**
ERETH
ILETH

Bell-wether, nether, tether, together, wether, whether

ETHER
see
EATHER
ER

Æsthetic, apathetic, arithmetic, **ETIC**
ascetic, athletic, cosmetic, emetic, *see*
energetic, frenetic, genetic, geodetic, IC
hermetic, homiletic, magnetic, noetic,
onomatopoetic, parenthetic, pathetic,
peripatetic, phonetic, phrenetic, poetic,
polysynthetic, prophetic, sympathetic,
synthetic

Leto, magneto, veto **ETO**
see
O*

Breton, Eton, phaeton, simpleton, **ETON**
skeleton *see*
ON

Kilometre, metre, saltpetre **ETRE**
see
ETER

Chronometry, coquetry, geometry, **ETRY**
marquetry, musketry, parquetry, po- *see*
etry, psychometry, symmetry, trigo- E**
nometry

Aigrette, anisette, barette, blan- **ETTE**
quette, briquette, brochette, brunette, *see*
chemisette, cigarette, collarette, co- ET
quette, corvette, cravenette, croquette,
curette, dinette, epaulette, etiquette,
flannelette, fourchette, gazette, gris-
ette, historiette, kitchenette, Lafay-
ette, layette, leatherette, lorgnette,
lunette, maisonnette, Marie Antoin-
ette, midinette, mignonette, moquette,

novelette, oubliette, palette, parquette, pipette, planchette, poussette, quartette, quintette, rosette, roulette, satinette, serviette, silhouette, soubrette, statuette, suffragette, toilette, vedette, vignette, vinaigrette, voiturette, wagonette

ETTE

Begetter, better, dead letter, fetter, getter, letter, red-letter, Roman letter, setter, typesetter, uncial letter, unfetter, wetter, whetter

ETTER
see
ER

Confetti, Rossetti, spaghetti

ETTI
see
I**

Fettle, kettle, mettle, nettle, settle, tea-kettle

ETTLE
see
EL
.LE

Allegretto, amoretto, falsetto, ghetto, libretto, palmetto, Rigoletto, stiletto, terzetto, Tintoretto

ETTO
see
O*

Betty, jetty, petty, pretty

ETTY
see
E**

Crotchety, fidgety, nicety, ninety, pernickety, rackety, rickety, safety, subtlety, surety, velvety

ETY
see
E**

Epictetus, impetus, quietus

ETUS
see
US

Feud

EUD
see
UDE

Pseudo

EUDO
see
O*

Athenaeum, Colosseum, Herculane- **EUM**
um, linoleum, lyceum, mausoleum, *see*
museum, odeum, petroleum, rheum, IUM
Te Deum OM

Amateur, bonheur, chauffeur, coif- **EUR**
feur, connoisseur, enterpreneur, fleur, *see*
grandeur, liqueur, masseur, monsieur, IR
raconteur, seigneur, sœur, voyageur OUR**
UR

Alpheus, Asmodeus, Briareus, cadu- **EUS**
ceus, coleus, hic liber est meus, Mor- *see*
pheus, nucleus, Orpheus, Peleus, Per- UCE
seus, Prometheus, Proteus, scarabæus, US
Smintheus, Theseus, Zeus

Berceuse, Betelgeuse, chartreuse, **EUSE**
danseuse, masseuse *see*
ERS
URS

Sleuth

EUTH
see
UTH

Kislev

EV
see

Coeval, medieval, primeval	**EVAL** *see* AL
Eve, Midsummer eve	**EVE** *see* EAVE IEVE
Bevel, dishevel, level, revel, sea-level, spirit-level	**EVEL** *see* EL
Eleven, even, seven	**EVEN** *see* EN
Cantilever, dissever, ever, fever, forever, lever, never, retriever, sever, soever, whatever, whensoever, whoever, whomsoever, whosoever	**EVER** *see* ER
Dare-devil, devil, evil, printer's devil, she-devil	**EVIL** *see* IL
Brevity, levity, longevity	**EVITY** *see* ITY
Bevy, chevy, levy	**EVY** *see* E**
Anew, askew, bedew, beefstew, beshrew, bestrew, blew, brand-new, brew, corkscrew, crew, curfew, curlew, dew, drew, eschew, feverfew, few, Hebrew,	**EW** *see* AGUE*** IEW

hew, honey-dew, immew, Jew, knew, merry-andrew, mew, mildew, nephew, new, pew, phew, renew, screw, sew, shrew, sinew, skeleton crew, skew, slew, smew, spew, St. Andrew, St. Bartholomew, stew, strew, threw, thumbscrew, unscrew, Wandering Jew, whew, withdrew, yew

EW
o**
ou*
u
ue*
ed-EWD
s-OSE**
USE*

Lewd, shrewd

EWD
see
UDE

Bejewel, crewel, jewel, newel

EWEL
see
EL

Ewer, fewer, hewer, reviewer, sewer, skewer

EWER
see
ER

Hewn, rock-hewn, rough-hewn, sewn, strewn, unhewn

EWN
see
OON

King's Mews, news

EWS
see
EW-*s*

Newt

EWT
see
OOT**

Chewy, dewy, mildewy, screwy, sinewy, skewy

EWY
see
E**

Annex, apex, biconvex, circumflex, codex, complex, convex, duplex, flex, haruspex, ibex, ilex, index, inflex, multiplex, murex, perplex, pollex, pontifex, reflex, rex, sex, silex, simplex, vertex, vex, vortex

EX
see
ECK-*s*
ECT-*s*
EQUE-*s*
ed-EXT

Next, pretext, text, vex't, what-next

EXT
see
EX-*ed*

Abbey, Alderney, alley, attorney, barley, bey, blarney, bluey, bogey, bowling-alley, burley, chimney, choosey, chop-suey, chutney, clayey, cockney, convey, covey, courtsey, darkey, dingey, disobey, Dombey, donkey, dopey, fluey, flunkey, galley, gin rickey, gluey, grey, Guernsey, gulley, hackney, Hennessey, hey, jersey, jitney, jockey, journey, key, Killarney, lackey, lamprey, linsey-woolsey, malmsey, master-key, medley, monkey, Monterey, motley, obey, Odyssey, okey, Orkney, osprey, palfrey, parley, parsley, pass-key, phoney, phooey, Pompey, posey, pulley, purvey, Shelley, shimmey, Sidney, skeleton-key, surrey, survey, they, tourney, trey, trolley, turkey, turnkey, valley, volley, watchkey, Westminster Abbey, whey, whimsey, whiskey, Wolsey

EY
see
A*
AY
E**
s-IES**

All-seeing Eye, buckeye, bull's eye, cock-eye, evil-eye, eye, needle's eye, ox-eye, sheep's eye, wall-eye

EYE
see
I*
IE**

Cortez, fez, oyez, Suez, Velasquez

EZ
see
EACH-*es*
OICE-*s*

Trapeze

EZE
see
EEZE
ESE

Intermezzo, mezzo

EZZO
see
O*

I SOUNDS

Alibi, alkali, alumni, Delphi, demi,
Eli, fungi, genii, I, Magi, Malachi,
modus operandi, pi, rabbi, semi,
Shang-ti, vox populi

I*

   see

AI
EFY
EYE
IE**
IFY
IGH
ISFY
ULY**

Agni, Amalfi, Amenti, Ani, Assisi,
bacardi, banditti, Bartholdi, beri-beri,
bhakti, Buonarotti, Cabiri, cadi, Capri,
chianti, Chili, conoscenti, Cotopaxi,
daiquiri, Disraeli, do-re-mi, droshki,
effendi, ennui, Fascisti, Fiji, Firdausi,
Fo-hi, frangipani, Gandi, Garibaldi,
Gehazi, Gobi, Hadji, hari-kari, Hawaii,
Hopi, houri, Jami, khaki, kiwi, Lak-
shmi, lapis lazuli, Leonardo da Vinci,
Loki, Machiavelli, Mahdi, Maori,
Medici, Miami, Midi, mufti, Nagasaki,
Nazami, Nazi, obi, okapi, Parvati,
patchouli, peccavi, Pehlevi, peri, picca-
lilli, Pompeii, potpourri, quasi, Rishi,
Saadi, salmagundi, sans-souci, saki,
sakti, sbirri, scudi, ski, soldi, sperma-
ceti, sri, Sufi, Tauri, taxi, Tiki, Tishri,
Trimurti, tutti-frutti, Uffizi, Valmiki,

I**

   see

ALI
ATI
E*
EE
ETTI
IE*
IGREE
INI
IORI
ITI
OLI
ONI

287

Vasari, Verdi, vermicelli, visconti, voici, Yogi **I****

Abyssinia, acacia, Aglaia, Alexandria, ambrosia, Andalusia, aphrodisia, apologia, Arabia, Arcadia, artemisia, Assyria, Bessarabia, Bœotia, Bohemia, Bolivia, braggadocia, Britannia, Calabria, California, Cambodia, camellia, Cappadocia, cassia, Circassia, claustrophobia, Columbia, cyclopedia, Cynthia, Czecho-Slovakia, dahlia, deutzia, Dionysia, Discordia, dyspepsia, encyclopedia, Etruria, emphorbia, fuchsia, gilia, godetia, Hibernia, hydrophobia, Hypatia, hypochrondia, India, inertia, insignia, insomnia, intelligentsia, Ischia, Ismailia, kleptomania, Lemuria, loggia, Lucrezia Borgia, Malaysia, Manchuria, memorabilia, Mesopotamia, militia, minutia, misericordia, Moravia, neuralgia, nostalgia, Nubia, Olympia, onomatopœia, paranoia, Patricia, Persia, Perugia, petunia, phantasmagoria, phobia, Phoenicia, Phrygia, pointsettia, Portia, Prussia, Pythia, raffia, rudbeckia, Russia, salvia, Scandinavia, Scythia, sedilia, sepia, sequoia, stadia, stevia, St. Sofia, symposia, Syria, Thalia, tibia, Transcaucasia, Trinosophia, via, via media, Zenobia

IA
see
A**
ALIA
ANIA
ARIA
ASIA
EIA
ELIA
ENIA
ENTIA
ERIA
ESIA
OLIA
ONIA
OPIA
ORIA

Amiable, inexpiable, insatiable, invariable, justifiable, liable, pitiable, pliable, reliable, satiable, sociable, undeniable, variable

IABLE
see
ABLE
EL
LE

Ammoniac, aphrodisiac, cardiac, celeriac, demoniac, elegiac, hypochondriac, kleptomaniac, maniac, pericardiac, symposiac, Syriac, theriac, Zodiac

IAC
see
AC

Iliad, jeremiad, myriad, naiad, Olympiad, Pleiad, triad

IAD
see
AD

Carriage, foliage, gun carriage, horseless carriage, marriage, verbiage

IAGE
see
AGE*

Jeremiah, Messiah, Mount Moriah, pariah, Zedekiah

IAH
see
AH

Actuarial, alluvial, ambrosial, antimonial, antisocial, Belial, bestial, biennial, burial, celestial, centennial, ceremonial, circumferential, circumstantial, colonial, coloquial, commercial, congenial, connubial, consequential, convivial, cordial, courtmartial, credential, crucial, decennial, deferential, denial, dial, differential, diluvial, entente cordial, equatorial, equinoctial, Escurial, essential, evidential, facial, filial, financial, finial, fluvial, glacial, impartial, imperial, inconsequential, industrial, inessential, inferential, influential, initial, jovial, labial, manorial, martial, matrimonial, memorial, menial, mercurial, non-essential, nuptial, official, palatial, parochial, partial, patrimonial, penitential, perennial, pestilential, phial, pluvial, post-pran-

IAL
see
AL
ERIAL
ICIAL
ORIAL

dial, potential, Prairial, prandial, pre- **IAL**
glacial, presidential, primordial, pro-
verbial, providential, provincial, pru-
dential, racial, radial, residential, re-
trial, reverential, secretarial, self-
denial, social, spatial, special, substan-
tial, sundial, terrestrial, testimonial,
torrential, trial, triennial, trivial, uncial, uncongenial, unsocial, venial, vial

In memoriam, Miriam, Priam, Siam, **IAM**
sweet-William *see*
AM
EM

Amphibian, Andalusian, antedilu- **IAN**
vian, antinomian, Arcadian, artesian, *see*
Assyrian, Bacchanalian, bathycolpian, AN*
beautician, Bodleian, Bohemian, Brob- ARIAN
dingnagian, Carthusian, Castilian, EDIAN
Christian, Cimmerian, Circassian, Cis- ICAN
tercian, Confucian, Corinthian, custo- ICIAN
dian, Cyprian, Dickensian, diluvian, IDIAN
Draconian, durian, Eleusinian, Ely- ORIAN
sian, Ephesian, equestrian, Essenian,
Ethiopian, fringed-gentian, fustian,
guardian, Hanoverian, Hertzian, Hi-
bernian, Indian, Ionian, isthmian,
Itrurian, Justinian, Lilliputian, Luca-
dian, Lydian, Machiavellian, magian,
Manchurian, Merovingian, metaphysi-
cian, Midian, Midlothian, Norwegian,
Nubian, Olympian, Ossian, Parisian,
Parthian, pedestrian, Peloponnesian,
Persian, Perugian, Peruvian, Pierian,
plebian, Pomeranian, Pythian, Ra-
belaisian, reptilian, riparian, ruffian,

salarian, Saturnalian, saurian, Shake- **IAN**
sperian, Siberian, simian, Spenserian,
St. Sebastian, Stygian, Sumerian, Swa-
bian, Tasmanian, tertian, theologian,
Thespian, Titian, tragedian, Umbrian,
Uranian, Utopian, valerian, Venetian,
Wagnerian, Zoroastrian

Affiance, allegiance, alliance, appli- **IANCE**
ance, brilliance, compliance, dalliance, *see*
defiance, insouciance, invariance, lux- ANCE
uriance, radiance, reliance, variance

Chateaubriand, viand **IAND**
  see
  AND*

Brilliant, compliant, defiant, giant, **IANT**
luxuriant, mediant, pliant, principiant, *see*
radiant, reliant, suppliant, valiant, ANT*
variant

Briar, familiar, friar, liar, peculiar, **IAR**
sweetbriar, unfamiliar, Whitefriar *see*
  AR*
  ER
  IRE

Tiara **IARA**
  see
  A**

Billiard, galliard, poniard, Spaniard **IARD**
  see
  ARD

Apiary, auxiliary, aviary, benefi-
ciary, breviary, diary, incendiary, in-
termediary, judiciary, pecuniary, peni-
tentiary, plenipotentiary, subsidiary,
tertiary

IARY
see
AIRY
E**
IE*
UARY

Alias, Ananias, bias, Deo gratias,
Elias, paterfamilias, Phidias, Tiresias,
Zacharias

IAS
see
AS*

Commissariat, fiat, lariat, proletar-
iat

IAT
see
AT*

Abbreviate, affiliate, alleviate, ap-
preciate, appropriate, associate, colle-
giate, conciliate, denunciate, depreci-
ate, deviate, dissociate, excruciate, ex-
patiate, expatriate, expediate, expiate,
expropriate, filiate, foliate, humiliate,
immediate, inappropriate, infuriate,
ingratiate, insatiate, intercollegiate,
intermediate, luxuriate, mediate, mis-
appropriate, negotiate, noviciate, ob-
viate, officiate, opiate, palliate, prin-
cipiate, propitiate, radiate, repatriate,
repudiate, retaliate, satiate, striate,
substantiate, transubstantiate, trifoli-
ate, vitiate

IATE
see
ATE
ITATE

Abbreviation, appreciation, aviation,
denunciation, expatriation, initiation,
negotiation, principiation, pronuncia-
tion, renunciation

IATION
see
ATION
ION

Ad lib., bib, Carib, corn-crib, crib, dib, drib, fib, glib, jib, nib, Ninib, rib, sahib, Sennacherib, sparerib, turbid, umbrella-rib

IB
see
UIB

Cannibal, Hannibal, intertribal, tribal

IBAL
see
AL

Dribble, fribble, nibble, quibble, scribble

IBBLE
see
EL
LE

Ascribe, bribe, circumscribe, describe, imbibe, inscribe, jibe, oversubscribe, prescribe, proscribe, scribe, subscribe, transcribe, tribe

IBE
see

Exhibit, inhibit, prohibit

IBIT
see
IT

Accessible, audible, Bible, collapsible, combustible, comprehensible, compressible, contemptible, convertible, corrigible, corruptible, credible, crucible, dirigible, discernible, divisible, edible, eligible, exhaustible, fallible, feasible, flexible, forcible, frangible, fusible, gullible, horrible, illegible, impassible, imperceptible, impossible, inaccessible, inaudible, incombustible, incompatible, incomprehensible, incontrovertible, inconvertible, incorrigible, incorruptible, incredible, indefensible, indestructible, inedible,

IBLE
see
EL
LE

inexhaustible, infallible, inflexible, in- **IBLE**
sensible, intangible, intelligible, invin-
cible, invisible, irascible, irresistible,
irresponsible, legible, mandible, neg-
ligible, ostensible, partible, passible,
perceptible, permissible, plausible, pos-
sible, reducible, refrangible, repress-
ible, resistible, responsible, reversible,
risible, sensible, susceptible, tangible,
terrible, thurible, vendible, visible

Audibly, forcibly, glibly, indelibly, **IBLY**
invisibly, possibly, terribly, visibly   *see*
                                          E**

Calibre, fibre   **IBRE**
                                          see
                                          ER

Attribute, contribute, distribute,   **IBUTE**
tribute   *see*
                                           UTE

Accoustic, acrostic, agnostic, agres-   **IC**
tic, akashic, alembic, allopathic, an-   *see*
electric, anopisthographic, angelic,   ACTIC
Antarctic, anthropographic, antiseptic,   AIC
anti-toxic, Arabic, Arctic, asbestic,   AMIC
aspic, attic, authentic, azoic, baldric,   ANIC
barbaric, basic, benefic, bishopric,   ANTIC
black magic, cambric, cataclysmic,   ASTIC
cathartic, caustic, Celtic, cherubic,   ATIC
chic, chivalric, civic, classic, concen-   ENIC
tric, Coptic, cosmic, cryptic, cubic,   ERIC
cynic, decasyllabic, Delphic, diagnos-   ETIC
tic, diametric, domestic, eccentric, ec-   ICK
lectic, ecliptic, egocentric, elliptic, em- IFIC
piric, endemic, eolithic, epic, epidemic, INIC

ethic, eupeptic, eurythemic, evangelic, fabric, forensic, formic, frozen music, Gaelic, Gallic, garlic, geocentric, geodesic, geometric, gnostic, Gothic, graphic, gum arabic, hectic, heliocentric, hermeneutic, heroic, hieroglyphic, hierographic, homopathic, hydraulic, hydroelectric, iambic, Icelandic, idyllic, intrinsic, Ionic, Islamic, italic, karmic, lethargic, lyric, magic, majestic, malic, metallic, metamorphic, metric, mimic, monolithic, monosyllabic, mystic, mythic, natureopathic, neolithic, Nordic, obstetric, Olympic, optic, Orphic, orthopedic, orthorhombic, oxalic, palæstric, paleolithic, panegyric, patronymic, phallic, physic, picnic, picric, Pindaric, polytechnic, polytheistic, pragmatic, prognostic, prussic, psychiatric, psychic, psychoanalytic, public, Punic, pyrotechnic, relic, republic, rhombic, rubric, runic, rustic, salic, salicylic, sapphic, satiric, seismic, seraphic, Slavic, sic, skeptic, spic, stenographic, stoic, strategic, sulphuric, styptic, syllabic, symmetric, syndic, technic, telepathic, telestic, thalassic, therapeutic, thermometric, theurgic, tombic, toreutic, toxic, traffic, tunic, tyrannic, unauthentic, Vedic

IC
ISTIC
ITIC
ODIC
OGIC
OLIC
OMIC
ONIC
OPIC
ORIC
OTIC
ed-ICT
s-IX

Africa, America, angelica, arnica, Attica, basilica, Britannica, Corsica, harmonica, hepatica, Jamaica, japonica, majolica, materia medica, mica, nux vomica, pica, replica, sciatica, silica, veronica

ICA
see
A**

Delicacy, efficacy, indelicacy, in- **ICACY**
tricacy
see
ACY
E**

Aeronautical, allegorical, anthropo- **ICAL**
logical, artistical, biblical, biograph- *see*
ical, biological, canonical, chemical, AL
chronological, clerical, comical, con-
ical, cosmical, cosmogonical, critical,
cylindrical, cynical, diabolical, ecclesi-
astical, emblematical, empirical, en-
cyclical, ethnological, etiological, ety-
mological, evangelical, farcial, finical,
genetical, geographical, grammatical,
heretical, hermeneutical, hierarchical,
historical, horological, hypercritical,
hypocritical, hypothetical, hysterical,
identical, illogical, inimical, ironical,
lackadaisical, logical, lyrical, magical,
majestical, medical, meteorological,
methodical, metrical, mimical, mor-
phological, musical, mystical, myth-
ological, nautical, nonsensical, numer-
ical, ontological, optical, paradoxical,
pathological, periodical, philosophical,
physical, piratical, poetical, pontifical,
practical, pragmatical, psychical, quiz-
zical, radical, rhetorical, sabbatical,
satirical, semi-tropical, skeptical, so-
phistical, spherical, stoical, surgical,
symbolical, symmetrical, technical,
technological, theatrical, theoretical,
tragical, tropical, typical, tyrannical,
unsophistical, vertical, vortical, whim-
sical

African, American, angelican, Mexican, pan-american, pelican, publican, republican, Vatican

ICAN
see
IAN

Applicant, communicant, insignificant, lubricant, mendicant, significant, supplicant

ICANT
see
ANT*

Abdicate, certificate, communicate, complicate, dedicate, delicate, domesticate, duplicate, eradicate, excommunicate, extricate, fabricate, fornicate, imbricate, implicate, indelicate, indicate, intoxicate, intricate, lubricate, masticate, pontificate, predicate, prevaricate, prognosticate, reduplicate, rusticate, sophisticate, supplicate, syndicate, vindicate

ICATE
see
ATE

Advice, allspice, beggar-lice, bice, device, dice, entice, field-mice, high-price, ice, interslice, low-price, mice, nice, not-nice, price, rice, sacrifice, slice, spice, splice, suffice, thrice, trice, twice, vice

ICE*
see
ISE**

Accomplice, apprentice, armistice, artifice, auspice, avarice, Beatrice, benefice, box-office, cantatrice, caprice, chalice, cicatrice, cornice, cowardice, crevice, dentifrice, hospice, injustice, justice, lattice, licorice, malice, malpractice, mounted-police, notice, novice, office, police, poultice, practice, precipice, prejudice, pumice, summer solstice, service, surplice, winter solstice

ICE**
see
IFICE
IS*
ISE****
ISS
ed-IST
s-IES**

Magnificent, munificent, reticent **ICENT**
see
ENT

Enrich, Greenwich, Ipswich, ostrich, **ICH**
rich, sandwich, which *see*
ICHE
ITCH

Niche **ICHE**
see
ICH

Artificial, beneficial, judicial, official, **ICIAL**
prejudicial, sacrificial, superficial, un- *see*
official IAL

Geometrician, magician, musician, **ICIAN**
optician, patrician, Phœnician, physi- *see*
cian, politician, statistician, technician IAN

Fratricide, germicide, infanticide, **ICIDE**
matricide, parricide, regicide, suicide, *see*
vermicide IDE

Agnosticism, Catholicism, criticism, **ICISM**
didacticism, empiricism, eroticism, fa- *see*
naticism, gnosticism, mysticism, ro- ISM
manticism, witticism

Deficit, explicit, illicit, implicit, licit, **ICIT**
solicit *see*
IT

Authenticity, causticity, domestic- **ICITY**
ity, duplicity, eccentricity, electricity, *see*
ellipticity, felicity, lubricity, periodic- E**
ity, publicity, rusticity, sphericity, ITY
simplicity

Bailiwick, beggar-tick, Benedick, brick, broomstick, candlestick, chick, chopstick, click, cowlick, crick, derrick, dirty trick, double-quick, drop-kick, drumstick, fiddle-stick, flick, glass-brick, goldbrick, hayrick, Herrick, homesick, joss-stick, kick, lick, limerick, lipstick, maulstick, maverick, Moby Dick, niblick, nick, pick, Pickwick, pinprick, polostick, prick, quick, rick, rollick, seasick, sick, slapstick, slick, St. Patrick, swizzle-stick, thick, tick, toothpick, trick, walkingstick, wick, yardstick, Yorick

ICK
see
IK
ed-ICT
ly-E**
s-IX

Bicker, dicker, flicker, pricker, rag-picker, slicker, snicker, sticker, thicker, wicker

ICKER
see
ER

Cricket, picket, thicket, ticket, wicket

ICKET
see
ET

Fickle, mickle, pickle, prickle, sickle, tickle, trickle

ICKLE
see
EL
LE

Finicky, panicky

ICKY
see
E**

Auricle, canticle, chicle, chronicle, conventicle, cubicle, cuticle, icicle, particle, pendicle, radicle, vehicle, ventricle, versicle

ICLE
see
EL
LE
YCLE

Calico, medico, Mexico, Pimlico, portico, Porto Rico, pro bono publico

ICO
see
O*

Harmonicon, Helicon, icon, irenicon, lexicon, Rubicon, silicon

ICON
see
ON

Academics, analytics, classics, dogmatics, dynamics, eclectics, empirics, ethics, genetics, kinetics, mathematics, metaphysics, metrics, physics, politics, psychics, statistics, tactics, thermodynamics, topics

ICS
see
IC-*s*

Addict, afflict, benedict, conflict, constrict, contradict, convict, depict, derelict, district, edit, evict, inflict, interdict, predict, relict, restrict, strict, verdict

ICT
see
IC-*ed*
ICK-*ed*
ed-ED

Benediction, diction, fiction, friction, interdiction, jurisdiction, malediction, prediction

ICTION
see
ION

Epicure, manicure, pedicure

ICURE
see
URE

Icy, impolicy, policy, spicy

ICY
see
E**

Acid, acrid, amid, Andromedid, aphid, avid, bi-cuspid, bid, candid, Cid, coverlid, David, did, Euclid, fervid, fetid, flaccid, florid, forbid, frigid, gelid, gravid, Haroun al-Rashid, hid,

ID
see
ALID
ED
EID

horrid, hybrid, ibid, id, insipid, in-
trepid, invalid, katydid, kid, Leonid,
lid, limpid, livid, lucid, lurid, Madrid,
masjid, mid, morbid, non-skid, orchid,
outbid, outdid, Ovid, pallid, pellucid,
placid, prussic acid, putrid, pyramid,
rabid, rancid, rapid, rid, rigid, sayid,
skid, slid, solid, sordid, splendid, stolid,
taurid, timid, torpid, torrid, turbid,
turgid, underbid, undid, valid, Valla-
dolid, vapid, viscid, vivid

ID
IED**
UID
UMID
UPID
YD

Bridal, cotidal, tidal, suicidal

IDAL
see
AL

Candidate, delapidate, elucidate, in-
timidate, invalidate, lapidate, liquid-
ate, validate

IDATE
see
ATE

Diddle, fiddle, griddle, middle, rid-
dle, twiddle, unriddle

IDDLE
see
EL

Abide, alongside, aside, astride,
autumn-tide, backslide, bedside, be-
side, betide, bona fide, bride, broad-
side, bromide, carbide, chide, coincide,
collide, confide, countryside, cyanide,
decide, deride, dioxide, divide, ebb-
tide, eventide, fireside, floodtide, gar-
den-side, glide, hayride, hide, hillside,
homicide, imbibe, ingleside, inside,
landslide, lopside, neap tide, noontide,
ocean-tide, outride, outside, over-ride,
oxhide, oxide, peroxide, preside, pride,
provide, rawhide, reside, ride, ringside,

IDE
see
EYE-*d*
ICIDE
IED*
UIDE
ed-ED
s-IDES**

roadside, seaside, set-aside, Shrovetide, **IDE**
side, slide, stand aside, stride, subside,
sulphide, summertide, tide, wayside,
Whitsuntide, wide, worldwide, yule-
tide

Accident, coincident, confident, in- **IDENT**
cident, occident, over-confident, presi- *see*
dent, provident, resident, strident, ENT
trident

Backslider, cider, circusrider, glider, **IDER**
outrider, outsider, provider, rider, *see*
roughrider, spider, wider ER

Aristides, cantharides, caryatides, **IDES***
Eumenides, Eumolpides, Hebrides, *see*
Hesperides, Maimonides, Oceanides, ES*
Thucydides

Besides, bestrides, coincides, Ides, **IDES****
Old Ironsides *see*
IDE-*s*

Abridge, auction bridge, bridge, **IDGE**
cartridge, Coleridge, covered bridge, *see*
drawbridge, footbridge, low bridge, AGE
partridge, pepperidge, porridge, ridge, EGE
tollbridge

Bridget, fidget, midget **IDGET**
see
ET

Antemeridian, meridian, nullifidian, **IDIAN**
Numidian, ophidian, quotidian *see*
IAN

Acidity, aridity, avidity, cupidity, fluidity, humidity, insipidity, intimity, intrepidity, lucidity, placidity, rapidity, sapidity, solidity, stupidity

IDITY
see
E**
ITY

Bridle, idle, sidle, unbridle

IDLE
see
EL
LE

Frigidly, idly, languidly, rigidly, timidly, vividly

IDLY
see
E**

Corridor, cuspidor, Fructidor, humidor, Messidor, Thermidor

IDOR
see
OR

Didst, midst

IDST
see

Width

IDTH
see

Bowie, brie, brownie, calorie, cap-à-pie, collie, coolie, coterie, dearie, Dixie, dominie, fantasie, gillie, girlie, kelpie, kiltie, lassie, lorrie, mashie, Mme. Curie, movie, nixie, organdie, parapluie, porgie, prairie, prima facie, rookie, sharpie, sortie, specie, talkie, Valkyrie

IE*
see
E**
ERIE
I**
S-EASE
E*-*s*
IES**

Belie, die, hie, huckleberry-pie, humble-pie, lie, magpie, mince-pie, necktie, pie, potpie, tie, untie, vie

IE**
see
EYE˙
I*

IE**
ed-IED*
s-ISE*

Altar-piece, fowling-piece, frontis-piece, itty-bitty piece, mantelpiece, masterpiece, mouthpiece, niece, piece, tailpiece

IECE
see
EASE**
ISE***

Allied, amplified, atrophied, certi-fied, citified, complied, countryfied, cried, crucified, defied, deified, denied, died, dried, espied, fortified, fried, glorified, gratified, hog-tied, implied, intensified, justified, lied, liquefied, magnified, mortified, multiplied, mum-mified, occupied, ossified, petrified, pied, pre-occupied, pried, purified, qualified, relied, replied, sanctified, satisfied, shied, spied, stupefied, sun-dried, supplied, tongue-tied, tried, un-occupied, unsatisfied, unversified, ver-sified

IED*
see
EYE-*d*
IDE
IE**-*d*

Ablebodied, astonied, buried, candid, dallied,. ivied, levied, mutinied, pal-sied, parodied, serried, Siegfried, studied, taxied, travestied, varied, wearied

IED**
see
ED
ID

Bas-relief, belief, brief, chief, dis-belief, grief, handkerchief, kerchief, mischief, relief, thief, unbelief

IEF
see
EAF*
EEF
s-EAVE-*s*

Besiege, liege, siege

IEGE
see
IGE

Shriek

IEK
see
EAK*
EEK

Abdiel, Ariel, cocker-spaniel, Daniel, Gamaliel, oriel, spaniel, spiel, Uriel

IEL
see
EL

Afield, cornfield, field, infield, outfield, paddyfield, shield, stubblefield, wield, windshield, yield

IELD
see
ed-ED
EAL*-*ed*
EEL-*ed*

Carpe diem, per diem, requiem

IEM
see
EM

Alien, St. Julien, T'ien

IEN*
see
EAN**

Lien, mien

IEN**
see
EEN

Audience, clairaudience, conscience, convenience, experience, faience, inconvenience, inexperience, nescience, obedience, omniscience, patience, prescience, resilience, sapience, science, subservience

IENCE
see
ENCE

Ambient, ancient, client, convenient, deficient, desipient, ebullient, efficient, emollient, esurient, expedient, gradi-

IENT
see
ENT

ent, incipient, inconvenient, inexpedi-
ent, ingredient, insufficient, lenient,
nescient, obedient, omniscient, Orient,
patient, percipient, proficient, pruri-
ent, recipient, reorient, resilient, sal-
ient, sapient, sentient, subservient,
sufficient

IENT

Angrier, atelier, barrier, bier, brazier,
brigadier, carrier, cashier, cavalier,
chandelier, chiffonier, chillier, collier,
courier, courtier, croupier, crozier,
dossier, duskier, easier, fancier, farrier,
financier, fox terrier, frontier, glacier,
glazier, grenadier, heavier, hoosier,
lordlier, manlier, merrier, mightier,
Montpellier, moodier, osier, pannier,
pier, prettier, premier, rapier, ruddier,
soldier, sorrier, terrier, tier, toy soldier,
town crier, vizier, Whittier, Xavier

IER*
see
ER
EAR*
ERE*

Amplifier, brier, flier, magnifier,
plier, purifier, sweet-brier

IER**
see
IRE
S-IRES

Fierce, pierce, tierce

IERCE
see

Arrière, boutonière, jardinière, por-
tière

IERE
see
ERE**

Apple pies, cries, dragon-flies, fire-
flies, flies, fortifies, lies, pies, plies,
ratifies, skies, squash pies, supplies,
tries, wailing-cries

IES*
see
IE**-s
ISE*
Y-s

Absurdities, argosies, Aries, arteries, Caesar's Commentaries, cavities, centuries, charities, cities, comedies, congeries, courtesies, curiosities, darbies, dictionaries, doweries, duties, Early Nineties, East Indies, economies, eddies, effigies, Eleusinian Mysteries, exigencies, fairies, fallacies, fantasies, fillies, fisheries, flag-lilies, frailties, Furies, gullies, harpies, idolatries, miseries, monies, Notes and Queries, obsequies, oddities, orgies, pansies, peonies, pickaninnies, pigmies, pixies, ponies, quanderies, rareties, remedies, reveries, roaring forties, rubies, scurries, series, species, strawberries, superficies, superfluities, theories, trophies, Tuileries

IES**
see
E**-*s*
EEZE
EY**-*s*
ICE**-*s*
IE*-*s*
IS**

Airiest, driest, earliest, flabbiest, funniest, leakiest, lowliest, prettiest, ricketiest, rustiest, scantiest, sorriest, stateliest, swankiest, tidiest, trickiest, wittiest, worthiest

IEST*
see
EST
UEST

High-priest, priest

IEST**
see
EASE**-*d*
EAST*
ISTE

Diet, disquiet, quiet, Soviet

IET
see
ET

Anxiety, contrariety, gaiety, impiety, moiety, noteriety, piety, propriety, satiety, sobriety, society, variety

IETY
see
E**

Adieu, lieu, prie-dieu, purlieu, Riche-
lieu

IEU
see
U

Achieve, believe, disbelieve, grieve,
make-believe, relieve, reprieve, re-
trieve, St. Genevieve, thieve

IEVE*
see
EAVE
EIVE
S-IEVES

Sieve

IEVE**
see
IVE**

Forty Thieves, retrieves, thieves

IEVES
see
IEVE*-S

Interview, mountain-view, pre-view,
purview, review, view

IEW
see
EW
O**

Frieze

IEZE
see
EASE*
EE-S
ESE

Alif, aperitif, calif, Chateau d'If, if,
khalif, motif

IF
see
IFE
YPH

Alewife, bowie-knife, fife, housewife,
inner-life, jack-knife, life, loosestrife,
midwife, pocket-knife, rife, strife, wife,
wild-life

IFE
see
S-IVE*-S

Fifer, lifer, Lucifer, thurifer	**IFER** *see* ER
Bailiff, biff, caitiff, Cardiff, cliff, hippogriff, jiff, mastiff, midriff, miff, Pecksniff, plaintiff, pontiff, sheriff, skiff, sniff, stiff, tariff, tiff, whiff	**IFF** *see* IF IPH YPH
Teneriffe	**IFFE** *see* IFF
Horrific, omnific, pacific, prolific, scientific, soporific, specific, sudorific, terrific, transpacific, unprolific	**IFIC** *see* IC
Edifice, orifice, sacrifice	**IFICE** *see* ICE**
Rifle, stifle, trifle	**IFLE** *see* EL LE
Anguilliform, cruciform, cuneiform, oviform, triform, uniform, vermiform	**IFORM** *see* ORM
Adrift, chimney-swift, drift, gift, lift, makeshift, rift, shift, shoplift, sift, snowdrift, spendthrift, swift, thrift, uplift	**IFT** *see* *ed*-ED

Beautiful, bountiful, dutiful, fanciful, merciful, pitiful, plentiful, overdutiful

IFUL
see
UL

Aerify, amplify, beautify, calcify, certify, clarify, classify, codify, crucify, deify, disqualify, diversify, dulcify, edify, electrify, falsify, fortify, fructify, gratify, horrify, identify, ignify, indemnify, intensify, justify, lapidify, lignify, liquify, magnify, modify, mollify, mortify, mummify, mystify, notify, nullify, ossify, pacify, personify, petrify, purify, qualify, ramify, ratify, rectify, requalify, revivify, salsify, sanctify, solidify, specify, speechify, stultify, terrify, testify, transmogrify, unify, verify, versify, vilify, vivify

IFY
see
I*
EFY
IGH
Y

Big, bigwig, brig, cat-rig, cig, dig, earwig, fig, gig, guinea-pig, jig, lady-pig, nig, periwig, phennig, pig, prig, rig, scratch-wig, swig, thimblerig, thingumajig, trig, twig, whig, whirli-gig, wig

IG
see

Cardigan, hooligan, ptarmigan

IGAN
see
AN*

Frigate, fumigate, fustigate, instigate, investigate, irrigate, litigate, mitigate, navigate, obligate, profligate

IGATE
see
ATE

Prestige, vestige

IGE*
see
IEGE

Oblige

IGE**
see

Bigger, digger, gold-digger, jigger, nigger, outrigger, rigger, square-rigger, trigger

IGGER
see
ER

Higgle, jiggle, niggle, wiggle, wriggle

IGGLE
see
EL
LE

Anigh, high, knee-high, nigh, sigh, thigh, wellnigh

IGH
see
I*

Affright, after-sight, airtight, alight, all-right, arc-light, aright, beacon-light, bedight, benight, bight, birth-right, blight, bright, bull-fight, candle-light, copyright, daylight, delight, dimlight, downright, drop-light, eye-bright, eyesight, fight, flashlight, flight, floodlight, fly-by-night, footlight, fore-sight, fortnight, fright, frosty-night, gaslight, goodnight, headlight, hind-sight, honor-bright, insight, Isle of Wight, knight, light, limelight, lusty-knight, midnight, might, moonlight, night, outright, overnight, oversight, pilot-light, playwright, plight, prize-fight, purple-night, rapid-flight, red-light, right, rush-light, sea-fight, searchlight, second-sight, shining light, sidelight, sight, sit-tight, skylight, slight, spotlight, stagefright, starlight, sticktight, summer's night, sunlight,

IGHT
see
EIGHT**
ITE*
YTE
ed-ED

tail-light, taper-light, tight, tonight, traffic-light, Twelfth-night, twilight, upright, watertight, wheelwright, wight, wright, yesternight
IGHT

Almighty, blighty, flighty, high and mighty, highty-tighty, mighty, nighty
IGHTY
see
E**

Enigma, sigma, stigma
IGMA
see
A**

Align, assign, benign, condign, consign, design, ensign, malign, resign, sign, traffic-sign
IGN
see
INE*
ed-IND*

Amigo, indigo, vertigo
IGO
see
O*

Bigot, spigot
IGOT
see
OT

Filigree, pedigree, perigee
IGREE
see
EE

Effigy, prodigy
IGY
see
E**

Batik, Bolshevik, mujik, sheik
IK
see
EAK
IK

Paprika, swastika

IKA
see
A**

Alike, aspen-like, belike, bike, child-like, dike, dislike, fanlike, ghostlike, gnomelike, gooselike, hitch-hike, homelike, hunger-strike, ladylike, marline-spike, mike, pike, proboscis-like, saintlike, sphinxlike, spike, sportsmanlike, statue-like, strike, suchlike, swanlike, tike, trance-like, turnpike, unlike, viselike, wandlike, war-like

IKE
see
AIK

Anvil, April, argil, Azrafil, basil, Boabdil, boll weevil, Brazil, cavil, cheveril, civil, codicil, council, coutil, daffodil, distil, fibril, fossil, fulfil, fusil, instil, lentil, nil, nostril, pencil, Salsabil, slatepencil, stencil, sweetbasil, tendril, tonsil, tumbril, uncivil, until, utensil, vigil, Virgil, Vril, weevil

IL
see
ERIL
ERYL
EVIL
ILE**
ILL
ILLE
UIL
ed-ILD*

Jubilant, sibilant, vigilant

ILANT
see
ANT*

Dissimilar, similar

ILAR
see
AR*

Annihilate, dilate, jubilate, mutilate, ventilate

ILATE
see
ATE

Filch, milch **ILCH**
see

Brunhild, gild, regild **ILD***
see
IL-*ed*
UILD

Child, godchild, grandchild, mild, **ILD****
wild
see
ILE*-*d*

Bewilder, builder, guilder **ILDER**
see
ER

Anile, awhile, camomile, compile, **ILE***
crocodile, defile, erstwhile, exile, file, *see*
Gentile, juvenile, meanwhile, mile, ISLE
Nile, pile, profile, reconcile, red-tile, UILE
reptile, revile, scissile, seldomwhile, YLE
senile, single-file, smile, statute mile, *ed*-ILD**
stile, tile, turnstile, vile, while, wile,
woodpile

Anglophile, automobile, bastile, bib- **ILE****
liophile, bissextile, Castile, cortile, *see*
docile, domicile, ductile, facile, febrile, EAL*
fertile, flexile, fluviatile, fragile, futile, EEL
hostile, imbecile, immobile, mercantile, IL
missile, mobile, pensile, prehensile,
projectile, puerile, servile, sextile, ster-
ile, subtile, tactile, tensile, textile,
virile, versatile, volatile

Campanile, facsimile, primum- **ILE*****
mobile, simile
see
E*

Compiler, tiler   **ILER**
see
ER

Merciless, penniless, pitiless   **ILESS**
see
ESS

Availeth, bewaileth, broileth, faileth, **ILETH**
soileth   *see*
ETH

Bilge   **ILGE**
see

Pavilion, postilion, vermilion   **ILION**
see
ION

Ability, anility, applicability, com- **ILITY**
patability, capability, civility, culpa-   *see*
bility, debility, dependability, disabil-   E**
ity, dividibility, durability, eligibility,
facility, fallibility, fertility, flexibility,
fraility, gentility, gullibility, immuta-
bility, impenetrability, inability, in-
civility, incompatibility, indefatigabil-
ity, indefectibility, indelibility, inev-
itability, infallibility, instability, in-
visibility, liability, mutability, negli-
gibility, nobility, notability, plausibil-
ity, possibility, probability, responsi-
bility, senility, servility, stability,
susceptibility, tangibility, tensibility,
utility, virility, visibility, volubility,
vulnerability

Asses' milk, bilk, buttermilk, ilk, milk, rawsilk, silk, skim milk

ILK
see

Ant-hill, bill, Bunker Hill, cambric-frill, chill, cranes-bill, dill, distill, door-sill, drill, duckbill, dunghill, fill, fire-drill, foothill, frill, fulfill, gill, goodwill, frill, gristmill, handbill, hill, hornbill, ill, ill-will, kill, mandrill, mill, mole-hill, pill, playbill, powder-mill, refill, rill, sandhill, sawmill, shrill, sill, skill, spill, spoonbill, standstill, still, stock-still, swill, thill, thrill, till, treadmill, trill, twill, uphill, whippoorwill, will, windmill, window-sill, Yggdrasill

ILL
see
IL
UILL
ed-ILD*
y-ILLY

Camilla, cedilla, chinchilla, Cinder-illa, flotilla, gorilla, guerilla, mantilla, Myrtilla, Priscilla, pulsatilla, sapodilla, sarsaparilla, scintilla, vanilla, villa

ILLA
see
A**

Bastille, chenille, dishabille, esca-drille, grille, Hotel de Ville, quadrille, Seville, soyez tranquille, vaudeville

ILLE
see
ILE**

Filler, miller, shriller, stiller, tiller, thriller

ILLER
see
ER

Billion, cotillion, million, pillion, trillion, vermillion

ILLION
see
ION

Armadillo, Murillo, negrillo, pecca-dillo

ILLO
see
O*

Billy, chilly, evilly, filly, hillbilly, hilly, Piccadilly, silly, stilly, willy nilly

ILLY
see
E**
ILL-*y*

Film, sound-film

ILM
see

Brickkiln, kiln, limekiln

ILN
see

Full-tilt, gilt, hilt, jilt, kilt, lilt, silt, spilt, stilt, tilt, wilt

ILT
see
UILT

Filth, spilth, tilth

ILTH
see

German silver, quicksilver, silver, solid silver

ILVER
see
ER

Bodily, busily, cannily, clammily, clumsily, craftily, daily, daintily, doily, dreamily, drearily, drowsily, easily, eerily, family, faultily, gaudily, gloomily, greedily, guiltily, homily, lazily, lily, luckily, lustily, merrily, mightily, moodily, pluckily, pondlily, primarily, scantily, shabbily, Sicily, speedily, spunkily, stealthily, temporarily, uncannily, unluckily, verily, voluntarily, waterlily, wily, wittily

ILY
see
E**
EE

Bedim, brim, broadbrim, cherubim, dim, Elohim, grim, him, interim, maxim, megrim, Mount Gerizim, passim, pilgrim, prim, Purim, rim,

IM
see
ATIM
ITHM

seraphim, skim, slim, swim, teraphim, **IM**
Thummim, trim, Urim, victim, whim ONYM
YMN
YTHM

Bellissima, Cloaca Maxima, Fatima, **IMA**
lacrima, Lima, quadragesima, septua- *see*
gesima, sexagesima, Yima A**

Animal, decimal, infinitesimal, max- **IMAL**
imal, millesimal, primal *see*
AL

Animate, antipenultimate, approxi- **IMATE**
mate, climate, decimate, estimate, in- *see*
animate, intimate, legitimate, over- ATE
estimate, penultimate, primate, proxi-
mate, reanimate, sublimate, ultimate

Limb **IMB***
see

Climb **IMB****
see

Limber, tall-timber, timber **IMBER**
see
ER

Nimble, thimble, wimble **IMBLE**
see
EL
LE

Aforetime, bedtime, begrime, be- **IME***
time, cherry-time, chime, classtime, *see*
clime, crime, dime, grime, lifetime, YME

lilac-time, lime, mealtime, meantime, **IME***
ofttime, overtime, pantomime, pas-
time, prime, quicklime, ragtime, rime,
seedtime, slime, sometime, sparetime,
springtime, sublime, summer-time,
swingtime, time, wartime

Intime, maritime, mime, régime   **IME****
see
EAM

Regimen, specimen   **IMEN**
see
EN

Accompaniment, aliment, compli-   **IMENT**
ment, condiment, crack regiment,   *see*
detriment, embodiment, experiment,   ENT
habiliment, impediment, liniment,
merriment, nutriment, orpiment, pre-
sentiment, raiment, regiment, re-em-
bodiment, rudiment, sediment, sentiment

Dimity, equanimity, magnanimity,   **IMITY**
proximity, sublimity, unanimity   *see*
E****
ITY

Dimmer, glimmer, shimmer, simmer,   **IMMER**
slimmer   *see*
ER

Centimo, duodecimo, Eskimo, for-   **IMO**
tissimo, generalissimo, Geronimo, pia-   *see*
nissimo, prestissimo, primo, proximo,   O*
ultimo

Blimp, crimp, imp, limp, pimp, primp, scrimp, shrimp, simp, skimp

IMP
see
UIMP

Dimple, pimple, simple, wimple

IMPLE
see
EL
LE

Glimpse

IMPSE
see

A-cluckin' adrenalin, a-grin, akin, Aladdin, all in, antitoxin, assassin, a-throbbin', bareskin, basin, bearskin, begin, belaying pin, bewitchin', bin, bodkin, bowfin, Brahmin, break-in, buckskin, built-in, bulletin, bumpkin, buskin, cabin, calfskin, Capuchin, catkin, chagrin, chin, chinquapin, Chopin, clavecin, clothespin, cock-robin, coffin, cousin, creeping-in, cretin, cruisin', cryin', cumin, Darwin, dauphin, deerskin, din, doeskin, dolphin, Dublin, duckpin, dunlin, exceedin', Fagin, feelin', fetchin', fin, firkin, fit-in, florin, gelatin, gherkin, gin, goblin, griffin, grimalkin, grin, herein, highfalutin, hin, hobgoblin, in, insulin, interruptin', Jacobin, jasmin, jerkin, kaolin, khamsin, kin, king-pin, Kremlin, lambskin, linchpin, listen-in, logcabin, Lohengrin, lupin, mandarin, mannikin, margin, martin, matin, maudlin, Mazarin, mechlin, Merlin, metheglin, moccasin, moleskin, muezzin, muffin, muslin, napkin, nine-pin, nothin', nubbin, Odin, oilskin, origin,

IN
see
AMIN
ATIN
ELIN
ERIN
INN
OLIN
UIN
al-AL
ed-IND**
s-INS

paladin, paraffin, Pekin, Pepin, pepsin, pidgin, pigskin, pin, pippin, poplin, prevailin', protein, puffin, pumpkin, push-in, rabbin, ragamuffin, raisin, ramekin, Redskin, replevin, resin, rolling-pin, round robin, running-in, Ruskin, saccharin, safety-pin, Saladin, Sanhedrin, scarf-pin, sculpin, sealskin, sea-urchin, sheepskin, shin, sin, skin, sloe gin, spadassin, spavin, spillikin, spin, St. Swithin, tailspin, tannin, tarpaulin, tellin', terrapin, therein, Theremin, thin, thole-pin, Tientsin, tiffin, tocsin, toxin, tune-in, twin, underpin, urchin, vermin, virgin, wanderin', washbasin, welkin, wherein, win, within, Yin

IN

Ægina, Agrippina, ballerina, Carolina, Catalina, cavatina, China, Cochin China, concertina, czarina, lamina, Maria Farina, Medina, Messalina, ocarina, Proserpina, regina, retina, saltina, Salva Regina, stamina, vina

INA
see
A**

Aboriginal, cardinal, criminal, final, germinal, latitudinal, libidinal, longitudinal, marginal, matutinal, nominal, original, paginal, Quirinal, subliminal, terminal, virginal

INAL
see
AL
IN-*al*

Culinary, extraordinary, imaginary, luminary, ordinary, preliminary, sanguinary, seminary, veterinary

INARY
see
ARY

Assassinate, culminate, determinate, disseminate, dominate, eliminate, exterminate, fascinate, fulminate, germi-

INATE
see
ATE

nate, hallucinate, illuminate, incrimi-
nate, indeterminate, insubordinate,
nominate, obstinate, originate, pere-
grinate, predominate, procrastinate,
recriminate, ruminate, subordinate,
terminate, vaccinate

INATE

Zinc

INC
see
INK

Black Prince, convince, evince,
mince, prince, province, quince, since,
wince

INCE
see
INT-*s*

Bullfinch, chaffinch, cinch, clinch,
finch, flinch, goldfinch, inch, pinch,
winch

INCH
see
YNCH

Distinct, extinct, indistinct, pre-
cinct, succinct

INCT
see
INK-*ed*

Behind, bind, blind, colorblind,
grind, humankind, kind, mankind,
master mind, mind, never-mind, pur-
blind, remind, rind, unkind, unwind,
wind, window-blind

IND*
see
IGN-*ed*
INE*-*d*

Etesian wind, night-wind, rescind,
second wind, tamarind, trade-wind,
west-wind, whirlwind, wind

IND**
see
IN-*ed*

Binder, blinder, cinder, cylinder,
grinder, hinder, path-finder, reminder,
stem-winder

INDER
see
ER

Brindle, dwindle, kindle, rekindle, spindle, swindle

INDLE
see
EL
LE

Airline, alkaline, Alpine, aniline, Apennine, aquiline, asinine, balloon vine, bovine, Brandywine, bread line, brine, canine, chalk-line, clothesline, coalmine, columbine, combine, concubine, confine, crystalline, decline, define, dine, disincline, divine, eglantine, enshrine, entwine, feline, fine, fishline, gadding vine, goldmine, grapevine, greedy-swine, headline, incline, intertwine, iodine, kine, leonine, line, lordly pine, lupine, mine, monkeyshine, moonshine, nine, opine, outline, Palatine, Palestine, pine, pitch-pine, plumbline, porcupine, port wine, quinine, ratline, recline, redwine, refine, repine, Rhine, rush line, saltmine, seabrine, sea-line, serpentine, shine, shoreline, shrine, side-line, sine, skyline, spine, streamline, strychnine, superfine, supine, swine, tapeline, thine, tine, trellised-vine, turbine, twine, undermine, valentine, vine, vulpine, water-line, whine, white wine, wine, woodbine

INE*
see
IGN
YNE
ed-IND*
s-INES

Adamantine, adrenaline, alexandrine, amaranthine, aquamarine, Argentine, atropine, Aventine, bandoline, Benedictine, benzine, brigantine, caprine, carmine, chlorine, clandestine, Constantine, crinoline, cuisine, destine,

INE**
see
AZINE
EAN
EEN
ENE

determine, discipline, doctrine, ele-
phantine, engine, ermine, Euxine,
Evangeline, famine, feminine, figurine,
fluorine, gaberdine, gamine, gasoline,
Ghibelline, grenadine, guillotine, heroine, horse marine, hyaline, illumine,
imagine,' incarnadine, intestine, jessa-
mine, latrine, leporine, levantine, lib-
ertine, limousine, machine, margarine,
marine, masculine, mazarine, medi-
cine, mezzanine, muscadine, nectarine,
opaline, ovine, palatine, paraffine,
pelerine, peregrine, Philippine, Philis-
tine, phocine, pilot-machine, porcine,
praline, predestine, pristine, quaran-
tine, rapine, ravine, routine, Sabine,
saccharine, saline, Sibylline, Sistine,
slot-machine, submarine, tambourine,
tangerine, tourmaline, transpontine,
ultramarine, undine, ursine, vaccine,
vaseline, vitamine

INE**
ERINE
IENE
UIN
UINE

Continent, eminent, imminent, im-
pertinent, incontinent, pertinent, pre-
eminent, prominent

INENT
see
ENT

Ancient Mariner, diner, finer, forty-
niner, liner, mariner, milliner, miner,
moonshiner, ocean-liner, refiner, shiner,
shriner

INER
see
ER

Bulkiness, business, cloudiness, cozi-
ness, dinginess, dowdiness, emptiness,
fussiness, fustiness, ghastliness, giddi-
ness, guiltiness, happiness, haughti-
ness, headiness, holiness, loneliness,
loveliness, mightiness, mistiness, petti-

INESS
see
ES**
ESS

ness, readiness, silliness, steadiness, **INESS**
sultriness, surliness, tidiness, uneasi-
ness, weariness, wordiness, worthiness

Bassinet, bobbinet, cabinet, clarinet, **INET**
martinet, spinet   *see*
                                        ET

Absorbing, according, a-Maying, **ING**
amazing, ambling, amusing, angling,   *see*
anything, apronstring, a-wing, awning, ARING
baffling, bee-keeping, beetling, befit- ATING
ting, begrudging, belting, bing, bless- EING
ing, bloodcurdling, blueing, bombing,   OMING
boring, bowling, bowstring, boxing,   ER-*ing*
bring, Browning, building, bungling,   *ly*-E**
bunting, bustling, carding, carting,   *s*-INGS
casing, ceiling, central-heating, chafing,
charming, chattering, cling, clinging,
closing, cod-fishing, coming, cotton-
batting, crystal-gazing, cruising, cun-
ning, curdling, damning, dancing, dar-
ling, dazzling, directing, dismantling,
diverting, do-nothing, drawing, dress-
ing, drifting, duckling, dumpling, dur-
ing, dwelling, dying, easy-going, en-
circling, ending, Erl-king, etching,
everlasting, face-lifting, far-reaching,
far-seeing, farthing, fawning, feeling,
flapping, fledgling, fleeting, flinching,
fling, flouting, flowing, foregoing, foun-
dling, fringing, frisking, gangling, glis-
tening, glowing, going, goodbreeding,
gosling, grilling, gurgling, gushing,
hamstring, harrowing, hasty pudding,
hazel-sapling, heat-lightning, heckling,
hedging, herring, Highland fling, hik-

ing, hireling, hobnobbing, hooting, howling, huddling, hustling, hymning, ill-feeling, imposing, incoming, indwelling, ingrowing, inkling, jarring, jolting, jostling, juggling, key-ring, kidding, kindling, king, Kipling, kneeling, knitting, landscaping, lapwing, lashing, lasting, latchstring, law-abiding, leave-taking, libelling, lightning, liking, lining, lodging, log-rolling, longing, long-standing, longsuffering, lunging, luring, lurking, lutestring, lying, mainspring, marshaling, mass meeting, matting, maying, mellowing, merry-making, mining, moiling, mooring, morning, motoring, mumbling, Nanking, necking, nestling, never-ending, nothing, notwithstanding, nursling, obliging, offing, offspring, oncoming, opening, out-building, outlying, outpouring, outstanding, overlooking, padding, painstaking, painting, paling, parting, Peiping, pervading, pettifogging, petting, piffling, playing, poor-thing, prevailing, priming, princeling, prize-ring, prompting, prying, pudding, purling, ranking, rattling, reckoning, redwing, rigging, ring, rising, ruching, rustling, sacking, sapling, scantling, screaming, sea-faring, sea-going, sea-king, seal-ring, seasoning, seedling, seething, self-denying, sewing, shambling, shelving, shepherd-king, shocking, shoestring, shortening, shrouding, sidesplitting, sightseeing, signet-ring, shilling, simpling, sing, singing, skulking, sling, smattering, snarling, soothing, spooning, spraying, spring, star-gazing, starling, startling, sterling, stilling, sting, stocking, string, strutting, sucking, suckling, swaddling, swelling, swing, swirling, swooping, tantalizing, Tao-Teh-King, tap-dancing, teeming, teething, thanksgiving, thing, thorough-going, thronging, time-serving, tingling, town-meeting, trekking, twinkling, ugly-duckling, underling, underpinning, undying, unending, unfeeling, unflinching, unknowing, untiring, unveiling, upbuilding, uplifting, upstanding, upswing, upyearning, using, vanishing, varnishing, Viking, wainscoting, waning, warning, waxing, webbing, wedding, well-being, wending, whaling, whirling, whiting, wing, winning, witling, worldling, wring, writing, yawning, yearling, yearning

ING

Astringe, binge, constringe, cringe, fringe, hinge, impinge, infringe, intertinge, singe, syringe, tinge, twinge, unhinge

INGE
see

Finger, ginger, harbinger, lady-finger, linger, minnesinger, porringer, singer, slinger, wringer

INGER
see
ER

Commingle, ingle, intermingle, jingle, Kris Kringle, mingle, shingle, single, surcingle, tingle

INGLE
see
EL
LE

Bingo, dingo, flamingo, gringo, jingo, lingo, San Domingo

INGO
see
O*

Apronstrings, armorial bearings, blessings, dwellings, innings, invisible wings, playthings, shillings, stockings, strings, things, wings

INGS
see
ING-*s*

Meringue

INGUE
see
ANG

Anno Domini, Benvenuto Cellini, contadini, Gemini, martini, Mussolini, Paganini, Puccini, Rimini, Rossini

INI
see
I**

Actinic, clinic

INIC
see
IC

Dominion, minion, opinion, pinion

INION
see
ION

Consanguinity, femininity, infinity, trinity, vicinity, virginity

INITY
see
E**
ITY

Bethink, blink, bobolink, brink, chewink, chink, clink, clovepink, drink, hoodwink, India-ink, interlink, jink, kink, link, mink, pen-and-ink, pink, prink, rink, rinky-dink, river-brink, shell pink, shrink, sink, slink, stink, think, wink

INK
see
INC
ed-INCT
s-INKS
INX
YNX

Blinker, diesinker, drinker, pinker, stinker, thinker, tinker

INKER
see
ER

Crinkle, periwinkle, Rip van Winkle, sprinkle, twinkle, wrinkle

INKLE
see
EL
LE

Cuff-links, golf-links, methinks

INKS
see
INK-*s*

Dinky, inky, kinky, pinky

INKY
see
E**

Inn, jinn, Tabard Inn, Wayside Inn

INN
see
IN

Dinner, inner, sinner, spinner, thinner, tinner, winner

INNER
see
ER

Finny, hinny, ninny, picaninny, shinny, tinny, whinny

INNY
see
E**

Albino, bambino, casino, domino, Filipino, maraschino, merino, Solferino

INO
see
O*

Bituminous, heinous, libidinous, luminous, mucilaginous, multitudinous, mutinous, ominous, platitudinous, resinous, ruinous, villainous, voluminous

INOUS
see
OUS

Asvins, fins, gherkins, ins, muggins, ninepins, nubbins, Redskins, shins, sins, skins, step-ins, Tom Collins, water-skins, wins

INS
see
IN-*s*

Rinse **INSE**
see
INCE

Blueprint, cuckoopint, dint, finger- **INT**
print, flint, footprint, glint, hint, hoof- *see*
print, imprint, lint, mezzotint, mint, s-INCE
peppermint, print, reprint, Septaugint,
skinflint, sodamint, spearmint, splint,
sprint, squint, stint, tint, varmint

Inter, printer, splinter, sprinter, **INTER**
winter *see*
ER

Absinth, Corinth, hyacinth, jacinth, **INTH**
labyrinth, plinth, terebinth *see*

Faintly, quaintly, saintly **INTLY**
see
E**

Chintz **INTZ**
see
INT-s

Linus, minus, Ninus, Plotinus, Qui- **INUS**
rinus, sinus, Tarquinus, terminus *see*
US

Jinx, minx, sphinx, Syrinx **INX**
see
INK-s
YNX

Briny, destiny, hominy, ignominy, **INY**
mutiny, Pliny, scrutiny, shiny, tiny *see*
E**

Adagio, addio, agio, arpeggio, Bellagio, Boccaccio, braggadocio, cheerio, Clio, Correggio, curio, ex-officio, finochio, Horatio, imbroglio, intaglio, internuncio, Io, nuncio, oratorio, patio, pistachio, Ponte Vecchio, presidio, punctilio, radio, ratio, Rio, Scipio, Scorpio, seraglio, solfeggio, studio, tertio, Tokio, trio

IO
see
ARIO
O*
OLIO

Hesiod, period

IOD
see
OD

Viol, vitriol

IOL
see
OL

Axiom, idiom

IOM
see
OM

Abjection, abortion, absorption, accordion, action, adhesion, adjunction, affection, air condition, Albion, Amphion, anthelion, ant lion, ascension, assertion, assumption, attention, battalion, benefaction, bisection, boon companion, bullion, carrion, caution, centurion, champion, circumscription, circumspection, coercion, Coeur de Lion, collection, collodion, companion, compulsion, conception, concoction, concretion, concussion, confection, congestion, conjunction, connection, contagion, contortion, contraction, contraption, convention, conversion,

ION
see
ASION
ATION
EGION
EON
ESSION
IATION
ICTION
ILION
ILLION
INION
ISION
ISSION
ITION

correction, corruption, counteraction, criterion, crucifixion, cushion, dandelion, deception, decoction, defection, dejection, description, Deucalion, dimension, discretion, discussion, disruption, distention, distortion, diversion, election, emotion, emulsion, enchiridion, Endymion, erection, exception, excursion, expansion, extension, extortion, extroversion, faction, fashion, film-version, fourth dimension, function, gammadion, ganglion, gumption, high tension, Hyperion, Ilion, inaction, inattention, incorruption, incursion, indigestion, indiscretion, induction, infraction, inhesion, injunction, inquisition, insertion, insurrection, intention, interjection, interruption, intervention, introspection, introversion, invention, inversion, Ion, irruption, Ixion, junction, lesion, lion, maladaption, mansion, Marmion, medallion, mention, mullion, objection, oblivion, old-fashion, onion, oppression, option, orchestrion, Orion, passion, pension, perception, percussion, perfection, perihelion, perversion, petrifaction, pincushion, portion, precaution, predilection, prelection, presumption, prevention, proportion, proscription, protection, putrefaction, Pygmalion, quaternion, question, rapscallion, reaction, recollection, redaction, redemption, reflection, reflexion, refraction, rejection, religion, repercussion, resumption, resurrection, revulsion, sanction, scion, scorpion, scul-

ION
ON
OSION
OTION
UCTION
UN
UNION
USION
UTION
al-AL
IONAL

lion, section, selection, stallion, stan- **ION**
chion, subjection, subscription, sugges-
tion, suspension, suspicion, tension,
traction, transaction, transfixion, unc-
tion, version, vivisection

Confessional, conventional, dimen- **IONAL**
sional, emotional, exceptional, frac- *see*
tional, functional, intentional, inter- AL
national, irrational, national, notional,
occasional, optional, precessional, pro-
fessional, proportional, rational, recessional, sectional, sensational, traditional, transitional, vocational

Anterior, behavior, excelsior, exte- **IOR**
rior, inferior, interior, junior, Melchior, *see*
mother-superior, posterior, prior, sen- OR
ior, superior, ulterior, warrior ORE

A fortiori, a posteriori, a priori **IORI**
 see
 I**

Adios, Helios **IOS**
 see
 OS

Grandiose, otiose **IOSE**
 see
 OSE

Chariot, cheviot, compatriot, idiot, **IOT**
Judas Iscariot, patriot, riot *see*
 OT

Abstemious, acrimonious, adsciti-
tious, adventitious, amphibious, anx-
ious, atrocious, auspicious, bilious,
bumptious, calumnious, capricious,
captious, cautious, ceremonious, com-
modious, compendious, conscientious,
conscious, contagious, contentious, co-
pious, curious, delicious, delirious,
disputatious, dubious, egregious, en-
vious, expeditious, fastidious, feloni-
ous, ferocious, fictitious, flagitious,
furious, glorious, gregarious, harmoni-
ous, hilarious, ignominious, impecuni-
ous, imperious, impervious, impious,
inauspicious, industrious, infectious,
ingenious, inglorious, inharmonious,
injudicious, injurious, insidious, invidi-
ous, irreligious, judicious, laborious,
licentious, lugubrious, luscious, luxuri-
ous, malicious, melodious, meretricious,
meritorious, multifarious, mysterious,
nefarious, notorious, noxious, nutri-
tious, oblivious, obnoxious, obsequious,
obvious, odious, officious, opprobrious,
ostentatious, overcurious, parsimoni-
ous, penurious, perfidious, pernicious,
pious, pluvious, precarious, precious,
precocious, pretentious, previous, pro-
digious, propitious, punctilious, rebel-
lious, religious, sacrilegious, salubrious,
sanctimonious, scrumptious, seditious,
self-conscious, serious, specious, spuri-
ous, studious, subconscious, supercili-
ous, superstitious, surreptitious, suspi-
cious, tedious, unceremonious, uncon-
scious, uxorious, vainglorious, various,
vexatious, vicarious, vicious, victorious

IOUS
see
ACIOUS
AMUS
EUS*
OUS
UOUS
US
ly-E**
OUSLY

Adeptship, apostleship, battleship, buggy-whip, catnip, celery-tip, censorship, championship, chip, clip, clubship, companionship, cork-tip, courtship, cowslip, dictatorship, dip, drip, equip, fellowship, finger-tip, flip, gossip, grip, guardianship, harc-lip, hardship, hero-worship, hip, horsewhip, kinship, ladyship, lightship, leadership, lip, lordship, marksmanship, midship, nip, outstrip, ownership, parsnip, partnership, penmanship, phantom-ship, pillowslip, pleasure-trip, potato-chip, quip, round trip, ruby-lip, sailingship, scholarship, scrip, ship, showmanship, sip, skip, slip, snip, strip, tallowdip, tree-worship, trip, troop-ship, tulip, turnip, warship, whaleship, whip, worship, zip

IP
see
ed-IPT
YPT
s-IPSE

Assurbanipal, municipal, principal

IPAL
see
AL

Anticipate, dissipate, emancipate, participate

IPATE
see
ATE

Bagpipe, blowpipe, briar-pipe, cobpipe, gripe, guttersnipe, hornpipe, organpipe, over-ripe, pipe, pitchpipe, rareripe, reedpipe, ripe, sideswipe, snipe, stovepipe, stripe, swipe, tomahawk-pipe, tripe, unripe, windpipe, wipe

IPE
see
YPE

Juniper, pen-wiper, Pied Piper, piper, sandpiper, sniper, swiper, viper

IPER
see
ER

Caliph **IPH**
see
IFF

Disciple, multiple, participle, principle, triple **IPLE**
see
EL
LE

Big Dipper, clipper, dipper, flipper, gallinipper, lady's-slipper, ripper, shipper, skipper, slipper, tripper, worshipper, zipper **IPPER**
see
ER

Cripple, nipple, ripple, stipple, tipple **IPPLE**
see
EL
LE

Eclipse, ellipse **IPSE**
see
IP-*s*

Gipsy, tipsy **IPSY**
see
E**

Conscript, manuscript, nipt, nondescript, postscript, script, transcript **IPT**
see
IP-*ed*
YPT
s-IPSE

Antique, bezique, cacique, clique, critique, lyrique, Mozambique, oblique, perique, physique, pique, pneumatique, pratique, technique, unique **IQUE**
see
EAK*
EEK

Astir, bestir, decemvir, elixir, Elzevir, emir, fakir, fir, Guadalquivir, kaffir, Kashmir, Mimir, nadir, Ophir, sir, souvenir, stir, tapir, triumvir, Vladimir, Ymir

IR
see
ARTYR
ERE**
IRR
UR
YRRH

Ça ira, Hegira, lira, Sapphira, Sephira

IRA
see
A**

Conspiracy, piracy

IRACY
see
ACY
E**

Irate, pirate, triumvirate

IRATE
see
ATE

Besmirch, birch, smirch

IRCH
see
URCH

Arctic Circle, circle, encircle, semicircle, sewing-circle

IRCLE
see
EL
LE

Bird, blackbird, catbird, gird, jailbird, jaybird, lovebird, mockingbird, night-bird, railbird, reedbird, secretary bird, third

IRD
see
ORD**
IR-*ed*
IRE-*d*

Admire, afire, aspire, attire, Ayrshire, back-fire, barb-wire, bonfire, campfire, conspire, cross-fire, crosswire, desire, Devonshire, dire, empire, expire, fire, for-hire, grandsire, gunfire, haywire, hire, inspire, ire, live wire, mire, mis-fire, perspire, pismire, quagmire, re-spire, retire, samphire, sapphire, satire, shire, spare-tire, spitfire, suspire, tire, transpire, umpire, vampire, watch-fire, wildfire, wire

IRE
 see
 ER
 IAR
 IER***
 OIR*
 UIRE
 YRE
 ed-EARD*
 S-IRES

Dirge

IRGE
 see
 OURGE

Dirk, irk, kirk, quirk, shirk, smirk

IRK
 see
 ERK
 ORK

Flower-girl, girl, old-girl, skirl, swirl, twirl, whirl

IRL
 see
 EARL
 URL
 ed-ORLD

Affirm, confirm, firm, infirm, squirm

IRM
 see
 ORM**

Andiron, castiron, Chiron, curling-iron, environ, flatiron, grappling-iron, gridiron, iron, midiron, pig-iron, sad-iron, wrought-iron

IRON
 see
 ON

Whirr | **IRR**
see
IR

First, thirst | **IRST**
see
ORST
URST

Begirt, black shirt, dirt, flirt, girt, hobble-skirt, hoopskirt, outskirt, red shirt, seagirt, shirt, skirt, steel-girt, stuffed-shirt, undershirt | **IRT**
see
UIRT
URT

Birth, firth, girth, mirth, rebirth | **IRTH**
see
ORTH**

Inquiry, miry, spiry, wiry | **IRY**
see
E**

Aegis, amaryllis, analepsis, analysis, Annus Mirabilis, Anubis, aphis, Apis, Artemis, Atlantis, Attis, axis, Bubastis, caddis, Chablis, Charybdis, Clovis, Colchis, crisis, De Profundis, Dis, Eblis, Eleusis, ephemeris, epidermis, Fenris, finis, hamamelis, Harmachis, houris, ibis, Iblis, ichthyornis, iris, Isis, Lake Moeris, laryngitis, mantis, marquis, Memphis, morris, myosotis, non compos mentis, Nunc Dimittis, ora pro nobis, orris, Osiris, parvis, pelvis, Phyllis, portcullis, proboscis, prognosis, Propontis, psycho-analysis, rara avis, sacred-ibis, Salamis, Salmacis, salpiglossis, Sardis, Semiramis, | **IS***
see
AIS
ALIS
ARIS
ASIS
ATIS
ESIS
ICE**
ISE****
ISS
OLIS
ONIS
OPSIS
OSIS
UCE**

semper fidelis, Serapis, Sesostris, Smerdis, stephanotis, tennis, Thamyris, Themis, thesis, Thetis, this, Tiflis, Tigris, trellis, Tunis, Walpurgis

IS*

Chassis, his, is, 'tis, this-is

IS**
see
IZ
ACE-*S*
EACH-*S*

Ambergris, verdigris

IS***
see
EESE****

Artisan, Nisan, non-partisan, partisan

ISAN
see
AN*

Disc

ISC
see
ISK

Advise, anywise, apprise, arise, catechise, chastise, circumcise, coastwise, comprise, compromise, contrariwise, corner-wise, crosswise, demise, despise, devise, edgewise, enterprise, exercise, exorcise, franchise, improvise, incise, leastwise, lengthwise, likewise, merchandise, moonrise, mortal-wise, nowise, otherwise, penny-wise, revise, rise, slant-wise, suchwise, sunrise, supervise, surmise, surprise, thuswise, unwise, weatherwise, wise

ISE*
see
IZE
EYE-*S*
IE**-*S*
IES*

Concise, Paradise, precise

ISE**
see
ICE*

Cerise, chemise, Heloise, marquise, valise

ISE***
see
EASE**
EESE**
ESE

Anise, mortise, practise, premise, promise, treatise

ISE****
see
ISS

Appetiser, despiser, Kaiser, miser, wiser

ISER
see
ER

Accomplish, admonish, apish, astonish, backshish, banish, blemish, bluefish, bookish, boorish, boyish, brackish, brandish, British, brutish, bulldoggish, burnish, butterdish, cat-fish, cattish, chafing-dish, churlish, cloddish, clownish, coltish, Cornish, crawfish, dervish, devilish, disrelish, elfish, embellish, English, establish, famish, fetish, finish, fish, Flemish, flourish, foolish, freakish, furbish, furnish, garish, garnish, girlish, goldfish, grayish, greenish, hashish, heathenish, hellish, hoggish, horseradish, hoydenish, impish, Irish, jelly-fish, Jewish, knavish, lavish, loutish, mannish, mawkish, minish, modish, monkish, Moorish, mulish, oafish, offish, ogreish, outlandish, paganish, parish, peevish, pilot-fish, pound-fool-

ISH
see
EESH
ERISH
OLISH
UISH
ly-E**

ish, priggish, prudish, publish, punish, **ISH**
radish, rakish, ravish, reddish, relish,
replenish, rubbish, sawfish, selfish,
sheepish, shellfish, shrewish, skirmish,
skittish, slavish, sluggish, snobbish,
Spanish, squeamish, starfish, stiffish,
sunfish, swish, swordfish, tarnish, Tar-
shish, ticklish, undiminish, vanish,
varnish, waggish, waspish, whirling
dervish, whitish, wish, womanish, Yid-
dish

Fisher, garnisher, kingfisher, pub- **ISHER**
lisher, well-wisher *see*
ER

Decision, derision, division, elision, **ISION**
envision, incision, indecision, precision, *see*
prevision, provision, revision, super- ION
vision, television, vision

Asterisk, basilisk, bisk, brisk, disk, **ISK**
frisk, obelisk, risk, tamarisk, whisk *see*
ISQUE

Frisky, risky, whisky **ISKY**
see
E**

Aisle, blessed-isle, Carlisle, Emerald **ISLE**
Isle, fairy-isle, lisle, safety-isle, sea- *see*
swept-isle ILE*

Actinism, altruism, analogism, an- **ISM**
thropomorphism, aphorism, asterism, *see*
atavism, baptism, barbarism, Bolshe- AISM
vism, Brahmanism, Buddhism, cate- ALISM
chism, chauvinism, chrism, collecti- ICISM
vism, conservatism, despotism, dyna- ONISM

mism, egoism, egotism, empiricism, epicurism, exorcism, Fascism, galvanism, gormandism, henotheism, heroism, hyperbolism, incendiarism, Islamism, magnetism, mannerism, mechanism, mesmerism, metabolism, micro-organism, modernism, monotheism, Nazism, nepotism, nihilism, occultism, Ophism, optimism, organism, ostracism, pacifism, paganism, pantheism, pedagogism, pessimism, phallicism, polytheism, prism, proletarianism, propagandism, pugilism, purism, quietism, recidivism, red-tapism, republicanism, rheumatism, rowdyism, Sabæanism, sabbatism, Sadism, savagism, schism, Shiism, sinapism, skepticism, solecism, somnambulism, sophism, Sufism, surrealism, sybaritism, syllogism, symbolism, theism, totemism, vandalism, voodooism, witticism

ISM
UISM
YSM

Benison, bison, caparison, comparison, garrison, imprison, jettison, Kyrie eleison, liaison, orison, poison, prison, unison, venison

ISON
see
ON

Crisp, lisp, will-o'-the-wisp, wisp

ISP
see

Bisque, odalisque

ISQUE
see
ISK

Amiss, bliss, cumiss, dismiss, hiss, kiss, miss, Swiss, remiss

ISS
see
IS*
YSS
ed-IST

Admission, emission, intermission, mission, omission, permission, remission, submission, transmission

ISSION
see
ION

Fissue, issue, tissue

ISSUE
see
UE

Alarmist, alchemist, apiculturist, artist, atheist, atomist, atwist, autoist, balladist, banjoist, Baptist, bicyclist, bigamist, Bonapartist, caricaturist, cartoonist, chemist, cist, colonist, columnist, Communist, computist, conformist, consist, copyist, cubist, cyclist, deist, dentist, desist, druggist, egoist, egotist, equilibrist, enlist, eucharist, evangelist, exist, exorcist, fabulist, Fascist, fatalist, feminist, fist, florist, futurist, gist, glossarist, grist, herbalist, hist, hobbyist, homilist, humorist, insist, journalist, jurist, leftist, list, lobbyist, loyalist, Methodist, miniaturist, mist, moralist, motorist, naturalist, nihilist, non conformist, novelist, nudist, obscurantist, occultist, Oliver Twist, opportunist, optimist, optometrist, organist, orientalist, pacifist, palmist, parodist, Paulist, persist, pessimist, pharmaceutist, pharmacist, philatelist, physicist, physiognomist, physiologist, pianist, plagiarist, polytheist, propagandist, psalmist, psychist, pugilist, purist, pyramidologist, Quietist, realist, resist, revivalist, rhapsodist, rightist, ritualist, Romanist, royalist, Sadist, satirist, scientist, Scotch-mist,

IST*
see
OGIST
ONIST
UIST
YST*
ICE**-*ed*

shortist, soloist, somnambulist, sophist, specialist, strategist, stylist, subsist, surrealist, taxlist, thaumaturgist, theist, theurgist, tourist, Trappist, twist, violinist, vocalist, whist, wrist, wist

IST*

Christ

IST**
see

Ballista, genista, vista

ISTA
see
A**

Artiste, batiste, modiste

ISTE
see
EAST*
YST**

Administer, barrister, blister, canister, minister, mister, register, sinister, sister

ISTER
see
ER

Altruistic, anachronistic, animistic, anomalistic, artistic, cabalistic, Calvinistic, casuistic, characteristic, chremastistic, deistic, egoistic, egotistic, Elohistic, euphuistic, fatalistic, inartistic, Jehovistic, linguistic, militaristic, modernistic, optimistic, pantheistic, pessimistic, phlogistic, realistic, ritualistic, sadistic, spiritistic, statistic

ISTIC
see
IC

Bristle, epistle, gristle, peanut whistle, thistle, whistle

ISTLE
see
EL
LE

Artistry, chemistry, ministry, palmistry, papistry, registry, sophistry

ISTRY
see
E**

Accredit, adit, admit, affidavit, audit, bandit, befit, benefit, bit, bottomless pit, bowsprit, chit, coalpit, cock-pit, comfit, commit, cubit, culprit, davit, debit, decline-it, decrepit, deposit, digit, discomfit, dispirit, emigravit, emit, exit, explicit, fit, flit, grit, habit, half-wit, hermit, hit, Holy Writ, howbeit, illicit, inhabit, intermit, ipse-dixit, it, jack-in-the-pulpit, kit, knit, lamplit, licit, lickety-split, limit, lit, make-up kit, manumit, misfit, moonlit, nimble-wit, nit, nit-wit, no-hit, obit, omit, orbit, outfit, outwit, permit, pit, plaudit, posit, profit, prohibit, prosit, pulpit, pundit, rabbit, refit, remit, revisit, Sanskrit, sit, skit, slit, so-be-it, spirit, spit, split, sprit, starlit, stonepit, submit, summit, Tashmit, tidbit, tit, to wit, transit, twit, unfit, unit, visit, vomit, welsh-rabbit, whit, wit, writ

IT
see
EDIT
EIT**
ERIT
IBIT
ICIT
ITE**
UIT*
ed-ED
s-ITS

Amrita, per capita, Sita

ITA
see
A**

Charitable, habitable, hospitable, illimitable, indubitable, inevitable, inhospitable, inimitable, profitable, suitable, veritable

ITABLE
see
ABLE

Capital, hospital, marital, non-commital, orbital, recital, requital, vital

ITAL
see
AL

Cosmopolitan, metropolitan, Neapolitan, puritan, Samaritan

ITAN
see
AN*

Annuitant, concomitant, exorbitant, habitant, inhabitant, irritant, militant, visitant

ITANT
see
ANT*

Agitate, cogitate, felicitate, gravitate, gurgitate, hesitate, imitate, incapacitate, irritate, meditate, necessitate, precipitate, premeditate, regurgitate, rehabilitate, solicitate

ITATE
see
ATE
ed-ED

Auction pitch, backstitch, bewitch, bitch, czarevitch, ditch, featherstitch, flitch, hemstitch, hitch, itch, lockstitch, low pitch, pitch, stitch, switch, twitch, whipstitch, witch

ITCH
see
ICH

Aconite, Adamite, aerolite, Amalekite, Ammonite, anchorite, anthracite, Aphrodite, appetite, apposite, Areopagite, ashy-white, backbite, bite, blatherskite, bobwhite, box-kite, Canaanite, Carmelite, cenobite, cite, contrite, cyanite, despite, dolomite, dynamite, ebonite, Edomite, eremite, erudite, excite, expedite, finite, frostbite, Gilroy's kite, graphite, Hepplewhite, hermaphrodite, hoplite, hyposulphite, incite, incondite, indite, invite, Israelite, Jacobite, kite, labradorite, lazulite, lignite, lyddite, malachite, meteorite, midshipmite, milkwhite, mite, Muscovite, Nazarite, niccolite, parasite, phosphite, plebiscite, polite, poor white,

ITE*
see
EIGHT**
IGHT
YTE

quite, recite, recondite, requite, rite, satellite, Semite, Sethite, Shiite, Shunammite, site, smite, socialite, spite, sprite, stalactite, stalagmite, suburbanite, sulphite, Sybarite, termite, thalmite, theodolite, trite, underwrite, unite, vulcanite, white, widow's mite, write **ITE***

Definite, exquisite, favorite, granite, indefinite, infinite, marguerite, opposite, perquisite, preterite, requisite **ITE**** *see* IT

Arbiter, ghost writer, Jupiter, liter, miter, niter, scimiter, typewriter, writer **ITER** *see* ER

Aerolith, blacksmith, crith, forthwith, frith, goldsmith, Judith, kith, Lilith, locksmith, megalith, Meredith, monolith, Neith, neolith, pith, silversmith, smith, Tanith, with, zenith **ITH** *see* YTH

Blithe, lithe, tithe, writhe **ITHE** *see* YTHE

Dither, nowhither, slither, thither, whither, wither, zither **ITHER** *see* ER

Logarithm **ITHM** *see* YTHM

Haiti, prakriti, Tahiti, wapiti **ITI** *see* I**

Critic, mephitic, parasitic, politic   **ITIC**
see
IC

Abolition, admonition, air-condition, **ITION**
ambition, apparition, apposition, attri- *see*
tion, audition, coalition, coition, com- ION
petition, composition, condition, con-
trition, decomposition, disposition,
ebullition, edition, exhibition, expedi-
tion, exposition, extradition, fruition,
ignition, imposition, inhibition, Inquisition, intuition, juxtaposition, muni-
tion, nutrition, opposition, partition,
perdition, petition, position, predispo-
sition, premonition, prohibition, recog-
nition, recondition, rendition, repeti-
tion, requisition, sedition, special edition, superstition, supposition, tradi-
tion, tuition, volition

Auditive, competitive, fugitive, gen- **ITIVE**
itive, infinitive, inquisitive, partitive, *see*
primitive, prohibitive, punitive, sensi- IVE**
tive, transitive, volitive

Gitche Manito, incognito, mosquito, **ITO**
Quito *see*
O*

Auditor, city-editor, competitor, **ITOR**
creditor, depositor, inquisitor, janitor, *see*
monitor, progenitor, servitor, solicitor, OR
suitor, traitor, visitor

Calamitous, circuitous, felicitous, **ITOUS**
gratuitous, iniquitous, solicitous, ubiq- *see*
uitous OUS
US

Bitter, flitter, fritter, glitter, jitter, litter, outfitter, quitter, sitter, titter, transmitter, twitter

ITTER
see
ER

Belittle, brittle, lickspittle, little, spittle, tittle, vittle, whittle

ITTLE
see
EL
LE

Ditty, gritty, kitty, witty

ITTY
see
E**

Altitude, amplitude, aptitude, attitude, beatitude, certitude, decrepitude, exactitude, fortitude, gratitude, habitude, inaptitude, incertitude, ineptitude, infinitude, ingratitude, lassitude, latitude, longitude, magnitude, multitude, nigritude, platitude, plenitude, promptitude, rectitude, servitude, similitude, solicitude, solitude, turpitude, vicissitude, virisimilitude

ITUDE
see
UDE

Ad libitum, infinitum

ITUM
see
UM

Discomfiture, expenditure, forfeiture, furniture, garniture, geniture, investiture, portraiture, primogeniture

ITURE
see
URE

Emeritus, Hermaphroditus, St. Vitus, Tacitus, Theocritus, Titus, Unigenitus

ITUS
see
US

Constitute, destitute, institute, prostitute, substitute   **ITUTE**
see
UTE
ed-ED

Absurdity, alacrity, amity, anonymity, benignity, caducity, calamity, cavity, celebrity, chastity, city, comity, complexity, concavity, conformity, corporeity, credulity, deformity, density, depravity, dignity, enmity, enormity, entity, eternity, fatality, fecundity, fidelity, fraternity, frivolity, gravity, heredity, identity, immensity, indemnity, indignity, infidelity, infirmity, integrity, intensity, jollity, laity, laxity, maternity, necessity, nonconformity, nonentity, nudity, nullity, obesity, oddity, paucity, perplexity, perversity, pity, polity, probity, profundity, prolixity, propensity, quantity, Radio City, rotundity, salubrity, sanctity, sanity, scarcity, self-pity, solemnity, spontaneity, suavity, taciturnity, tensity, uniformity, university, varsity, velocity   **ITY**
see
ACITY
ALITY
ANITY
ARITY
E**
EITY
ENITY
ERITY
EVITY
ICITY
IDITY
ILITY
IMITY
INITY
IVITY
OCITY
ORITY
OSITY
UITY
UNITY
URITY

Fritz, seidlitz, sitz   **ITZ**
see

Howitzer, kibitzer   **ITZER**
see
ER

Alluvium, aquarium, atrium, bdellium, Belgium, Byzantium, calcium, chromium, compendium, cranium, decennium, delirium, delphinium, diluvium, effluvium, elysium, encomium, eulogium, euphorbium, exordium, geranium, gymnasium, harmonium, helium, herbarium, iridium, magnesium, medium, megatherium, millennium, nasturtium, odium, opium, opprobrium, osmium, palladium, pandemonium, peculium, pericranium, planetarium, polonium, potassium, premium, principium, proscenium, protevangelium, radium, rose-geranium, scholium, selenium, sodium, stadium, stramonium, symposium, tedium, trifolium, trillium, trivium, uranium

IUM
see
EUM
OM*
OME*
ORIUM
UM
UMN

Æsculapius, Apuleius, Aquarius, Athanasius, Boëthius, Cassius, Confucius, Dionysius, Erichthonius, expurgatorius, genius, Helvetius, Lucretius, Marcus Aurelius, Mencius, nisi prius, Pluvius, Polonius, Procopius, radius, Sagittarius, Sirius, Stradivarius, Suetonius, Tiberius, Titus Livius, Vesuvius

IUS
see
US

Arrival, carnival, festival, outrival, revival, rival, survival

IVAL
see
AL

Activate, cultivate, motivate, private, recidivate, titivate

IVATE
see
ATE

Alive, archive, arrive, beehive, chive, connive, contrive, deprive, dive, five, hive, revive, scared-alive, strive, survive, thrive

IVE*
see
YVE
S-IFE-S
IVES

Active, adhesive, aggressive, attentive, captive, cohesive, collective, compressive, consumptive, convective, convictive, cursive, decisive, defective, descriptive, destructive, detective, diminutive, directive, elective, endive, eruptive, executive, exhaustive, expansive, expensive, expressive, extensive, festive, forgive, furtive, give, housewive, impassive, inactive, incentive, inexpensive, inoffensive, instinctive, intensive, invective, inventive, irrespective, Khedive, live, massive, misgive, missive, objective, obstructive, offensive, ogive, olive, oppressive, outlive, passive, pendentive, pensive, perceptive, perspective, persuasive, pervasive, perversive, plaintive, presumptive, progressive, projective, prospective, qui vive, radioactive, receptive, reflective, respective, restive, retentive, retrogressive, secretive, selective, skive, sportive, suasive, subjective, submissive, substantive, subversive, suggestive, susceptive, vindictive, votive, wive

IVE**
see
ATIVE
IEVE**
ITIVE
OSIVE
OTIVE
USIVE

Drivel, shrivel, snivel, swivel

IVEL
see
EL
LE

Deliver, diver, driver, giver, law-giver, liver, purling-river, quiver, receiver, river, screw driver, slave-driver, shiver, sliver, waiver

IVER
see
ER

Delivery, livery

IVERY
see
E**

Archives, hives, housewives, pocket-knives

IVES
see
IVE*-s

Civet, privet, rivet, trivet

IVET
see
ET

Acclivity, activity, captivity, declivity, festivity, inactivity, nativity, objectivity, passivity, proclivity, receptivity, relativity, selectivity

IVITY
see
E**
ITY

Administratrix, affix, Aix, appendix, betwixt, calix, cicatrix, crucifix, felix, fix, infelix, intermix, janitrix, matrix, mix, nix, Phoenix, prefix, prolix, radix, semper felix, six, spadix, suffix, testatrix, transfix, Vercingetorix

IX
see
YX
IC-s
ICK-s
ed-IXT

Betwixt, 'twixt

IXT
see
IX-ed

Agassiz, biz, Cadiz, friz, Hafiz, phiz, rheumatiz, viz , whiz

IZ
see
IES**
IS**
IZZ
UIZ

Advertize, affinitize, anathematize, anglicize, apologize, apotheosize, assize, atomize, attitudinize, authorize, baptize, barbarize, botanize, capsize, cauterize, centralize, civilize, criticize, crystallize, demobilize, demoralize, deodorize, emphasize, energize, epitomize, eulogize, evangelize, extemporize, familiarize, fertilize, foreignize, fossilize, fraternize, galvanize, gormandize, headsize, hybridize, idolize, itemize, jeopardize, latinize, lionize, memorize, mercerize, mesmerize, minimize, mobilize, modernize, monopolize, neutralize, Nobel prize, organize, ostracize, overemphasize, oxidize, particularize, plagiarize, polarize, popularize, ˙prize, proselytize, pulverize, rhapsodize, recognize, satirize, scandalize, scrutinize, sensitize, size, solemnize, soliloquize, stabilize, sterilize, stigmatize, syllogize, sympathize, synchronize, temporize, terrorize, theorize, tranquilize, undersize, utilize, vaporize, victimize

IZE
see
ALIZE
ONIZE
EYE-*S*
IES*
ISE*
UISE*

Bedizen, citizen, denizen, wizen

IZEN
see
EN

Appetizer, atomizer, criticizer, fertilizer, organizer, vocalizer

IZER
see
ER

Fizz, gin fizz

IZZ
see
IZ

Drizzle, fizzle, frizzle, sizzle, swizzle **IZZLE**
see
EL
LE

O SOUNDS

Accelerando, akimbo, Alamo, Aleppo, alfresco, allegro, ambo, antipasto, Apollo, Aquilo, Ariosto, arroyo, auto, autogyro, banjo, Banquo, basso, basso-profundo, basso relievo, bayamo, bilbo, bravo, broncho, burro, Cairo, Cagliostro, calabozo, Callisto, Calypso, certo, chiaroscuro, chromo, Co., Colombo, concerto, Consuelo, conto, corso, cui bono, de facto, Dido, ditto, dodo, Draco, dynamo, echo, ego, embryo, ergo, fiasco, Figaro, forego, fresco, fro, gaucho, gazebo, ginkgo, go, Gran Chaco, Guido, gusto, hidalgo, H_2O, Hoang-Ho, hobo, indigo, inferno, in toto, ipso facto, Jericho, Jethro, jocko, junco, Juno, kilo, kimono, lasso, let-go, libido, Lido, limbo, lo, Lorenzo, maestro, major-domo, Manchukuo, manifesto, mestizo, Michael Angelo, Monaco, Monte Carlo, Monte Cristo, Morocco, mulatto, Mumbo-Jumbo, Navajo, negro, no, octavo, oho, Orinoco, Palermo, papagayo, papyro, perfecto, Pernambuco, peso, photo, pico, Pizarro, placebo, Pluto, Po, poncho, pro, Prosilipo, proviso, pueblo, quarto, Quasimodo, rancho, recto, re-echo, righto, rococo, Salerno, salvo, San Diego, San Francisco, Sappho, Sargasso, secundo,

O*

see

ADO
AGO
ALO
ANGO
ANO
ANTO
AO
ARGO
ATO
EAU
EDO
EGO
ELLO
ENDO
ENTO
EO
ERO
ESTO
ETO
ETTO
ICO
ILLO
IMO
INGO
INO
IO
ITO
OE**

shako, Shinto, silo, sirocco, so, so and so, so-ho, so-so, status quo, St. Elmo, stucco, tabasco, tally-ho, tardo, taro, Tasso, tempo, Terra del Fuego, testudo, theorbo, to and fro, tobacco, torso, tufo, tyro, undergo, Valparaiso, verso, veto, Virgo, Yao, yo-ho, Zeno

O*
OLO
OSO
OTTO
OUGH*
OW*
OWE
s-OSE*
OWS

Ado, came-to, do, heave-to, hitherto, how-d'ye-do, lean-to, outdo, overdo, that-will-do, thereunto, to, to-do, two, underdo, undo, unto, well-to-do, we-two, who

O**
see
AGUE***
EW
IEW
OE*
OO
OU*
OUGH****
OUX
U
UE*

Balboa, boa, cocoa, Genoa, goa, proa, protozoa, Samoa, whoa

OA
see
A**

Accroach, approach, broach, coach, cockroach, encroach, poach, reproach, roach, slow coach, stage coach

OACH
see
OCHE

Abroad, broad, carload, corduroy-road, crossroad, goad, highroad, horned-toad, inroad, load, overload, railroad, road, shipload, toad, tree toad, unload, woad

OAD
see
ODE
OW*-*ed*

Loaf, oaf **OAF**
see
OPHE**

Bathcloak, Charter Oak, cloak, croak, holm-oak, live-oak, oak, scrub-oak, soak, uncloak, white-oak **OAK**
see
OKE
s-OAX

Cannel coal, charcoal, coal, foal, goal, shoal **OAL**
see
OL
OUL**

Foam, gloam, loam, roam, Siloam, sea-foam **OAM**
see
OMB**
OME**

Bemoan, Darby and Joan, groan, loan, moan, roan **OAN**
see
ONE*

Soap **OAP**
see
OPE

Bezoar, boar, dripping-oar, hoar, muffled-oar, roar, soar, torrent's-roar, uproar, wild-boar **OAR**
see
OOR*
ed-OARD
s-OR-s

Aboard, above board, all aboard, billboard, blackboard, board, bristol board, buckboard, cardboard, chequer-board, chess board, clapboard, cupboard, dashboard, hoard, inboard, **OARD**
see
ORD*
OAR-*ed*
OR-*ed*

keyboard, lapboard, larboard, mop-board, mortarboard, ouija-board, out-board, overboard, pasteboard, running-board, school-board, shipboard, shuffle-board, sideboard, signboard, sounding-board, starboard, switch-board

OARD

Boast, cinnamon toast, coast, corn-roast, dry-toast, milktoast, pot-roast, roast, toast

OAST
see
OST**
ed-ED

Afloat, bloat, blue-coat, boat, bum-boat, canal boat, coat, cut-throat, ferryboat, float, fur-coat, gloat, goat, great-coat, gunboat, jolly-boat, life boat, moat, motorboat, nanny-goat, oat, overcoat, packet-boat, petticoat, police boat, red coat, rowboat, sailboat, scapegoat, shoat, speedboat, steam-boat, surcoat, throat, topcoat, torpedo boat, turncoat, U-boat, waistcoat, whaleboat

OAT
see
OTE
s-OATS

Inchoate

OATE
see
ATE

Loath, oath

OATH
see
OTH*

Wild-oats

OATS
see
OAT-*s*

Blob, bob, cob, corncob, fob, gob, heart-throb, hob, hobnob, Jacob, job, knob, lob, mob, nabob, rob, slob, snob, sob, soft job, thingumbob, throb
OB*
see
AB**
UAB

Job
OB**
see
OBE

Approbate, probate, reprobate
OBATE
see
ATE

Dobber, jobber, robber, slobber
OBBER
see
ER

Cobble, gobble, hobble, wobble
OBBLE
see
EL
LE

Blobby, bobby, hobby, knobby, lobby
OBBY
see
E**

Disrobe, globe, lap-robe, lobe, microbe, nightrobe, probe, robe, wardrobe
OBE
see
OB**

October, sober
OBER
see
ER

Ennoble, ignoble, noble
OBLE
see
EL
LE

En bloc, havoc, langue d'Oc, Medoc, opodeldoc, roc, Tlaloc

OC
see
OCH

Bifocal, equivocal, focal, local, reciprocal, vocal

OCAL
see
AL

Allocate, dislocate, equivocate, invocate, locate, reciprocate, suffocate

OCATE
see
ATE

Antioch, Enoch, epoch, loch, Moloch, pibroch

OCH
see
OC
OCK

Troche

OCHE
see
OACH

Ochre

OCHRE
see
ER

Atrocity, ferocity, precocity, reciprocity, velocity

OCITY
see
E**
ITY

Alpenstock, bedrock, block, bock, bullock, burdock, buttock, cassock, chock-a-block, chopping-block, clock, cock, crock, deadlock, dock, fetlock, firelock, flintlock, flock, forelock, frock, game-cock, grandfather's clock, haddock, hammock, hassock, haycock,

OCK
see
OC
OCH
ed-OCT
s-OX

hemlock, hillock, hock, hollyhock, **OCK**
hummock, interlock, jabberwock,
joint-stock, knock, laughing-stock,
livestock, lock, lovelock, mattock,
minster-clock, mock, moss-grown-
rock, oarlock, o'clock, overstock, pad-
dock, padlock, peacock, pock, pollock,
poppy-cock, Plymouth Rock, Rappa-
hannock, rowlock, shaddock, sham-
rock, shell-shock, shock, shuttlecock,
Shylock, smock, sock, stock, stopcock,
stumbling-block, Tarpeian Rock, tick-
tock, town-clock, traprock, tussock,
unfrock, unlock, warlock, weathercock,
wedlock, white rock, woodcock

Knickerbocker, knocker, locker, **OCKER**
rocker, shilling shocker   *see*
                            ER

Crocket, docket, locket, pickpocket, **OCKET**
pocket, rocket, sky-rocket, socket,   *see*
sprocket   ET

Mediocre   **OCRE**
                            see
                            ER

Concoct, decoct   **OCT**
                            see
                         OCK-*ed*

Crocus, focus, hocus-pocus, locus   **OCUS**
                            see
                            US

Aaron's rod, Cape Cod, clod, coal-hod, cod, decapod, demigod, divining-rod, downtrod, dryshod, ephod, gastropod, God, goldenrod, Herod, hexapod, hod, land-o-Nod, lightning-rod, megapod, method, Nimrod, nod, Novgorod, od, pea-pod, platypod, plod, pod, prod, ramrod, rod, roughshod, sea-god, shod, slipshod, sod, sun-god, synod, tripod, trod, unshod, well-shod

OD
see
IOD
ODD
UAD

Bi-carbonate of soda, coda, pagoda, sal soda

ODA
see
A**

Odd

ODD
see
OD

Abode, à la mode, anode, bestrode, bode, cathode, code, commode, corrode, decode, discommode, episode, epode, erode, explode, forebode, incommode, lode, mode, monopode, node, ode, outmode, rode, strode

ODE
see
OAD
ow*-*ed*

Dislodge, dodge, hodge-podge, lodge

ODGE
see

Anodic, episodic, melodic, odic, parodic, periodic, prosodic, spasmodic

ODIC
see
IC

Coryphodon, glyptodon, mastodon

ODON
see
ON

Heterodox, orthodox

ODOX
see
OX

Anybody, body, chiropody, custody, disembody, embody, everybody, melody, monody, nobody, parody, prosody, psalmody, rhapsody, somebody, threnody, torpedo body

ODY
see
E**

Canoe, horseshoe, overshoe, shoe, snowshoe, Tippecanoe

OE*
see
O**
s-USE*

Aloe, Arapahoe, Crusoe, Defoe, doe, floe, foe, John Doe, mistletoe, oboe, pekoe, roe, shadroe, sloe, throe, tip-toe, toe, woe

OE**
see
O*
OW*
ed-OAD
OW*-*ed*
s-OSE

Poem, proem

OEM
see
EM

Boer, church-goer, doer, evil-doer, good-doer, o'er, shoer

OER
see
ER

Of, unheard of, thereof, whereof

OF
see
OVE**

Cast-off, cut-off, doff, far-off, kick-off, off, palm-off, ring-off, Romanoff, scoff, send-off, show-off, stand-off, take-off, tee-off, toff

OFF
see
OUGHT*****
ed-OFT

Coffer, offer, proffer, scoffer

OFFER
see
ER

Aloft, cockloft, croft, hayloft, how-oft, loft, Lowestoft, oft, soft

OFT
see
OFF-*ed*

Agog, backlog, befog, bog, bullfrog, clog, cog, cranberry bog, dog, egg-nog, firedog, flog, fog, frog, Gog, golliwog, grog, ground-hog, hedgehog, hog, hot dog, house-dog, incog., jog, knotty-log, lapdog, leapfrog, log, Magog, megafog, peat-bog, polly-wog, prairie-dog, river-hog, roadhog, sand-hog, sea-dog, sea-hog, spitz-dog, sundog, under-dog, watch-dog

OG
see
OGUE*

Saratoga, toga, yoga

OGA
see
A**

Abrogate, arrogate, interrogate, sur-rogate

OGATE
see
ATE

Doge, horologe, gamboge

OGE
see

Cyanogen, hydrogen, nitrogen, oxy-hydrogen

OGEN
see
EN

Boggle, goggle, horn-swoggle, joggle, woggle

OGGLE
see
EL
LE

Boggy, doggy, foggy, groggy, soggy **OGGY**
see
E**

Geologic, logic, pedagogic, philologic **OGIC**
see
IC

Anthologist, apologist, bacteriologist, biologist, craniologist, entomologist, etymologist, fossilologist, geologist, graphologist, neurologist, ontologist, ornothologist, philologist, phrenologist, physiologist, psychologist, sinologist, teratologist **OGIST**
see
IST

Bologne, Bourgogne, eau de Cologne **OGNE**
see
ONE*

Ideogram, kilogram, monogram, parallelogram, program, radiogram, seismogram **OGRAM**
see
AM

Ogre **OGRE**
see
ER

Analogue, apologue, catalogue, Decalogue, demagogue, dialogue, duologue, eclogue, epilogue, monologue, mystagogue, pedagogue, prologue, prorogue, sinologue, theologue, travelogue **OGUE***
see
OG

Brogue, rogue, vogue **OGUE****
see

Amphilogy, analogy, eulogy, fogy, genealogy, logy, mineralogy, pedagogy, stogy, tetralogy, trilogy **OGY**
see
E**
OLOGY

Oh, Pharaoh, Shiloh **OH**
see
O*

Kohl **OHL**
see
OL

Demi-john, Prester John **OHN**
see
ON

Hoi polloi, Borzoi, Tolstoi **OI**
see
OY

Choice, invoice, joice, rejoice, voice **OICE**
see
ed-OIST
S-EZ

Alkaloid, aneroid, anthropoid, aster- **OID**
oid, avoid, celluloid, deltoid, devoid, *see*
ichthyoid, mattoid, negroid, ornithoid, OY-*ed*
planetoid, rhomboid, spheroid, tab-
loid, thyroid, typhoid, void

Coif **OIF**
see
OFF

Coign **OIGN**
see
OIN

Boil, broil, cinquefoil, coil, despoil, **OIL**
embroil, foil, free-soil, fusel oil, hard- *see*
boil, midnight-oil, oil, panbroil, par- OYLE

boil, quatrefoil, recoil, roil, salad-oil, soil, spark coil, spoil, subsoil, tinfoil, toil, trefoil, turmoil, uncoil **OIL**

Benzoin, coin, disjoin, enjoin, groin, heroin, join, loin, purloin, rejoin, sirloin, subjoin, tenderloin **OIN** *see* OIGN

Heroine, Macedoine **OINE** *see* INE

Anoint, appoint, dewpoint, disappoint, fingerpoint, joint, needlepoint, point, spear-point, standpoint, starting-point, vanishing-point, viewpoint, vowel point, West Point **OINT** *see* ed-ED

Choir **OIR*** *see* IRE

Boudoir, memoir, peignoir, recevoir, rouge et noir **OIR**** *see* AR*

Armoire, bête noire, Directoire, escritoire, Grimoire, pourboire, repertoire **OIRE** *see* OIR**

Avoirdupois, chamois, Marguerite de Valois, patois **OIS** *see*

Counterpoise, equipoise, noise, poise, porpoise, tortoise, turquoise **OISE** *see* OY-s

Foist, hoist, joist, moist

OIST
see
OICE-*d*

Adroit, exploit, maladroit, quoit

OIT
see

Amok, O.K., Ragnarok, Zadok

OK
see
OCK

Artichoke, awoke, bespoke, bloke, broke, choke, coke, convoke, downstroke, evoke, fog-smoke, invoke, joke, moke, poke, provoke, revoke, Roanoke, smoke, spoke, stoke, stroke, sunstroke, upstroke, woke, yoke

OKE
see
OAK
OLK
OQUE
en-OKEN
s-OAX

Bespoken, betoken, broken, Hoboken, outspoken, plainspoken, spoken, token, unspoken

OKEN
see
EN

Broker, choker, croker, joker, pawnbroker, poker, soker, stockbroker, stoker

OKER
see
ER

Alcohol, Bath kol, carol, consol, control, entresol, extol, fal-de-rol, frijol, gambol, horse-pistol, idol, lysol, menthol, old Sol, parasol, patrol, petrol, pistol, protocol, Sebastopol, self-control, symbol, systol, Tyrol

OL
see
IOL
OLE
ULL**
ed-OLD

Cupola, dongola, gondola, gorgonzola, Loyola, parabola, pergola, pianola, Pico della Mirandola, Romola, Savonarola, victrola, viola, Zola

OLA
see
A**

Chocolate, desolate, disconsolate, etiolate, inviolate, isolate, percolate, violate

OLATE
see
ATE

Age-old, behold, blindfold, bold, Childe Harold, Cloth of Gold, cold, cuckold, enfold, finegold, fold, foot-hold, foretold, fourfold, gold, hold, household, hundredfold, kobold, mani-fold, marigold, marsh marigold, mold, molten-gold, ninefold, old, scaffold, scold, sevenfold, sheepfold, sold, stone-cold, stranglehold, stronghold, tenfold, thousandfold, threefold, threshold, told, unfold, untold, uphold, withhold, wold

OLD
see
OULD*
OL-*ed*
OLE-*d*
y-E**

Bolder, cigarette-holder, colder, folder, holder, landholder, older, share-holder, smolder

OLDER
see
ER

Air-hole, aureole, barberpole, bar-carole, blowhole, bunghole, cajole, camisole, casserole, cigarette-hole, cole, condole, console, Creole, cubby-hole, dole, drole, girandole, glory-hole, groundmole, hole, keyhole, loophole, manhole, mole, North Pole, Old King Cole, oriole, parole, peephole, pigeon-hole, pin-hole, pistole, pole, port-hole, ridge-pole, rigmarole, role, Seminole, sole, South Pole, tadpole, tent-pole, thole, totem-pole, whole

OLE*
see
OAL
OL
OLL*
OUL**
ed-OL-*ed*
OLD

Hyperbole, frijole

OLE**
see
E**

Indolent, insolent, malevolent, redolent, somnolent, violent

OLENT
see
ENT

Golf, werewolf, wolf

OLF
see

Argoli, broccoli, Gallipoli, Rivoli,
tivoli

OLI
see
I**

Anatolia, magnolia, melancholia,
Mongolia

OLIA
see
IA

Alcoholic, bucolic, carbolic, catholic,
colic, diabolic, frolic, non-alcoholic,
parabolic, symbolic

OLIC
see
IC

Semi-solid, solid, stolid

OLID
see
ID

Etiolin, lanolin, mandolin, violin

OLIN
see
IN

Folio, olio, portfolio

OLIO
see
IO

Acropolis, Annapolis, anolis, Heliop-
olis, metropolis, necropolis, Persepolis

OLIS
see
IS*

Abolish, coolish, demolish, foolish,
polish

OLISH
see
ISH

Country-folk, fisher-folk, folk, gentle-folk, kinsfolk, yolk

OLK
see
OQUE
S-OAX

Boll, breakfast-roll, droll, enroll, knoll, mossy-knoll, muster-roll, payroll, roll, scroll, stroll, toll, troll, unroll

OLL*
see
OLE
OUL**

Doll, loll, moll, poll

OLL**
see

Collar, dollar, trade dollar

OLLAR
see
AR

Dolly, folly, holly, jolly, polly, sea holly

OLLY
see
E**

Coco-bolo, Fra Diavolo, gigolo, Marco Polo, piccolo, polo, solo, tremolo, water polo

OLO
see
O*

Anthology, apology, archæology, astro-theology, biology, bryology, Christology, chronology, cryptology, dactylology, demonology, dermatology, doxology, Egyptology, eschatology, ethnology, etymology, geology, glossology, graphology, hagiology, homology, horology, ichthyology, ideology, lexicology, martyrology, meteorology, metrology, morphology, mythology, neology, nephology, nostology, numerology, odontology, ontology,

OLOGY
see
OGY

oölogy, ornithology, orthology, osteol- **OLOGY**
ogy, pathology, penology, philology,
photology, phraseology, phrenology,
physiology, psychology, pyramidology,
seismology, sinology, tautology, tech-
nology, teleology, teratology, termi-
nology, theology, toxicology, zoölogy

Ben Bolt, bolt, colt, dolt, iron-bolt, **OLT**
jolt, king-bolt, micro-volt, molt, revolt, *see*
thunderbolt, volt

Absolute, dissolute, irresolute, reso- **OLUTE**
lute, volute *see*
UTE

Absolve, devolve, dissolve, evolve, **OLVE**
involve, resolve, revolve, solve *see*

Absolver, dissolver, resolver, re- **OLVER**
volver *see*
ER

Holy, melancholy, moly, monopoly, **OLY**
roly-poly, unholy *see*
E**

Accustom, besom, blossom, bore- **OM***
dom, bosom, bottom, buxom, carda- *see*
mom, carom, Christendom, Chrysos- EUM
tom, cockneydom, custom, Edom, em- IUM
bosom, envenom, Epsom, fathom, free- OME*
dom, from, hansom, heathendom, king- OSM
dom, lissom, maelstrom, martyrdom, UM
officialdom, Om, Peeping Tom, phan-
tom, Pithom, pogrom, random, ransom,
rock bottom, rush-bottom, serfdom,

Sodom, stardom, symptom, thralldom, tomtom, unbosom, venom, whilom, wisdom **OM***

Whom **OM*** *see* OOM

Aroma, coma, diploma, La Paloma, Oklahoma, pleroma, Point Loma, soma **OMA** *see* A**

Dragoman, Ottoman, toman, woman, yeoman **OMAN** *see* AN*

Aplomb, bomb, rhomb **OMB*** *see*

Catacomb, comb, coxcomb, curry-comb, hecatomb, honey-comb, tomb, uncomb, womb **OMB*** *see* UMB

Become, blithesome, burdensome, come, cumbersome, fearsome, four-some, frolicsome, gladsome, gruesome, handsome, income, irksome, lissome, loathsome, lonesome, meddlesome, mettlesome, noisome, outcome, over-come, quarrelsome, rollicksome, some, tiresome, toilsome, toothsome, trouble-some, venturesome, wearisome, well-come, wholesome, winsome **OME*** *see* IUM OM* UM UMN

Chrome, dome, gnome, hippodrome, home, metronome, monochrome, palin-drome, polychrome, Rome, St. Jerome, tome, vela-drome, Vendome **OME*** *see* OAM

Abdomen, cognomen, omen, women **OMEN**
see
EN

Astronomer, customer, Homer, in-comer, misnomer, newcomer, omer **OMER**
see
ER

Comet, Mahomet **OMET**
see
ET

Atomic, comic, economic, gastro-nomic, gnomic, serio-comic **OMIC**
see
IC

Blossoming, coming, homing, in-coming, on-coming, spring-blossoming, Wyoming **OMING**
see
ING

Chromo, Como, Ecce Homo, major-domo **OMO**
see
O*

Pomp, romp **OMP**
see
AMP**

Prompt **OMPT**
see

Anatomy, antinomy, economy, phle-botomy, physiognomy, zoötomy **OMY**
see
E**

Abandon, æon, Agamemnon, Ajalon, Anglo-Saxon, anon, antiphon, apron, Armageddon, Ascalon, Audubon, au-tomaton, Avalon, Avignon, Babylon, **ON**
see
AGON
AN**

backgammon, bacon, barbiton, baron, beckon, be-ribbon, blue-ribbon, bonbon, bon-ton, bouillon, Bourbon, boustrophedon, caisson, call-upon, cannon, canon, canton, capon, carbon, carillon, carry on, cauldron, cedar of Lebanon, Ccladon, Ceylon, chanson, Charon, chevron, chiffon, chiton, cinnamon, citron, colon, common, cordon, corydon, cotillon, cotton, coupon, crimson, crouton, damson, Demogorgon, Devon, dodecahedron, don, donjon, egg-on, eidolon, electron, emblazon, Emerson, epsilon, falcon, fanfaron, gallon, gibbon, gnomon, goings-on, gonfalon, Gorgon, grandson, griffon, gryphon, guerdon, guncotton, hanger-on, headon, Hebron, horizon, Huron, jargon, Jupiter Ammon, klaxon, Kwannon, Lacedæmon, Laocöon, Lisbon, London, Mammon, marathon, matron, Memnon, mescal button, mignon, Milton, Mme. de Maintenon, Mormon, moron, Mother Shipton, myrmidon, neuron, Nippon, non, Oberon, on, pardon, parson, patron, pennon, person, phaëton, phenomenon, Phlegethon, piston, plastron, pompon, Poseidon, Princeton, pro and con, prolegomenon, python, rayon, reckon, rhododendron, ribbon, Rimmon, sabbaton, saffron, salmon, salon, Samson, Sanchoniathon, Sandalphon, Sargon, Saxon, semi-colon, sermon, sexton, Sheraton, Sidon, Simple Simon, simpleton, siphon, Solomon, Solon, son, soupçon, squadron, Stevenson, summon, talon, tampon, tarpon,

ON

ASON
AZON
EACON
EASON
ELON
EMON
EON
ERON
ETON
ICON
ION
IRON
ISON
ODON
OHN
ONE***
OPHON
UAN
UN
UTTON
YLON
YON
ed-UND

tendon, Tennyson, tetragrammaton, thereupon, torchon, Trianon, trilithon, triton, trogon, Typhon, uncommon, upon, wagon, wanton, Washington, weapon, welsh-mutton, whereon, yon, Yukon, zircon

ON

Arizona, Barcelona, Bellona, chincona, corona, Cremona, Crotona, Desdemona, Dodona, Latona, madrona, Pomona, Verona

ONA
see
A**

Ammonal, conditional, confessional, congressional, coronal, denominational, devotional, diagonal, dimensional, emotional, fourth dimensional, functional, gravitational, hexagonal, impersonal, international, meridional, national, notional, occasional, octagonal, optional, precessional, processional, prohibitional, rational, recessional, regional, seasonal, septentrional, sulphonal, traditional, unconditional, vegetational, veronal, visional

ONAL
see
AL

Dictionary, legionary, missionary, pulmonary, reactionary, revolutionary, stationary, visionary

ONARY
see
ARY

Donate, detonate, impersonate, intonate, passionate, pulmonate

ONATE
see
ATE

Once

ONCE*
see
UNCE

Ensconce, nonce, sconce

ONCE**
see
ONSE

Conch

ONCH
see
ONK

Abscond, almond, baby bond, be-
yond, blond, bond, correspond, despond, diamond, fond, frond, Phara-
mond, pond, reedy-pond, respond,
Richmond, second, Slough of Despond,
split-second, Trebizond, vagabond

OND
see
AND**

Anaconda, Gioconda, Golconda

ONDA
see
A**

Fonder, ponder, wonder, yonder

ONDER
see
ER

Alcyone, alone, anti-cyclone, atone,
backbone, baritone, barkstone, blood-
stone, bone, breast-bone, brimstone,
brownstone, canzone, capstone, chap-
erone, cheekbone, cicerone, cobble-
stone, condone, cone, cornerstone,
crone, crossbone, curbstone, cyclone,
dethrone, dictaphone, doorstone,
drone, fir-cone, fishbone, foundation-
stone, freestone, frozen zone, funny-
bone, gramophone, graphophone,
gravestone, grindstone, half-tone,
headstone, hearthstone, herringbone,
holystone, hone, intone, jackstone,

ONE*
see
OWN*

jawbone, keystone, knucklebone, Ladrone, limestone, megaphone, memorial-stone, microphone, milestone, millstone, monotone, moonstone, neurone, oilstone, outshone, overtone, ozone, ozytone, padrone, paroxytone, philosopher's stone, phone, postpone, prone, rawbone, rolling-stone, Rosetta stone, sandstone, saxophone, scone, semitone, shin-bone, shone, soapstone, steppingstone, stone, throne, tombstone, tone, torrid-zone, tottering-throne, trombone, undertone, whalebone, whetstone, xylophone, Yellowstone, zone

ONE*

Agone, begone, bygone, gone, woebegone

ONE**
see
AWN

Done, none, one, outdone, overdone, someone, underdone, undone, welldone

ONE***
see
UN

Component, exponent, opponent

ONENT
see
ENT

Almoner, executioner, falconer, practitioner, wagoner

ONER
see
ER

Nones, sawbones

ONES
see
ONE-*s*

Baronet, bayonet, canzonet, clarionet, coronet

ONET
see
ET

Honey, money, papermoney, pin-money

ONEY
see
EY

Age-long, along, among, belong, cradle-song, ding-dong, erelong, even-song, folksong, furlong, gong, head-long, headstrong, Hong Kong, livelong, long, mah-jong, oblong, oolong, ping-pong, prolong, prong, sarong, sidelong, singsong, siren's song, so-long, song, strong, swan song, thong, throng, tong, warsong, wrong

ONG
see
ONGUE
UNG

Sponge

ONGE
see
UNGE

Mother-tongue, ox-tongue, sacred tongue, silver tongue, tongue

ONGUE
see
ONG
UGN

Macaroni, Marconi, Zanoni, yoni

ONI
see
I**

Ammonia, begonia, Caledonia, Franconia, Harmonia, Macedonia, Patagonia, pneumonia

ONIA
see
IA

Bubonic, chronic, cyclonic, demonic, diatonic, electronic, harmonic, histrionic, iconic, Ionic, ironic, laconic, mnemonic, moronic, Platonic, philharmonic, polyphonic, sardonic, Slavonic, symphonic, telephonic, Teutonic, tonic

ONIC
see
IC

Adonis, Coronis, Draconis

ONIS
see
IS*

Anachronism, antagonism, exhibitionism, hedonism, reactionism, synchronism, unionism

ONISM
see
ISM

Abolitionist, antagonist, cartoonist, hedonist, impressionist, protagonist

ONIST
see
IST

Agonize, canonize, carbonize, colonize, harmonize, lionize, patronize

ONIZE
see
IZE

Honk, monk

ONK
see
UNK

Commonly, matronly, only, wantonly

ONLY
see
E**

Belladonna, Madonna, primadonna, Vittoria Colonna

ONNA
see
A**

Carcassonne, Sorbonne

ONNE
see
ON

Absonous, anachronous, autochthonous, cacophonous, gluttonous, poisonous, synchronous

ONOUS
see
OUS

Blazonry, falconry, freemasonry, masonry, solid masonry

ONRY
see
E**

Response

ONSE
see
ONCE

Confront, dont, font, front, Hellespont, shirtfront, water-front, wont

ONT
see
ANT**
UNT

Billionth, millionth, month, trillionth, twelfth-month

ONTH
see

Acrimony, agony, agrimony, alimony, antimony, antiphony, balcony, betony, bony, bryony, cacophony, ceremony, chalcedony, colony, crony, disharmony, ebony, euphony, felony, gluttony, harmony, hegemony, inharmony, irony, Mark Anthony, monotony, nudist colony, parsimony, patrimony, peony, phony, pony, scammony, Shetland pony, testimony, theogony

ONY
see
E**

Anonym, caconym, pseudonym, synonym

ONYM
see
IM

Bonze, bronze

ONZE
see

Ballyhoo, bamboo, bazoo, boo, boohoo, Bronx-Zoo, cockatoo, coo-coo, cuckoo, goo-goo, halloo, hoodoo, hullaballoo, igloo, kangaroo, karoo, moo,

OO
see
ABOO
O**

shampoo, shoo, skidoo, tattoo, tick-tack-too, too, toodle-oo, voodoo, Waterloo, Whangpoo, woo, yoo-hoo, zoo

OO
OUGH****
U

Boob

OOB
see
UBE

Brooch, hooch, mooch, scooch

OOCH
see

Basswood, blueblood, boxwood, briarwood, brushwood, camphorwood, candlewood, childhood, cottonwood, cypress wood, deadwood, dogwood, driftwood, firewood, good, gopher wood, greenwood, hardihood, holyrood, hood, ironwood, kindling-wood, knighthood, likelihood, livelihood, logwood, matchwood, misunderstood, monkhood, motherhood, neighborhood, no good, priesthood, Red Riding Hood, redwood, Robin Hood, rosewood, sandal-wood, satinwood, selfhood, stood, teakwood, understood, Wedgwood, wildwood, withstood, wood

OOD*
see
OULD

Blood, blueblood, cold blood, flood

OOD**
see
UD

Brood, food, mood, rood, snood, solid food

OOD***
see
UDE

Broody, goody, moody, woody

OODY
see
E**

Aloof, bombproof, bulletproof, dis-
proof, fireproof, foolproof, galley-proof,
gas-proof, high-proof, hoof, proof, rain-
proof, reproof, roof, shadoof, spoof,
waterproof, woof

OOF
see

Scrooge, stooge

OOGE
see
UGE

Pooh-pooh

OOH
see
OO

Betook, book, brook, buttonhook,
cook, crook, doomsday book, fishhook,
forsook, guide-book, hook, Holy Book,
ingle-nook, log-book, look, minnowy-
brook, mistook, murmuring-brook,
nook, nuthook, outlook, overlook,
pocketbook, pothook, prayerbook,
psalm-book, Sandy Hook, school book,
scrapbook, shepherd's crook, shook,
sketch book, story-book, tenterhook,
textbook, took, undertook, unhook,
visitor's book

OOK*
see

Nansook, spook

OOK**
see
UKE

Gadzooks

OOKS
see

April-fool, campstool, cool, cotton-
wool, drool, ducking-stool, faldstool,
finishing-school, fool, footstool, Liver-
pool, millpool, mineral wool, pool, rock

OOL
see
OUL***
ULE

wool, school, spool, stool, Sunday school, swimming-pool, toadstool, tool, whirlpool, wool

OOL

Ante-room, bloom, book room, boom, bridegroom, broadloom, broom, club room, doom, elbow-room, foredoom, gloom, greenroom, grillroom, groom, guest-room, heirloom, jib-boom, keeping-room, loom, messroom, mushroom, show-room, smoke-room, spare-room, stateroom, store-room, taproom, waiting-room, zoom

OOM
see
OM**
OMB***
UME

Bloomer, roomer

OOMER
see
ER

Afternoon, anæmic-moon, aswoon, baboon, balloon, bassoon, boon, buffoon, cartoon, cocoon, coon, croon, curved-moon, doubloon, dragoon, eftsoon, festoon, forenoon, galloon, half-moon, harpoon, harvest moon, honeymoon, hunter's moon, lagoon, lampoon, loon, macaroon, maroon, monsoon, moon, mushroon, new moon, noon, octoroon, pale-moon, Pantaloon, picaroon, platoon, poltroon, pontoon, quadroon, raccoon, Rangoon, rigadoon, saloon, sandal-shoon, shalloon, shoon, silverspoon, simoon, soon, spittoon, spoon, swoon, teaspoon, typhoon, woodenspoon, zoon

OON
see
EWN
UNE

Crooner, honeymooner, schooner, spooner

OONER
see
ER

Coop, droop, goop, hen-coop, hoop, loop, nincompoop, poop, scoop, scroop, sloop, snoop, stoop, swoop, troop, war-hoop, whoop

OOP
see
OUP
OUPE**
UPE

Barndoor, door, floor, indoor, next-door, stage-door, threshing-floor, trap-door, waxed-floor

OOR*
see
OR

Blackamoor, boor, Kohinoor, land-poor, moor, poor, spoor

OOR**
see
URE

Burnoose, caboose, calaboose, choose, goose, loose, mongoose, moose, Mother Goose, noose, papoose, unloose, va-moose

OOSE
see
UCE*
USE*

Tarboosh

OOSH
see

Boost, roost

OOST
see

Afoot, alumroot, arrowroot, bandi-coot, barefoot, bitter-root, bloodroot, boot, cahoot, calamus-root, cheroot, coot, crowfoot, cube root, eryngo root, flagroot, flatfoot, forefoot, hoot, hot-foot, lightfoot, loot, moot, offshoot, overshoot, presser foot, pussyfoot, root, scoot, shoot, snakeroot, snoot, soot, splayfoot, square root, taproot, tenderfoot, toot, underfoot, uproot, webfoot

OOT
see
UIT**
UT*
ed-ED

Booth, buck-tooth, eye-tooth, for-sooth, smooth, sooth, tooth, walrus-tooth

OOTH
see
OUTH*

Booty, snooty, sooty

OOTY
see
E**

Behoove, groove

OOVE
see
OVE***

Booze, ooze, snooze

OOZE
see
USE*

Æsop, archbishop, bishop, bucket-shop, chimney-top, chop, cop, crop, Cyclop, develop, dewdrop, drop, ear-drop, eavesdrop, flop, forest-top, gal-lop, grogshop, gumdrop, hop, house-top, hyssop, lollypop, lop, milksop, mop, Mrs. Malaprop, non-stop, organ-stop, orlop, overdevelop, overtop, pawnshop, pegtop, plop, pop, pork-chop, prop, raindrop, scallop, shallop, shop, shortstop, slip slop, slop, snow-drop, stop, strop, sweatshop, sweetsop, swop, teardrop, tip-top, top, tree-top, trollop, wallop, whop, wild-hyssop, workshop

OP
see
AP**
UP
ed-OPT
s-OPS

Copal, episcopal, opal

OPAL
see
AL

Allopath, homeopath, neuropath, osteopath

OPATH
see
ATH

Antelope, bellrope, Cape of Good Hope, chromoscope, cope, cymoscope, dope, electroscope, elope, envelope, grope, guyrope, heliotrope, hope, horoscope, interlope, kaleidoscope, kinetoscope, microscope, mirrorscope, misanthrope, mope, moviescope, myope, ope, periscope, pope, pyrope, rope, scope, slope, stanhope, spectroscope, syncope, telescope, tight-rope, trope, wire-rope

OPE*
see
OAP

Calliope, Merope, Parthenope, Penelope

OPE**
see
E*

Catastrophe

OPHE*
see
E*

Antistrophe, strophe

OPHE**
see
OAF

Gopher, philosopher, St. Christopher

OPHER
see
ER

Bellerophon, colophon, Zenophon

OPHON
see
ON

Anthroposophy, atrophy, philosophy, theosophy, trophy

OPHY
see
E**

Cornucopia, Ethiopia, Utopia **OPIA**
see
IA

Canopic, Ethiopic, kaleidoscopic, **OPIC**
microscopic, myopic, philanthropic, *see*
telescopic, topic, tropic IC

Chopper, clodhopper, copper, corn- **OPPER**
popper, cropper, grasshopper, hopper, *see*
topper, whopper, woodchopper ER

Choppy, floppy, poppy, sloppy, **OPPY**
soppy *see*
E**

Cecrops, Cheops, cyclops, Ops, Pe- **OPS**
lops *see*
OP-*s*

Copse **OPSE**
see
OPE-*s*

Ampelopsis, calliopsis, coreopsis, **OPSIS**
synopsis, thanatopsis *see*
IS*

Adopt, coöpt, Copt, epopt, opt **OPT**
see
OP-*ed*

Canopus, magnum opus, octopus, **OPUS**
opus, Rhodopus *see*
US

Baroque, toque

OQUE
see
OKE

Colloquy, obloquy, soliloquy

OQUY
see
E**

Abettor, abhor, ancestor, anchor,
antecessor, arbor, armor, Asia Minor,
author, bachelor, boa-constrictor, cam-
phor, candor, cantor, captor, carbure-
tor, Castor, censor, chancellor, clangor,
color, condor, conductor, confessor,
councilor, counselor, conveyor, de-
meanor, discolor, doctor, done for,
donor, dor, endeavor, Endor, ephor,
error, father-confessor, favor, fervor,
flavor, for, governor, Hathor, honor,
horror, humor, ichor, impostor, in-
structor, inventor, labor, languor, liquor,
lor', louis d'or, Luxor, major, manor,
mayor, mentor, metaphor, meteor,
milor, minor, mirror, misdemeanor,
motor, Mount Tabor, neighbor, Nes-
tor, non-conductor, nor, odor, off-color,
oppressor, or, pallor, parlor, pastor,
phosphor, preceptor, predecessor, pre-
sentor, proctor, professor, proprietor,
protestor, purveyor, rancor, razor,
rector, reflector, rigor, rumor, sailor,
savor, sculptor, sector, señor, sheet
anchor, social error, splendor, sponsor,
squalor, straw-color, stupor, successor,
succor, suitor, supervisor, surveyor,
survivor, technicolor, tenor, terror,
Thor, tor, tormentor, tremor, tricolor,

OR
see
ACTOR
ADOR
AMOR
ATOR
AUR
ECTOR
IDOR
IOR
ITOR
OAR
OOR*
ORE
OUR**
UTOR
ed-OARD
ORD*
s-ORES
ORS

Tudor, unlooked-for, Ursa Major, **OR**
Ursa Minor, valor, vapor, vendor, vic-
tor, vigor, visor, watercolor, Windsor

Agora, amphora, angora, aurora, **ORA**
carnivora, Cora, Diaspora, fedora, flora, *see*
Leonora, mandragora, Marmora, Pan- A**
dora, plethora, signora, sora

Anchorage, borage, forage, harbor- **ORAGE**
age, storage *see*
AGE

Balmoral, caporal, chloral, choral, **ORAL**
coral, corporal, floral, immoral, littoral, *see*
moral, oral, pastoral, pectoral, tem- AL
poral

Anaxagoras, Pythagoras **ORAS**
see
AS

Ameliorate, commemorate, corpo- **ORATE**
rate, corroborate, deteriorate, directo- *see*
rate, elaborate, evaporate, expectorate, ATE
incorporate, invigorate, meliorate, pas-
torate, perforate, perorate, protecto-
rate, reinvigorate

Absorb, orb, resorb, sorb **ORB**
see

Divorce, enforce, force, perforce, re- **ORCE**
inforce, tour de force *see*
ORSE*

Blowtorch, porch, scorch, torch **ORCH**
see

Accord, afford, broadsword, chord, clavichord, concord, cord, discord, ford, harpsichord, Hartford, hexachord, lord, monochord, Norwegian fiord, overlord, Oxford, record, sword, war-lord, whipcord

ORD*
see
OARD
ORDE
ORE-*d*
ed-ED

By-word, catchword, crossword, foreword, one-word, password, watchword, word

ORD**
see
EARD*
ERD
IRD
URD

Horde

ORDE
see
ORD

Border, corder, disorder, order, recorder

ORDER
see
ER

Adore, afore, alongshore, ashore, battledore, before, bore, chain-store, chore, coldsore, commodore, core, deplore, drug-store, encore, evermore, explore, folk-lore, fore, foreshore, fourscore, furore, furthermore, galore, gore, hellebore, heretofore, ignore, implore, inshore, lore, more, nevermore, offshore, ore, pebbled-shore, pinafore, pore, restore, score, semaphore, shore, Singapore, snore, sophomore, sore, spore, stevedore, store, sycamore, Tagore, Terpsichore, therefore, threescore, tore, underscore, wherefore, whore, wore, yore

ORE
see
IOR
OAR
OOR*
OR
OUR**
ed-OARD
ORD*
s-ORES

Ad valorem, theorem   **OREM**
                                         see
                                          EM

Swedenborg   **ORG**
                                         see

Disgorge, drop-forge, St. George,   **ORGE**
gorge   *see*

Morgue   **ORGUE**
                                         see

Gloria, noria, phantasmagoria, Vic-   **ORIA**
toria   *see*
                                          IA

Armorial, consistorial, dictatorial,   **ORIAL**
editorial, gladiatorial, gubernatorial, *see*
immemorial, inspectorial, memorial,   IAL
phantasmagorial, pictorial, piscatorial,
purgatorial, sartorial, senatorial, sen-
sorial, territorial, tonsorial

Dorian, gregorian, historian, saluta- **ORIAN**
torian, stentorian, valedictorian   *see*
                                          IAN

Allegoric, Amoric, amphoric, boric,   **ORIC**
caloric, Doric, historic, paregoric, ple- *see*
thoric, prehistoric, rhetoric, toric   IC

Anteriority, authority, inferiority,   **ORITY**
majority, minority, priority, sonority, *see*
sorority, superiority   E**
                                          ITY

Auditorium, emporium, moratorium, sanatorium, scriptorium

ORIUM
see
IUM

Cork, fork, New York, pitchfork, pork, stork, tuning fork, York

ORK*
see

All-work, basketwork, brickwork, butcher-work, clock-work, earthwork, fancywork, field-work, framework, fretwork, frostwork, groundwork, guesswork, handiwork, hard work, needlework, network, open-work, overwork, schoolwork, scrollwork, stonework, trellis-work, trestlework, waxwork, welfare work, wickerwork, work

ORK**
see
ERK

Schorl, whorl

ORL
see
URL

Netherworld, underworld, upperworld, world

ORLD
see
IRL-*ed*
URL-*ed*

Barnstorm, chloroform, conform, deform, dust-storm, form, inform, iodoform, misinform, norm, perform, platform, reform, sandstorm, sea-storm, snowstorm, thought-form, thunderstorm, transform

ORM
see
ARM**
IFORM

Angleworm, armyworm, bookworm, earthworm, glow-worm, grubworm, inchworm, silkworm

ORM**
see
ERM
IRM

Formal, informal, normal, sub- **ORMAL**
normal, supernormal   *see*
                                              AL

Acorn, adorn, barleycorn, baseborn, **ORN**
bicorn, bighorn, blackthorn, born,   *see*
broomcorn, buckthorn, bugle-horn,   ARN**
Cape Horn, Capricorn, careworn, corn, OURN
drinking-horn, earthborn, firstborn,
foghorn, footworn, forsworn, freeborn,
goat's horn, greenhorn, hartshorn,
hawthorn, horn, inborn, Leghorn, long-
horn, lorn, manor born, morn, new-
born, Norn, outworn, overworn, pop-
corn, powder horn, pronghorn, ram's
horn, saxhorn, scorn, seaborn, shoe-
horn, shopworn, shorn, shorthorn,
staghorn, stubborn, suborn, sweetcorn,
sworn, thorn, twice-born, unborn, uni-
corn, unshorn, water-born, war-torn,
wayworn, worn

Amorous, carnivorous, dolorous, **OROUS**
glamorous, humorous, languorous, *see*
malodorous, odorous, omnivorous, OUS
phosphorous, porous, rancorous, rigorous, sonorous, stertorous, vigorous

Dorp, thorp   **ORP**
                                      see
                                      ARP**

Corpse   **ORPSE**
                                      see
                                      ORP-*s*

Lorry, sorry, worry   **ORRY**
                                      see
                                      E**

Scissors

ORS
see
OR-*s*

Clotheshorse, cockhorse, gorse, hobby-horse, horse, indorse, Norse, race-horse, remorse, rockinghorse, saw-horse, seahorse, stalking-horse, stud-horse, worse

ORSE
see
ORCE
OURCE

Worst

ORST
see
ERST
URST

Abort, assort, bellwort, cavort, co-hort, colewort, comfort, comport, con-sort, contort, davenport, deport, dis-comfort, disport, distort, effort, escort, exhort, export, extort, field-sport, fig-wort, fort, gipsywort, import, liver-wort, mugwort, passport, port, pur-port, report, resort, retort, ribwort, seaport, short, snort, sort, spiderwort, sport, support, transport, what sort

ORT
see
ART**
OURT
UART
ed-ED

Immortal, mortal, portal

ORTAL
see
AL

Ottoman Porte, Sublime Porte

ORTE
see
ORT

Exporter, importer, porter, reporter, shorter, sorter, supporter

ORTER
see
ER

Forth, go-forth, henceforth, Kenil-worth, north, thenceforth, Words-worth, worth

ORTH
see
ARTH
OURTH

Decorum, forum, pons asinorum, quorum, Roman Forum, sanctum sanctorum

ORUM
see
UM

Apollodorus, Bosphorus, chorus, hel-leborus, Horus, phosphorus

ORUS
see
US

Accessory, allegory, armory, audi-tory, category, chicory, compulsory, cursory, desultory, directory, dormi-tory, dory, evocatory, factory, fish-story, ghost-story, glory, gory, hickory, history, illusory, introductory, inven-tory, invocatory, ivory, lory, memory, morning-glory, non-compulsory, offer-tory, Old Glory, olfactory, peremp-tory, perfunctory, pillory, porphory, pre-inventory, priory, promissory, promontory, rectory, refectory, refrac-tory, repository, satisfactory, savory, sensory, short-story, story, succory, territory, theory, tory, transitory, vainglory, valedictory, vapory, victory

ORY
see
ATORY
E**

Abydos, Anteros, Argos, asbestos, Atropos, Barbados, bathos, Bucepha-los, caballeros, chaos, Chronos, cosmos, dithyrambos, Encelados, Eos, epos, Eros, Galapagos, Hyksos, Hypnos, Lemnos, Lesbos, logos, Minos, Mount Athos, naos, Ninon de l'Enclos, Om-

OS
see
IOS
OSS

phalos, os, Parthenos, pathos, Patmos, Patroclos, Pergamos, pharos, Psychopompos, pueblos, reredos, rhinoceros, Samos, S.O.S., Tantalos, Tenedos, thanatos, thermos, Triptolemos

OS

Amorosa, Formosa, Mater Dolorosa, mimosa, scabiosa, sub rosa, via dolorosa

OSA
see
A**

Adipose, albuminose, appose, aquose, arose, bellicose, bottlenose, cellulose, chose, close, comatose, compose, crystalose, damask rose, decompose, depose, disclose, dispose, dose, equipose, expose, frostnipt-nose, foreclose, glucose, hooknose, hose, impose, inclose, interpose, jocose, juxtapose, lachrymose, metamorphose, morose, Nivose, nose, oppose, overdose, overexpose, plumose, Pluviose, pope's nose, pose, predispose, presuppose, primrose, propose, prose, pruinose, purpose, repose, Roman nose, rose, scapose, 'spose, suppose, tea-rose, those, transpose, tuberose, unclose, Ventose, verbose, wildrose

OSE*
see
IOSE
O*-*es*
OE**-*s*
OTHE-*s*
OW*-*s*
OWS
OZE

Lose, whose

OSE**
see
USE

Closet, marmoset

OSET
see
ET

Bosh, cohosh, galosh, gosh, josh, kibosh, mackintosh, Oshkosh, slosh

OSH
see
ASH**
UASH

Corrosion, erosion, explosion

OSION
see
ION

Apodosis, apotheosis, diagnosis, hypnosis, kenosis, metamorphosis, metempsychosis, necrosis, prognosis, psychoneurosis, psychosis, sorosis, tuberculosis

OSIS
see
IS*

Anfractuosity, aquosity, curiosity, generosity, gibbosity, impetuosity, jocosity, luminosity, monstrosity, nebulosity, pomposity, ponderosity, sabulosity, sinuosity, tortuosity, verbosity, virtuosity

OSITY
see
ITY

Corrosive, erosive, explosive

OSIVE
see
IVE

Bosk, kiosk

OSK
see
OSQUE

Macrocosm, microcosm

OSM
see
OM*

Amoroso, capriccioso, gracioso, Orlando Furioso, so-so, virtuoso, whoso

OSO
see
O*

Kiosque, mosque

OSQUE
see
OSK

Across, albatross, boss, bugloss, Charing-Cross, criss-cross, cross, double-cross, dross, emboss, engross, Florida moss, floss, gloss, golden-cross, gross, hoss, iron cross, joss, loss, moss, peat-moss, Red Cross, Southern Cross, toss

OSS
see
AUCE
OS
OSSE

Fosse, lacrosse, posse

OSSE
see
OSS

Bossy, flossy, glossy, mossy

OSSY
see
E**

Accost, Bifrost, cost, defrost, embost, frost, hoarfrost, Jack Frost, long-lost, lost, Pentecost

OST*
see
AUST
ed-ED

Almost, easternmost, foremost, ghost, hindermost, host, impost, inmost, innermost, middlemost, milepost, most, nethermost, northernmost, outpost, parcel post, post, provost, signpost, southernmost, topmost, uppermost, utmost, westernmost, whipping-post

OST**
see
OAST

Apostle, jostle, throstle

OSTLE
see
EL
LE

Closure, composure, disclosure, enclosure, exposure, foreclosure, inclosure, overexposure, underexposure

OSURE
see
URE

Argosy, nosy, posy, prosy, rosy

OSY
see
E**

Euphrosyne, Mnemosyne

OSYNE
see
E*

All-hot, allot, apricot, ballot, begot, bergamot, bloodshot, blot, bowknot, bowshot, buckshot, Camelot, carrot, coffee-pot, co-pilot, cot, despot, diglot, divot, dot, dryrot, earshot, ergot, fagot, fairy-grot, fleshpot, flowerpot, forget-me-not, forgot, foxtrot, gallipot, Gordian-knot, got, grapeshot, grot, harlot, helot, hot, hotspot, Hottentot, ingot, jackpot, jogtrot, jot, knot, lot, loveknot, maggot, marmot, marplot, mascot, monoglot, not, paletot, parrot, pilot, piping hot, pivot, plot, polyglot, pot, redhot, reef-knot, rot, ryot, sabot, Scot, shot, slingshot, slipknot, slot, snapshot, sot, spot, teapot, tender spot, tommyrot, topknot, tot, touch-me-not, trot, turbot, turkeytrot, try-pot, unguent-pot, upshot, wainscot, wateringpot, whatnot, wildcarrot, wot, zealot

OT*
see
ACHT
AT**
ATT
IGOT
IOT
OTT
OTTE

Argot, bon mot, depot, Huguenot, jabot, matelot, Pierrot, robot, tarot

OT**
see
O*

Dakota, iota, Minnesota, quota, rota

OTA
see
A**

Dotage, flotage, sabotage•

OTAGE
see
AGE

Annotate, connotate, rotate

OTATE
see
ATE

Blotch, botch, crotch, hopscotch, hot-Scotch, notch, Scotch, splotch, top-notch

OTCH
see
ATCH**

Anecdote, antidote, banknote, ca-pote, chorus-note, connote, cote, coy-ote, creosote, demote, denote, devote, dote, dovecote, footnote, keynote, mis-quote, mote, note, quote, promote, redingote, remote, rote, sheepcote, smote, straw vote, table d'hote, tote, treasury note, vote, wrote

OTE
see
OAT
s-OATS

Both, quoth, Sabbaoth, sloth, Suc-coth

OTH*
see
OATH
OWTH

Ashtaroth, azoth, behemoth, beroth, betroth, broadcloth, broth, cheese-cloth, cloth, fishbroth, froth, Goth, mammoth, moth, neckcloth, oilcloth, sackcloth, Sephiroth, Thoth, troth, Visigoth, wroth

OTH**
see

Clothe

OTHE
see
OATH

Another, bother, brother, foster-mother, grandmother, half-brother, mother, other, pother, smother, step-mother, tother

OTHER
see
ER

Chaotic, demotic, despotic, epizoötic, exotic, hypnotic, idiotic, narcotic, neurotic, patriotic, quixotic

OTIC
see
IC

Commotion, devotion, emotion, locomotion, lotion, love potion, motion, notion, perpetual motion, potion, promotion, slow-motion

OTION
see
ION

Automotive, locomotive, motive, promotive

OTIVE
see
IVE

Boycott, Scott

OTT
see
OT
OTTE

Calotte, charlotte, cocotte, gavotte, sans culotte, Wyandotte

OTTE
see
OT
OTT

Bluebottle, bottle, mottle, throttle, smelling-bottle

OTTLE
see
EL
LE

Blotto, Giotto, grotto, lotto, motto, Otto, risotto, sotto

OTTO
see
O*

Anjou, bayou, bijou, caribou, frou-frou, loup garou, marabou, sou, you

OU*
see
UE*

Thou

OU**
see
OUGH
OW**

Doubt, misdoubt, redoubt

OUBT
see
OUT

Caoutchouc

OUC
see
OOK*

Avouch, bridal-couch, couch, crouch, game-pouch, grouch, ouch, pouch, slouch, vouch

OUCH*
see

Retouch, touch

OUCH**
see
UCH*

Barouche, cartouche, douche, Scaramouche

OUCHE
see

Aloud, becloud, cloud, enshroud, loud, overcloud, overloud, proud, purse-proud, shroud, stroud, thunder-cloud

OUD
see
OWD
OW**-*ed*

Rouge **OUGE**
see

Although, borough, dough, furlough, **OUGH***
though, thorough
see
o*

Acacia-bough, apple-bough, bough, **OUGH****
Golden Bough, plough, slough, sough
see
ow**
s-ouse**

Enough, rough, slough, tough **OUGH*****
see
UFF

Through **OUGH******
see
U

Cough, hiccough, trough **OUGH*******
see
OFF

Afterthought, besought, bethought, **OUGHT**
bought, brought, drought, forethought,
see
fought, inwrought, methought, nought,
AUGHT*
ought, sought, take thought, thought,
AUT*
unsought, well-fought, wrought

Bedouin **OUIN**
see
UIN

Saint Louis **OUIS**
see
E**

Afoul, befoul, foul

OUL*
see
OWL

Over-soul, soul

OUL**
see
OL

Ghoul, Stamboul

OUL***
see
ULE

Mould

OULD*
see
OLD

Could, should, would

OULD**
see
OOD

Boulder, shoulder

OULDER
see
ER

Noun, pronoun

OUN
see
OWN**

Announce, bounce, cherrybounce, denounce, flounce, jounce, ounce, pounce, pronounce, renounce, trounce

OUNCE
see

Abound, aground, around, astound, background, blood-hound, bound, camping-ground, compound, dumb-found, expound, found, greyhound, harehound, hidebound, homeward-

OUND
see
OWN**-*ed*
ed-ED

bound, horehound, hound, impound, ironbound, merry-go-round, mound, musclebound, outward bound, playground, pound, profound, propound, rebound, redound, resound, round, sleuth-hound, snowbound, sound, spellbound, staghound, stamping-ground, surround, underground, vantage-ground, whimpering-hound, wound

OUND

Bounder, flounder, founder, grounder, rounder

OUNDER
see
ER

Coffee-grounds, fish pounds, zounds

OUNDS
see
OUND-*s*

Young

OUNG
see
UNG

Lounge

OUNGE
see

Account, amount, catamount, count, discount, dismount, fount, miscount, mount, paramount, recount, surmount, tantamount, viscount

OUNT
see

Bounty, county, mounty

OUNTY
see
E**

Croup, group, pea-soup, recoup, thick soup, soup, troup

OUP*
see
OOP
OUPE**
UPE

Coup   **OUP****
                                        see
                                        OU
                                        UE

Cantaloupe   **OUPE***
                                        see
                                        OPE

Troupe   **OUPE****
                                        see
                                        OUP
                                        UPE

Amour, armour, belabour, colour,   **OUR**
détour, devour, dour, downpour, fa-   *see*
vour, flavour, flour, four, giaour, glam- EUR
our, half-hour, honour, hour, ill-favour, OAR
labour, our, outpour, paramour, par-   OR
lour, Pompadour, pour, rumour, sav-   OWER
iour, scour, sour, splendour, succour,   URE
tambour, tour, troubadour, vigour,
your

Resource, source   **OURCE**
                                        see
                                        OURSE

Gourd   **OURD**
                                        see
                                        URD

Scourge   **OURGE**
                                        see
                                        ERGE
                                        IRGE
                                        URGE

Adjourn, bourn, sojourn   **OURN***
                                       see
                                       URN

Mourn   **OURN****
                                       see
                                       ORN

All fours, hours, ours, velours, yours **OURS**
                                        see
                                        OUR-*s*

Bourse, concourse, course, discourse, **OURSE**
intercourse, of-course, race-course, re- *see*
course, water-course   ORSE
                                        OURCE

Court, divorce court, police court,   **OURT**
Supreme Court   *see*
                                       ORT

Fourth   **OURTH**
                                       see
                                       ORTH

Ambidextrous, analogous, andro-   **OUS***
gynous, anepigraphous, anonymous,   *see*
barbarous, bibulous, blasphemous,   ALOUS
bulbous, callous, chivalrous, cumbrous, EOUS
declivous, desirous, diaphanous, dis- EROUS
astrous, enormous, famous, frivolous, INOUS
gibbous, gluttonous, hazardous, homol- IOUS
ogous, idolatrous, infamous, joyous,   ITOUS
lithophagous, ludicrous, magnanimous, ONOUS
mischievous, molluscous, momentous,   OROUS
monstrous, multifidous, murmurous,   ULOUS
nervous, nitrous, nubilous, ominous,   UOUS

parlous, pendulous, perilous, pompous, portentous, posthumous, prognathous, pusillanimous, rapturous, raucous, ravenous, rigorous, riotous, scurrilous, stupendous, sulphurous, synonymous, torturous, tremendous, troublous, tyrannous, unanimous, venomous, venous, venturous, viscous, wondrous

OUS*
US
ly-E**
OUSLY

Entre nous, rendevous

OUS**
see
U

Almshouse, blue-titmouse, bughouse, chapterhouse, chophouse, coach-house, custom-house, dormouse, douse, farmhouse, flitter-mouse, full-house, greenhouse, grouse, hot house, house, lighthouse, log-house, louse, meeting-house, mouse, penthouse, playhouse, poorhouse, power-house, rough-house, roundhouse, schoolhouse, shrew-mouse, souse, state house, storehouse, summerhouse, titmouse, wheel-house, White House, workhouse

OUSE*
see

Arouse, blouse, carouse, espouse, rouse, spouse

OUSE**
see
OUGH**-*s*
OWSE

Assiduously, continuously, copiously, curiously, furiously, instantaneously, joyously, previously, simultaneously, viciously

OUSLY
see
E**
IOUS-*ly*
OUS-*ly*

Joust, oust, roust **OUST**
see

About, blow-out, bout, boyscout, **OUT***
clout, cut-out, devout, dugout, eke out, *see*
fingerling trout, flatten-out, flout, gad- AUT**
about, gout, hereabout, in and out, OUBT
knockout, knout, layout, long-drawn-
out, lookout, lout, out, out and out,
pig's-snout, pout, right-about, root-
out, roundabout, rout, salmon trout,
scout, set-out, shout, snout, spout,
sprout, stout, thereabout, throughout,
tout, trout, try-out, turn-out, walkout,
wash-out, waterspout, whereabout,
without, worn-out

Mahout, marabout, surtout **OUT****
see
OOT**

Passe partout, ragout **OUT*****
see
OU*

Route **OUTE**
see
OUT*

Couth, Plymouth, uncouth, ver- **OUTH***
mouth, Yarmouth, youth *see*
UTH

Drouth, mouth, south **OUTH****
see

Billet-doux, Sioux   **OUX**
see
O**

Approval, disapproval, oval, removal   **OVAL**
see
AL

Innovate, ovate, renovate   **OVATE**
see
ATE

Alcove, clove, cove, drove, grove,   **OVE***
hove, interwove, Jove, mangrove, rove,   *see*
shrove, stove, strove, throve, treasure   AUVE
trove, trove, wove

Above, belove, boxing-glove, dove,   **OVE****
foxglove, glove, kid-glove, ringdove,   *see*
self-love, shove, turtledove, unglove   OF

Approve, disapprove, disprove, im-   **OVE*****
prove, move, prove, remove, reprove   *see*
OOVE

Grovel, hovel, novel, shovel   **OVEL**
see
EL
LE

Beethoven, cloven, disproven, inter-   **OVEN**
woven, oven, proven, sloven, woven   *see*
EN

Clover, cover, discover, four-leaved   **OVER**
clover, hang-over, Hanover, hover,   *see*
lover, moreover, over, Passover, plover,   ER

popover, recover, rover, runover, stop-over, turnover, uncover, undercover

OVER

After-glow, aglow, backflow, barge-tow, bellow, below, bestow, billow, blow, borrow, bungalow, burrow, cross-bow, crow, dormer-window, elbow, fan window, fiddlebow, flow, follow, fore-shadow, furbelow, Glasgow, glow, goodmorrow, grass-widow, hedge-row, inflow, Jim Crow, know, low, meadow, minnow, morrow, mow, outgrow, over-flow, overshadow, overthrow, peach-blow, peepshow, pillow, plow, pussy-willow, rainbow, roadshow, rose-win-dow, row, rum-row, saddlebow, scare-crow, shadow, show, show window, slow, snow, sorrow, stone's-throw, stow, throw, tomorrow, tow, undertow, widow, willow, window, winnow

OW*
see
ALLOW
ARROW
EAU
ELLOW
OE**
OUGH*
OWE
URROW
ed-OAD
ODE
er-ER
OUR*
ly-E**
OWLY
š-OSE*
OZE

Allow, anyhow, avow, bow, bow-wow, brow, Chinese-chow, chowchow, cow, dhow, disavow, endow, enow, ere now, eyebrow, for-now, Hankow, high-brow, how, kowtow, Moscow, Nankow, now, plow, pow-wow, row, scow, snow-plow, somehow, sow, trow, vow, wow

OW**
see
AU***
OU**
OUGH**
ed-OUD
OWD
š-OUSE**

Crowd, overcrowd

OWD
see
OUD

Chowder, gunpowder, powder

OWDER
see
ER

Crowdy, dowdy, howdy, rowdy   **OWDY**
see
E**

Owe   **OWE**
see
O*

Bowel, dowel, paper-towel, roller-towel, towel, trowel, vowel   **OWEL**
see
EL

Borrower, bower, candlepower, cauliflower, cornflower, cower, dower, embower, empower, flower, gilliflower, glower, horsepower, Leaning Tower, left-bower, lotus-flower, lower, mayflower, Mouse Tower, overpower, ower, passion flower, power, right-bower, shower, sunflower, tower, wallflower, watchtower, widower, wood-flower   **OWER**
see
ER
OUR*
ow*-*er*

Bowery, flowery, lowery   **OWERY**
see
ERY

Bowl, finger-bowl, pipe-bowl, wassail bowl   **OWL***
see
OUL**

Cowl, fowl, growl, howl, jowl, night-owl, prowl, river-fowl, scowl, screech-owl, sea-fowl, water-fowl, yowl   **OWL****
see
OUL*

Lowly, narrowly, slowly   **OWLY**
see
E**

Blown, disown, flown, fullblown, fullgrown, grown, highflown, known, mown, new-mown, outgrown, overblown, overthrown, own, self-sown, shown, sown, strown, thrown, unblown, unknown, unsown, well-known

OWN*
see
OAN
ONE*

A-down, brown, Cape Town, Chinatown, clown, comedown, crown, down, downtown, dressing-gown, drown, frown, gown, knock-down, let-down, low-down, marked-down, nightgown, plank down, renown, shakedown, showdown, shutdown, sit-down, Southdown, sun-down, swan's-down, thistledown, thrown-down, touch-down, town, tumbledown, uncrown, upsidedown, uptown

OWN**
see
OUN
*ed-*OUND

Bellows, gallows, overgrows, whoknows

OWS
see
OSE*
OW*-*s*

Browse, drowse

OWSE
see
OUSE**
OW**-*s*

Growth, overgrowth, undergrowth

OWTH
see
OATH
OTH*

Billowy, shadowy, willowy

OWY
see
E**

Ballot-box, bandbox, box, chatter-box, cowpox, deposit box, ditty-box, equinox, fox, letterbox, musicbox, muskox, Nox, ox, paddlebox, Pandora's box, paradox, pepperbox, phlox, pillbox, prowling-fox, rosewood box, saltbox, shooting-box, smallpox, snuffbox, soapbox, spitbox, strongbox, tinderbox

OX
see
OCK-*s*
ODOX

Doxy, foxy, heterodoxy, orthodoxy, proxy

OXY
see
E**

Ahoy, alloy, altar boy, annoy, babyboy, boy, bus boy, cabin-boy, charpoy, cloy, convoy, corduroy, coy, decoy, destroy, employ, enjoy, envoy, errand-boy, hautboy, Helen of Troy, highboy, joy, killjoy, lowboy, newsboy, old boy, overjoy, playboy, Rob Roy, savoy, sepoy, ship-ahoy, teapoy, tomboy, toy, viceroy

OY
see
UOY
ed-OID
s-OISE

Loyal, pennyroyal, royal, unloyal

OYAL
see
AL

Lloyd, sloyd

OYD
see
OID

Gargoyle, Hoyle

OYLE
see
OIL

Bulldoze, doze, froze **OZE**
see
OSE*
OW*-*s*

U SOUNDS

Babu, Bantu, bhikshu, Danu, emu, fichu, gnu, Hindu, Honolulu, impromptu, I.O.U., Jehu, ju-jitsu, juju, Khosru, Khufu, menu, Meru, Mu, Nu, ormolu, pari passu, parvenu, perdu, Peru, poilu, Shu, Timbuktu, Vishnu, zebu, Zulu

U

 see
 AGUE**
 EW
 IEU
 IEW
 INUE
 O**
 OO
 OU
 OUGH****
 UE*
 URU
 UT**
 S-EW-*S*
  OOSE**
  OOZE
  OSE**
  OUS**
  UISE**
  USE*

Aqua, Chatauqua, Gargantua, Joshua, Nicaragua, Padua, Papua

UA

 see
 A**

Equable, invaluable, valuable

UABLE

 see
 ABLE

Quad, squad	**UAD** *see* OD
Dissuade, overpersuade, persuade	**UADE** *see* ADE* EDE**
Quaff	**UAFF** *see* AFE**
Agglutinative language, assuage, language	**UAGE** *see* AGE*
Actual, annual, bi-annual, bilingual, casual, co-equal, contextual, continual, conventual, dual, effectual, eventual, gradual, habitual, homo-sexual, individual, ineffectual, intellectual, lingual, manual, mutual, perpetual, punctual, residual, ritual, sensual, sexual, spiritual, unusual, usual, victual, virtual, visual	**UAL** *see* AL *ly*-UALLY
Casually, eventually, habitually, mutually, perpetually, punctually, spiritually, unusually, usually, virtually	**UALLY** *see* ALLY E**
Qualm	**UALM** *see* ALM
Assuan, Don Juan, gargantuan, San Juan	**UAN** *see* AN**

Nuance, piquance, pursuance   **UANCE**
see
ANCE

Piquant, pursuant, truant   **UANT**
see
ANT

Blackguard, bodyguard, coastguard, guard, lifeguard, mud-guard, safe-guard, vanguard   **UARD**
see
ARD

Quarry   **UARRY**
see
ORY

Mary Stuart, quart   **UART**
see
ART**
ORT

Quartz   **UARTZ**
see
ORT-*s*

Actuary, antiquary, electuary, estuary, February, January, mortuary, obituary, ossuary, reliquary, residuary, sanctuary, statuary, voluptuary   **UARY**
see
AIRY
ARY
E**

Crookneck-squash, quash, musquash, squash   **UASH**
see
ASH**

Kumquat   **UAT**
see
AT**

Accentuate, actuate, adequate, anti-
quate, attenuate, devaluate, evacuate,
evaluate, extenuate, fluctuate, gradu-
ate, inadequate, individuate, infatuate,
insinuate, perpetuate, postgraduate,
punctuate, sinuate, situate, superannu-
ate, undergraduate

UATE
see
ATE

Suave, Zouave

UAVE
see

Cawquaw, musquaw, squaw

UAW
see
AW

Paraguay, quay, Uruguay

UAY
see
AY

Bathtub, Beelzebub, club, cub, dub,
grub, hubbub, Indian club, pub, rub,
rub-a-dub, scrub, shrub, sillabub, slub,
snub, strawberry shrub, stub, sub, tub,
yacht club

UB
see

Blubber, India-rubber, landlubber,
rubber, snubber

UBBER
see
ER

Chubby, fubby, grubby, hubby,
nubby, scrubby, snubby, tubby

UBBY
see
E**

Cube, inner-tube, jujube, rube,
speaking-tube, tube

UBE
see

Dissoluble, double, insoluble, re-double, resoluble, rouble, soluble, trou-ble, voluble

UBLE
see
EL
LE

Adduce, Bruce, conduce, deuce, educe, induce, introduce, lettuce, pro-duce, puce, reduce, reproduce, seduce, spruce, superinduce, traduce, truce

UCE
see
EUS
OOSE*
UICE

Forasmuch, inasmuch, much, non-such, overmuch, such

UCH*
see
OUCH**
UTCH

Eunuch, Pentateuch

UCH**
see
UKE

Ruche

UCHE
see

Amuck, awestruck, bestruck, buck, Calmuck, Canuck, chuck, cluck, duck, Friar Tuck, goodluck, horror-struck, luck, moonstruck, muck, muscovy duck, pluck, pot-luck, Puck, roebuck, sawbuck, shuck, struck, stuck, suck, tuck, truck, woodchuck

UCK
see
OK

Buckle, chuckle, honeysuckle, knuckle, muckle, shoebuckle, suckle

UCKLE
see
EL
LE

Lucre **UCRE**
see
ER

Abduct, conduct, construct, duct, **UCT**
induct, instruct, misconduct, obstruct, *see*
product, reconstruct, safe conduct, via- EDUCT
duct

Auction, deduction, destruction, in- **UCTION**
struction, obstruction, overproduction, *see*
production, reduction, reproduction, ION
ruction, seduction, suction

Bestud, bud, collar-stud, cud, dud, **UD**
mud, rosebud, scud, spud, stud, Tal- *see*
mud, thud OOD**

Rudder, shudder, udder **UDDER**
see
ER

Befuddle, fuddle, huddle, muddle, **UDDLE**
puddle *see*
EL
LE

Allude, collude, conclude, crude, **UDE**
delude, desuetude, dude, elude, etude, *see*
exclude, exude, include, inquietude, EUD
interlude, intrude, mansuetude, nude, ITUDE
obtrude, preclude, prelude, protrude, OOD***
prude, quietude, rude, seclude IEW-*ed*
UE*-*ed*
S-UDES

Begrudge, budge, drudge, fudge, grudge, judge, misjudge, nudge, sludge, smudge, trudge

UDGE
see

Soapsuds

UDS
see
UD-*s*

Accrue, argue, avenue, barbecue, blue, clue, construe, continue, cue, curlycue, due, ensue, flue, glue, hue, imbue, ingenue, marble-statue, misconstrue, out-argue, overdue, pursue, queue, rescue, retinue, revenue, revue, ring-true, robin's egg blue, rue, sky-blue, slue, statue, subdue, sue, true, true-blue, undervalue, undue, untrue, value, vendue, virtue

UE*
see
AGUE***
ISSUE
U
ed-EWD
UDE
s-EW-*s*
UISE**
USE

Fatigue, intrigue, overfatigue

UE**
see
AGUE**

Cruel, duel, fuel, gruel, Pantagruel, Samuel, sequel

UEL
see
EL

Guelph

UELPH
see

Affluence, congruence, consequence, effluence, eloquence, sequence

UENCE
see
ENCE

Minuend

UEND
see
END

Abluent, affluent, confluent, constit-
uent, delinquent, effluent, eloquent,
fluent, frequent, grandiloquent, incon-
sequent, influent, infrequent, refluent,
sequent, subsequent, unguent

UENT
see
ENT

Beleaguer, chequer, exchequer, lac-
quer, pursuer

UER
see
ER

Quern

UERN
see
ERN

Bequest, conquest, follow-guest,
guest, inquest, quest, request

UEST
see
EAST**

Banquet, bluet, cruet, duet, minuet,
paroquet, piquet

UET*
see
ET

Croquet, parquet, sobriquet, tourni-
quet

UET**
see
A*

Bluff, buff, cuff, dandruff, duff, fisti-
cuff, fluff, gruff, guff, handcuff, herbal
snuff, huff, luff, Macduff, muff, plum-
duff, puff, rebuff, ruff, scruff, scuff,
snuff, sob-stuff, stuff

UFF
see
OUGH**
ed-UFT

Candytuft, puft, tuft

UFT
see
UFF-*ed*

Bug, chug-chug, drug, dug, firebug,
fire-plug, hearth-rug, hug, humbug,

UG
see

jug, lady-bug, lightning-bug, lug, **UG**
mealy-bug, mug, plug, potato-bug,
pug, rug, shrug, slug, smug, snug,
spark-plug, thug, tug, vinegar jug,
wicker-jug

Kali Yuga, Satya Yuga **UGA**
see
A**

Centrifugal, frugal, fugal, Portugal **UGAL**
see
AL

Deluge, huge, refuge, subterfuge **UGE**
see

Drugget, nugget **UGGET**
see
ET

Juggle, smuggle, snuggle, struggle **UGGLE**
see
EL
LE

Buggy, muggy, puggy, sluggy **UGGY**
see
E**

Impugn, oppugn **UGN**
see
UNG

Alleluia **UIA**
see
IA

Squib **UIB**
see
IB

Juice, fruitjuice, grapejuice, sluice, **UICE**
tomato-juice *see*
USE**

Druid, fluid, languid, liquid, quid, **UID**
squid, tertian quid *see*
ID

Guide, misguide **UIDE**
see
IDE

Guayaquil, jonquil, tranquil **UIL**
see
IL

Build, guild, upbuild **UILD**
see
ILD*
ILL-*ed*

Beguile, guile **UILE**
see
ILE*

Goose-quill, quill, squill **UILL**
see
ILL

Bedquilt, built, clipper-built, guilt, **UILT**
quilt *see*
ILT
ed-ED

Guimp **UIMP**
see
IMP

Algonquin, Bedouin, beguin, bruin, **UIN**
harlequin, lambrequin, mannequin, *see*
palanquin, penguin, ruin, sequin, Tar- IN
quin UINE

Equine, genuine, sanguine **UINE**
see
INE**

Acquire, esquire, inquire, quire, re- **UIRE**
quire, squire *see*
IRE

Quirt, squirt **UIRT**
see
IRT
URT

Disguise, guise **UISE***
see
IZE

Bruise, cruise **UISE****
see
USE

Anguish, bluish, cliquish, distin- **UISH**
guish, extinguish, languish, relinquish, *see*
roguish ISH

Altruism, truism, ventriloquism **UISM**
see
ISM

Altruist, casuist, linguist, ventrilo-
quist

UIST
see
IST

Acquit, biscuit, circuit, conduit,
Jesuit, pilot-biscuit, quit, short-circuit

UIT*
see
IT

Breadfruit, bruit, dress-suit, follow
suit, fruit, grapefruit, lawsuit, pursuit,
recruit, suit, unionsuit

UIT**
see
UTE

Mesquite, suite, tout de suite

UITE*
see
EAT*

Quite, requite

UITE**
see
ITE*

Ambiguity, annuity, antiquity, con-
gruity, equity, gratuity, incongruity,
inequity, ingenuity, iniquity, longin-
quity, obliquity, perpetuity, perspicu-
ity, propinquity, superfluity, tenuity,
ubiquity

UITY
see
E**
ITY

Quiz

UIZ
see
IZ

Habakkuk, Kalmuk, Marduk, Sa-
rouk, Volapuk

UK
see
UCH**
UKE

Archduke, cuke, duke, fluke, Luke, Mameluke, peruke, rebuke

UKE
see
OOK**
UK

Annul, artful, awful, baleful, baneful, bashful, brimful, bulbul, caracul, careful, cheerful, consul, cupful, delightful, distrustful, doleful, doubtful, Elul, eyeful, faithful, fateful, fitful, forgetful, fretful, graceful, grateful, harmful, heartful, heedful, hurtful, ireful, lawful, lustful, masterful, mindful, mirthful, Mogul, mournful, mouthful, needful, pailful, painful, plateful, playful, powerful, prayerful, proconsul, purposeful, regretful, remorseful, reproachful, resentful, restful, revengeful, rueful, shameful, shovelful, slothful, sorrowful, tearful, thankful, thimbleful, thoughtful, tuneful, unfaithful, ungrateful, unmirthful, useful, vengeful, wakeful, watchful, wilful, wishful, wistful, woeful, wonderful, worshipful, wrathful, wrongful, youthful

UL
see
IFUL
ULL*

Calendula, Caligula, campanula, comatula, copula, fibula, formula, Gula, hula-hula, incunabula, nebula, peninsula, scapula, spatula, spicula, St. Ursula, tarantula

ULA
see
A**

Angular, binocular, cellular, circular, corpuscular, funicular, granular, globular, insular, irregular, jocular, jugular, lenticular, lobular, lunular, molecular, monocular, muscular, nebular,

ULAR
see
AR

oracular, orbicular, particular, peninsular, perpendicular, popular, rectangular, regular, secular, semi-circular, singular, spectacular, triangular, tubular, unpopular, valvular, vascular, vehicular, vernacular

ULAR

Articulate, calculate, circulate, coagulate, confabulate, congratulate, consulate, ejaculate, emulate, expostulate, formulate, granulate, immaculate, inarticulate, inoculate, insulate, jaculate, manipulate, matriculate, miscalculate, modulate, osculate, peculate, perambulate, populate, postulate, recapitulate, regulate, simulate, speculate, stimulate, stipulate, strangulate, tabulate, ululate, undulate

ULATE
see
ATE

Bulb, electric-light bulb, gladiola bulb, rubber-bulb

ULB
see

Mulch

ULCH
see

Animacule, capsule, cellule, corpuscule, crepuscule, ferrule, footrule, globule, golden-rule, granule, lobule, minuscule, misrule, module, molecule, mule, nodule, over-rule, plumbrule, pule, pustule, reticule, ridicule, rule, schedule, sumpter-mule, tule, vestibule, yule

ULE
see
OOL
OUL***

Corpulent, fraudulent, opulent, succulent, truculent, turbulent, virulent

ULENT
see
ENT

Amulet, Capulet, epaulet, rivulet	**ULET** *see* ET
Engulf, gulf	**ULF** *see*
Bulgar, vulgar	**ULGAR** *see* AR
Bulge, divulge, effulge, indulge, pro-mulge	**ULGE** *see*
Fulgent, effulgent, indulgent, over-indulgent	**ULGENT** *see* ENT
Bulk, hulk, skulk, sulk	**ULK** *see*
Bulky, sulky	**ULKY** *see* E**
Armfull, bull, chestfull, chock-full, cull, dull, full, gull, hull, jaw-full, jig-full, lull, mull, null numskull, pull, scull, sea-gull, skull, you'll	**ULL** *see* OL UL
Tulle	**ULLE** *see* ULE
Bully, carefully, dully, fully, gully, ruefully, spitefully, sully, truthfully, untruthfully, wilfully	**ULLY** *see* E**

Credulous, cumulous, fabulous, garrulous, homunculous, incredulous, meticulous, miraculous, nebulous, pendulous, populous, querulous, ridiculous, scrupulous, tremulous, tumulous, unscrupulous

ULOUS
see
OUS
US

Gulp, pulp

ULP
see

Pulse, impulse, repulse

ULSE
see
ULT-*S*

Adult, antepenult, catapult, consult, cult, difficult, exult, insult, occult, penult, result, semi-occult, tumult

ULT
see
ed-ED
S-ULSE

Difficulty, faculty, faulty

ULTY
see
E**

Calculus, convolvulus, ranunculus, Romulus, stimulus, tumulus

ULUS
see
US

Duly, patchouly, truly, unruly

ULY*
see
E**

July

ULY**
see
I*
Y

Addendum, adytum, alarum, album, alburnum, alum, annum, antidotum, arboretum, asylum, bay rum, begum, bum, bunkum, candelabrum, capsicum, cerebrum, chewing-gum, chrysanthemum, chum, colchicum, conundrum, corrigendum, curriculum, date-plum, doldrum, drum, E pluribus unum, ergastulum, factotum, Fatum, fe-fi-fo-fum, fulcrum, glum, gum, gypsum, harum-scarum, hokum, hoodlum, horrendum, hum, humdrum, index rerum, interregnum, kettledrum, Khartum, labarum, laburnum, lignum, magnum, maximum, memorandum, minimum, modicum, momentum, mum, nostrum, oakum, opossum, pabulum, panjandrum, pax vobiscum, pendulum, peplum, per-annum, platinum, plectrum, plum, quantum, referendum, regnum, rostrum, rum, sanctum, scrum, scum, scutum, sedum, serum, simulacrum, sistrum, slum, sorghum, spectrum, strum, sugar-plum, sum, summum bonum, sweet alyssum, tantrum, Targum, thrum, tintinnabulum, Tum, unguentum, unum, vade-mecum, vellum, viaticum, wampum, yum-yum

UM
see
ANUM
ATUM
AUM
EUM
ITUM
IUM
OM*
OME*
ORUM
OMB
UUM

Montezuma, Numa, puma, Satsuma, Uma

UMA
see
A**

Hanuman, human, inhuman, superhuman

UMAN
see
AN*

Benumb, crumb, dumb, numb, plumb, succumb, thumb, Tom Thumb

UMB
see
OMB**

Cucumber, cumber, encumber, lumber, number, slumber, outnumber

UMBER
see
ER

Bumble, crumble, fumble, grumble, humble, jumble, mumble, rumble, stumble, tumble

UMBLE
see
EL
LE

Gumbo, jumbo, Mumbo Jumbo

UMBO
see
O*

Penumbra, umbra

UMBRA
see
A**

Assume, brume, consume, costume, exhume, flume, fume, illume, legume, nom de plume, perfume, plume, presume, resume, quivering-plume, subsume, volume

UME
see
OOM

Acumen, albumen, bitumen, catechumen

UMEN
see
EN

Argument, document, emolument, instrument, integument, monument, wind-instrument

UMENT
see
ENT

Humid, tumid

UMID
see
ID

Drummer, hummer, Indian-summer, midsummer, mummer

UMMER
see
ER

Chummy, dummy, gummy, mummy, thingummy, tummy

UMMY
see
E**

Autumn, column, fluted column

UMN
see
UM

Air-pump, bump, chump, clump, dump, frump, hump, jump, lump, mugwump, plump, pump, rump, slump, stump, thump, trump

UMP
see
s-UMPS

Crumpet, trumpet, strumpet

UMPET
see
ET

Galumph, humph, triumph

UMPH
see

Dumps, mumps

UMPS
see
UMP-s

Air-gun, begun, Bull Run, bun, dun, fun, gun, homespun, hot-cross-bun, Hun, injun, machine gun, Maxim-gun, nun, out-run, over-run, popgun, pun, rising-sun, run, shotgun, spun, sun, tun

UN
see
ION
ON
ONE**

Arjuna, Fortuna, lacuna, luna, tuna, una, Varuna, vicuna

UNA
see
A**

Quidnunc	**UNC** *see* UNK
Dunce	**UNCE** *see* ONCE*
Bunch, crunch, hunch, lunch, munch, Planter's punch, punch, quick-lunch, scrunch	**UNCH** *see*
Adjunct, defunct	**UNCT** *see*
Bund, fecund, fund, furibund, gerund, jocund, moribund, orotund, refund, rotund, sinking-fund, Sigismund	**UND** *see*
Asunder, blunder, sunder, thunder, under	**UNDER** *see* ER
Foundry, laundry, sundry	**UNDRY** *see* E**
Bay of Fundy, Burgundy, maundy, Mrs. Grundy	**UNDY** *see* E**
Commune, demilune, dune, fortune, good-fortune, immune, importune, jejune, June, misfortune, Neptune, opportune, picayune, prune, rune, sandy-dune, triune, tune	**UNE** *see* EWN OON

Bung, clung, dung, far-flung, flag-strung, flung, high-strung, hung, lung, moss-hung, rung, slung, sprung, strung, stung, sung, swung, underhung, unhung, unstrung, unsung, wide-flung, wrung

UNG
see
ONG**

Expunge, lunge, plunge

UNGE
see
ONGE

Bunion, communion, non-union, re-union, union

UNION
see
ION

Community, immunity, impunity, opportunity, unity

UNITY
see
E**
ITY

Bunk, chipmunk, chunk, drunk, dunk, flunk, funk, hunk, junk, plunk, punk, Saratoga trunk, shrunk, skunk, slunk, spunk, stunk, sunk, tree-trunk, trunk

UNK
see

Funnel, runnel, tunnel

UNNEL
see
EL

Bunny, funny, gunny, sunny

UNNY
see
E**

Blunt, brunt, hunt, punt, runt, shunt, stunt

UNT
see
ONT*

Cluny, luny, puny   **UNY**
                                           see
                                           E**

Ambiguous, anfractuous, arduous,   **UOUS**
congruous, conspicuous, contemptu-   *see*
ous, contiguous, continuous, deciduous,   OUS
fatuous, flexuous, impetuous, incestu-   US
ous, incongruous, inconspicuous, inde-
ciduous, ingenuous, insinuous, mellif-
luous, presumptuous, promiscuous,
sensuous, sinuous, strenuous, sumptu-
ous, superfluous, supersensuous, tem-
pestuous, tumultuous, tenuous, tortu-
ous, unctuous, vacuous, virtuous, vo-
luptuous

Breeches-buoy, buoy, life-buoy   **UOY**
                                           see
                                           OY

Acorn-cup, buttercup, check-up,   **UP**
chirrup, clean-up, close-up, cup, dried-   *see*
up, drinkingcup, flare-up, frame-up,   OP
get-up, gold-cup, grown-up, hang-up,
het-up, hiccup, holdup, hook-up,
ketchup, keyed-up, kick-up, larrup,
let-up, line-up, lockup, loving-cup,
make-up, painted-cup, pent-up, pick-
me-up, pickup, puffed-up, pup, round-
up, scup, set-up, seven-up, shake-up,
shut up, smash-up, speed-up, standing-
up, step-up, stirrup, stirrup-cup, stuck-
up, sup, syrup, teacup, toss-up, up, up
and up, well-brought-up, wind-up

Dupe, Guadalupe   **UPE**
                                             see
                                             OOP

Cupid, stupid   **UPID**
                                             see
                                             ID

Abrupt, bankrupt, corrupt, disrupt,   **UPT**
erupt, interrupt   *see*

Ashur, augur, Baldur, concur, Côte   **UR**
d'Azur, cur, demur, fur, incur, King   *see*
Arthur, larkspur, lemur, murmur, Nip-   ERE***
pur, Nishapur, non sequitur, occur,   EUR
recur, slur, spur, sulphur, Ur, Vidur,   URE
Yom Kippur   URR
                                             ed-URD
                                             s-URS

Angostura, Asura, aura, camera-   **URA**
obscura, coloratura, datura, Estrema-   *see*
dura   A**

Augural, conjectural, guttural, in-   **URAL**
augural, intramural, mural, natural,   *see*
plural, preternatural, rural, scriptural,   AL
structural, subnatural, supernatural,
unnatural, Ural

Accurate, commensurate, curate, in-   **URATE**
accurate, inaugurate, incommensurate,   *see*
obdurate, saturate, triturate   ATE

Blurb, curb, disturb, perturb, sub-   **URB**
urb, uncurb   *see*
                                             ERB

Church, lurch

URCH
see
EARCH
ERCH
IRCH

Absurd, curd, Kurd, surd

URD
see
EARD*
ERD
URE-*d*

Curdle, hurdle

URDLE
see
EL
LE

Hurdy-gurdy, sturdy

URDY
see
E**

Abjure, adventure, agriculture, al-
lure, aperture, assure, azure, brochure,
capture, censure, cincture, cocksure,
coiffure, conjure, culture, cure, deben-
ture, demure, departure, disfigure, em-
bouchure, embrasure, endure, enrap-
ture, ensure, failure, faith-cure, figure,
fissure, fixture, floriculture, gesture,
gravure, high-pressure, horticulture,
imposture, impure, indenture, injure,
insecure, insure, inure, jointure, junc-
ture, lay figure, lecture, leisure, low-
pressure, lure, manufacture, manure,
mind cure, misadventure, mixture,
moisture, mure, nurture, obscure, over-
ture, pasture, pelure, peradventure,

URE
see
ASURE
ATURE
EUR
ICURE
ITURE
OOR**
OSURE
OUR**
ed-ERD
IRD
ORD**
URD

perjure, photogravure, picture, por- **URE**
traiture, posture, prefecture, prefigure,
premature, pressure, procedure, pro-
cure, puncture, pure, quadrature, rap-
ture, reassure, reinsure, Scripture, se-
cure, seizure, sepulture, sinecure, struc-
ture, sure, suture, tenure, texture,
tincture, tonsure, torture, transfigure,
venture, verdure, vesture, vulture, wax
figure, you're

Treasurer, usurer **URER**
see
ER

Surf, turf **URF**
see
ERF

Gettysburg, Strasburg, Vicksburg **URG**
see
ERG

Demi-urge, inner urge, Panurge, **URGE**
purge, scourge, splurge, spurge, surge, *see*
thaumaturge, urge ERGE
IRGE

Dramaturgy, liturgy, metallurgy, **URGY**
thaumaturgy, theurgy *see*
E**

Futurity, impurity, insecurity, ma- **URITY**
turity, obscurity, purity, security, semi- *see*
obscurity E**
ITY

Lurk, murk, Turk

URK
see
ERK
IRK

Churl, curl, furl, hurl, purl, unfurl

URL
see
EARL
IRL
ORL
ed-ORLD

Curly, burly, hurly-burly, surly

URLY
see
E**

Auburn, burn, churn, lecturn, mortuary-urn, nocturn, overturn, return, Saturn, spurn, sunburn, taciturn, turn, Tyburn, upturn, urn

URN
see
EARN
OURN*

Diurnal, journal, nocturnal

URNAL
see
AL

Burnt, sunburnt

URNT
see

Usurp

URP
see
ed-ERPT

Aaron Burr, blurr, burr, purr

URR
see
UR

Burrow, furrow

URROW
see
OW*

Curry, flurry, furry, hurry, scurry **URRY**
see
E**

Accurse, curse, cut-purse, disburse, **URSE**
impurse, nurse, purse, reimburse, shep- *see*
herd's-purse, wet-nurse EARSE
ERCE
ed-ED

Accurst, burst, cloudburst, curst, **URST**
durst, nurst, outburst, sunburst *see*
IRST
ed-ED

Blurt, curt, Frankfurt, hurt, spurt, **URT**
yurt *see*
ERT
IRT
UIRT

Hurtle, mockturtle, snapping turtle, **URTLE**
turtle *see*
EL
LE

Guru **URU**
see
U

Arcturus, Epicurus, Eurus **URUS**
see
AURUS
US

A-curve, curve, incurve **URVE**
see
ERVE

Augury, bury, Canterbury, century, **URY**
conjury, fury, injury, jury, luxury, *see*
Mercury, penury, perjury, tilbury, E**
treasury, usury

Abacus, Academus, acanthus, Æolus, **US**
agnus, ailanthus, Albertus Magnus, *see*
alumnus, amaranthus, angelus, animus, AGUS
ankus, Antæus, arbutus, Augustus, ALUS
Autolycus, Avernus, Bacchus, bacillus, AMPUS
Belus, bogus, bolus, bonus, Brutus, AMUS
bus, cactus, Cadmus, Catullus, Cau- ATUS
casus, caucus, Celsus, census, cholera- AURUS
morbus, cirrus, citrus, colossus, Co- EOUS
lumbus, Comus, consensus, conspectus, ERUS
Copernicus, Coriolanus, corpus, Crœ- ETUS
sus, Cronus, cultus, cuniculus, cyprus, EUS*
Cyrus, demiurgus, dianthus, Diodorus, INOUS
discobolus, discus, Duns Scotus, En- INUS
celadus, Ephesus, Erasmus, Erebus, IOUS
eucalyptus, exodus, faunus, fungus, ITOUS
habeas corpus, Halicarnassus, helian- ITUS
thus, Hephæstus, Herodotus, hibiscus, IUS
humus, Hyacinthus, Hymettus, Iam- OCUS
blicus, Icarus, ictus, ignis-fatuus, im- OPUS
petus, incubus, isthmus, Janus, Jesus, ORUS
Josephus, Judas Maccabæus, litmus, OUS
Leviticus, lotus, Lucullus, magnus, ULOUS
maybush, Menelaus, mittimus, modus, ULUS
Momus, mucus, narcissus, nautilus, URUS
negus, Nicodemus, Nilus, nimbus, USS
Ninus, nisus, nonplus, obolus, Oceanus, YLUS
Œdipus, Olympus, omnibus, onus, YRUS
opus, ornithorhynchus, Paracelsus, pa-
radus, Parnassus, Patroclus, Pegasus,
Peloponnesus, Pentelicus, Phœbus,
platypus, plexus, plus, polyanthus,

Polygnotus, Polyphemus, Pontus, Pri-　**US**
apus, prospectus, pus, Pyrrhus, raucus,
rebus, Remus, Rhadamanthus, rhom-
bus, rumpus, sanctus, Silenus, Sil-
vanus, Sisyphus, solus, Somnus, status,
strophanthus, stylus, surplus, syllabus,
Tacitus, Tarsus, Tartarus, tetanus,
thaumaturgus, Theophrastus, thesau-
rus, thus, thyrsus, Trismegistus,
uræus, Uranus, Ursus, U.S., us, Venus,
versus, virus, walrus, Xanthus

　　Anchusa. Arethusa, Medusa, Susa　**USA**
　　　　　　　　　　　　　　　　see
　　　　　　　　　　　　　　　　A**

　　Carousal, causal, espousal, perusal,　**USAL**
refusal　　　　　　　　　　　　　*see*
　　　　　　　　　　　　　　　　AL

　　Abstruse, abuse, accuse, amuse,　**USE**
bemuse, confuse, diffuse, disuse, Druse,　*see*
effuse, enthuse, exclude, excuse, fuse,　OOSE*
hypotenuse, infuse, interfuse, misuse,　OSE**
muse, obtuse, peruse, profuse, recluse,　UISE**
refuse, ruse, suffuse, transfuse, use,　EW-*s*
Vauclause　　　　　　　　　　　　OE*-*s*
　　　　　　　　　　　　　　　　U-*s*
　　　　　　　　　　　　　　　　UE*-*s*

　　Ambush, blush, brush, bulrush,　**USH**
bush, crush, flush, gush, hush, inrush,　*see*
lush, mush, onrush, plush, push, rush,
sagebrush, scrubbing-brush, shad-bush,
slush, spicebush, steeple-bush, thrush,
toothbrush, tush

Allusion, conclusion, confusion, delusion, disillusion, exclusion, fusion, illusion, inclusion, infusion, intrusion, obtrusion, profusion

USION
see
ION

Conclusive, delusive, elusive, exclusive, illusive, inclusive, intrusive, obtrusive, unobtrusive, preclusive

USIVE
see
IVE

Dusk, husk, mollusk, musk, rusk, tusk

USK
see
USQUE

Cusp

USP
see

Brusque

USQUE
see
USK

Blunderbuss, buss, cuss, discuss, fuss, muss, percuss, puss, sour puss, truss

USS
see
US

Adjust, anti-rust, august, brickdust, bust, combust, crust, disgust, distrust, dust, entrust, gold-dust, gust, incrust, intrust, just, locust, lust, mistrust, must, piecrust, portrait-bust, readjust, robust, rust, sawdust, star-dust, thrust, trust, unjust, wanderlust

UST
see

Adjuster, baluster, bluster, buster, cluster, duster, filibuster, fluster, luster, muster

USTER
see
ER

Bustle, hustle, rustle

USTLE
see
EL
LE

Crusty, dusty, fusty, gusty, lusty, musty, rusty, trusty

USTY
see
E**
UST-*y*

Abut, betelnut, brazil-nut, brut, but, butternut, catgut, chestnut, chut, clear-cut, cocoanut, Connecticut, crosscut, cut, doughnut, gamut, halibut, hut, jut, Lilliput, Mut, nut, output, put, peanut, rebut, rut, sackbut, scut, short-cut, shut, slut, smut, strut, tut, uncut, walnut, woodcut

UT*
see
OOT*

Début

UT**
see
U

Brutal, refutal

UTAL
see
AL

Clutch, crutch, Dutch, hutch, smutch

UTCH
see
UCH*

Acute, astute, brute, Canute, chute, commute, compute, confute, cute, deaf-mute, dilute, dispute, disrepute, electrocute, execute, flute, hirsute, jute, lute, minute, mute, parachute, persecute, pollute, prosecute, refute, repute, salute, transmute, tribute, Ute

UTE
see

Azimuth, bismuth, Ruth, truth, untruth, vermuth

UTH
see
EUTH
OOTH
OUTH*

Ablution, circumlocution, constitution, contribution, dissolution, distribution, elocution, evolution, involution, locution, persecution, pollution, prosecution, restitution, retribution, revolution, solution

UTION
see
ION

Contributor, distributor, executor, interlocutor, persecutor, prosecutor, tutor

UTOR
see
OR

Mutt, putt

UTT
see
UT*

Butter, clutter, cutter, flutter, gutter, mutter, peanut butter, putter, revenue cutter, shutter, sputter, stonecutter, stutter, utter

UTTER
see
ER

Button, glutton, mutton

UTTON
see
ON

Nutty, putty, smutty

UTTY
see
E**

Beauty, deputy, duty

UTY
see
E**

Meum et tuum, residuum, vacuum   **UUM**
                                 see
                                 UM

Chef d'œuvre, Louvre, manœuvre   **UVRE**
                                 see
                                 ER

Afflux, conflux, crux, efflux, fiat lux,   **UX**
flux, influx, Ku Klux, Pollux, reflux   *see*
                                 UCK-*s*
                                 UCT-*s*

Buy, guy   **UY**
                                 see
                                 Y

Santa Cruz, St. Jean de Luz, Tam-   **UZ**
muz, Uz, Vera Cruz   *see*
                                 OOZE

Guzzle, muzzle, nuzzle, puzzle   **UZZLE**
                                 see
                                 EL
                                 LE

Y SOUNDS

Apply, awry, blackfly, blue-sky, butterfly, by, by and by, cry, damsel fly, dragonfly, dry, espy, firefly, fly, fry, gad-fly, go-by, hereby, housefly, imply, lullaby, mayfly, mid-sky, misapply, multiply, my, nearby, occupy, outcry, passerby, Paul Pry, ply, preoccupy, pry, reply, satisfy, shoo-fly, shy, sky, sly, small fry, spanish fly, spry, spy, stand-by, sty, supply, thereby, thy, try, war-cry, whereby, why, wry

Y
see
EFY
EYE
I*
IFY
IGH
ULY**
UY
YE*

Cherimoya, Libya, Maitreya, Surya

YA
see
A**

Dryad, dyad, hamadryad

YAD
see
AD

Triptych

YCH
see
ECK

Bicycle, cycle, kilocycle, megacycle, Metonic Cycle, motorcycle, tricycle

YCLE
see
EL
LE

Jamshyd

YD
see
EED

Clepsydra, hydra

YDRA
see
A**

Aye, bye, dye, eye, goodbye, lye, rye, tye

YE*
see
I**
Y

Ye

YE**
see
E*

Oxygen

YGEN
see
EN

Dyke, tyke, Vandyke

YKE
see
IKE

Beryl, dactyl, idyl, methyl, sibyl

YL
see
EL

Adactyle, hypostyle, peristyle, pro-style, style

YLE
see
ILE*

Babylon, pylon

YLON
see
ON

Sylph	**YLPH** *see*
Rhyme, thyme	**YME** *see* IME*
Hymn	**YMN** *see* IM
Lymph, nymph, woodnymph	**YMPH** *see*
Lynch	**YNCH** *see* INCH
Anodyne, auld lang syne, dyne, heterodyne	**YNE** *see* INE*
Larynx, lynx, pharynx	**YNX** *see* INX
Amphictyon, amphitryon, Apollyon, canyon, halcyon	**YON** *see* ON
Gyp, polyp	**YP** *see* IP
Archetype, daguerreotype, linotype, monotype, prototype, stereotype, tintype, type	**YPE** *see* IPE

Anaglyph, glyph, hieroglyph, tri-glyph   **YPH**
see
IF

Apocalypse   **YPSE**
see
IP-*s*

Crypt, Egypt   **YPT**
see
IPT

Martyr, satyr, zephyr   **YR**
see
AR*
ER

Byre, gyre, lyre, pyre, Tyre   **YRE**
see
IRE

Myrrh   **YRRH**
see
IR

Papyrus, zephyrus   **YRUS**
see
US

Abysm, cataclysm, paroxysm   **YSM**
see
ISM

Chlamys   **YS**
see
IS*

Abyss	**YSS** *see* IS*
Amethyst, analyst, catalyst, cyst, tryst	**YST** *see*
Acolyte, neophyte, proselyte, troglodyte	**YTE** *see* IGHT ITE*
Myth	**YTH** *see* ITH
Scythe	**YTHE** *see* ITHE
Rhythm	**YTHM** *see* IM
Gyve	**YVE** *see* IVE*
Onyx, oryx, Pnyx, pyx, sardonyx	**YX** *see* IX